What Trouble I Have Seen

What Trouble I Have Seen

———

A History of Violence against Wives

David Peterson del Mar

Harvard University Press

Cambridge, Massachusetts
London, England
1996

Library of Congress Cataloging-in-Publication Data

Peterson del Mar, David, 1957–
    What trouble I have seen : a history of violence against wives /
David Peterson del Mar.
        p.   cm.
    Includes bibliographical references (p.   ) and index.
    ISBN 0-674-95076-3 (cloth : alk. paper)
    1. Wife abuse—Oregon—History.   I. Title.
HV6626.22.O7P47 1996
362.82′92′09795—dc20   95-46974

For those whose troubles will never be told

Contents

Acknowledgments

I would never have attempted this study without many years of support and inspiration from those whose interest in violence against wives is intensely personal. I am indebted to the people with whom I worked at Sitkans against Family Violence, the Clatsop County Women's Crisis Service, the Fergus Falls Women's Crisis Service, the Lane County Relief Nursery, Men against Rape, Womenspace, and ASAP Treatment Services.

Several organizations have provided crucial funding for this project: the Woodrow Wilson National Fellowship Foundation's Charlotte Newcombe dissertation fellowship; the Center for the Study of Women in Society, which very generously provided two grants; the University of Oregon; the Western History Association; and Oregon's chapter of the Colonial Dames of America.

Portions of Chapter 2 appeared first in two journals: the *Journal of Family Violence* 6 (March 1991): 1–15; and *The Journal of Interdisciplinary History* 23 (Summer 1992): 97–118, with the permission of the editors of *The Journal of Interdisciplinary History* and The MIT Press, Cambridge, Massachusetts, © 1992 by the Massachusetts Institute of Technology and the editors of *The Journal of Interdisciplinary History*.

The keepers of the archival records I used for this book were unusually helpful. I am particularly indebted to the late Jim Clark of the Oregon State Archives and to the Boys and Girls Aid Society. Those who oversee Oregon's voluminous circuit court records cheerfully accommodated my demanding and unconventional research needs. I am especially grateful to staff members at the Multnomah, Lane, Coos, and Deschutes County courthouses for their service and hospitality.

This book was first a dissertation, and a very active dissertation committee shaped it. I owe a great debt to Richard Maxwell Brown, who has given this project the benefit of his unstinting support, enthusiasm, and sagacity ever since we first discussed it. Jeffrey Ostler was a particularly exacting and generous reader. Miriam Johnson oversaw much of my early research and raised key theoretical concerns. Daniel Pope and Howard Brick prompted me to rethink and, I hope, to refine several central interpretive threads. Louise Wade identified some important sources and questions and freed up valuable research time.

I am indebted to many other scholars and friends. John Shurts, Tina Loo, Theresa Healy, James Mohr, Susan Armitage, Robert Johnston, Earl Pomeroy, Barrie Ratcliffe, Elizabeth Jameson, Betsy Downey, Clare V. McKanna, Jr., Glen Love, Ruth Barnes Moynihan, Nicole Smith, Gloria Myers, Eve Pankovitch, Dolores Smith, Liisa Penner, Armand Smith, John Mack Faragher, Harry Stein, Paul Semonin, Todd Carney, Marion Goldman, Jeff LaLande, Lizzie Reis, Matthew Dennis, Robert O'Brien, Barbara Corrado Pope, George Sheridan, and Anne Rushton took the time to help me at various stages and in various ways. Mary-Ellen Kelm and Robin Fisher shared their home with me while I finished the manuscript and told me about totalitizing meta-narratives and big ideas. Rick Harmon gave the manuscript a close reading at a critical point. These individuals, as well as Carl Dominey, Conrad Thomason, William Toll, Allan Winkler, Christie Farnham Pope, Michael Sherry, Josef Barton, Timothy Breen, Robert Wiebe, Stephen Recken, and Joseph Fracchia, taught me how to be a scholar.

I am also grateful to the people with whom I worked at Harvard University Press. Aïda Donald and Elizabeth Suttell were uniformly supportive and helpful. Donna Bouvier painstakingly ironed out my prose and spotted my mistakes, all with very good humor. David Johnson and Elizabeth Pleck combined critical and encouraging feedback as referees, and Regina Morantz-Sanchez understood and affirmed what I was trying to accomplish and told me how to do it.

I feel that I cannot begin to thank the dozens of friends and strangers who have nurtured me before and after I began working on this book. I chose this topic in part because I did not want to find myself in the middle of a project that I did not care deeply about. I did not then imagine that so many others would care so deeply about this book and its writer. Thank you for supporting the two of us.

I shall close by paying my respects to my family. Thanks to my mother, Bessie Barber Peterson, for teaching me about compassion, and to my father, the late Murl Peterson, for teaching me about hard work. I cannot think of two more important tools that you could have given me as a social historian or as a person. Thank you, Dolores Rich Smith and Armand Smith, for welcoming me so warmly. Thank you, Muril Helen, Jon, Bob, Lois, Lisa, Kanani, Nicole, Randy, and Scott, for being family. Thank you, Wendy, for understanding how much this book has meant to me and for remembering its purpose when I did not. What a marvelous act of grace, dear love, to join my life to yours while picking through the ashes of so many cruelties and tragedies.

Prologue

In 1869 James Head, a carpenter, recalled to an Oregon circuit court a conversation from three years before with his daughter, Sarah Moses. "I saw her with a very black eye," Head remarked, "and when I asked the cause, she said, 'Pa, the world will never know what trouble I have seen.'"[1]

The trouble that Sarah Moses had seen was a violent husband, and the world still knows precious little about such difficulties. There has been, to be sure, an explosion of scholarly and popular interest in contemporary wife beating in the United States, by sociologists and talk-show hosts alike. But historians have remained almost wholly aloof. Elizabeth Pleck and Linda Gordon are the major exceptions. Pleck's book, *Domestic Tyranny: The Making of American Social Policy against Family Violence from Colonial Times to the Present*, addresses the history of public policy regarding violence toward children and wives. Linda Gordon's *Heroes of Their Own Lives: The Politics and History of Family Violence, Boston, 1880–1960* focuses on violence toward wives and particularly children among the struggling working class and how professionals responded to that abuse.[2] These excellent studies have only begun to remedy scholars' failure to examine the history of one of our most pressing and stubborn social problems.

A paucity of sources partially explains why so few historians address wife beating. Domestic violence has commonly occurred in private,

1

and the shame surrounding it has made people reluctant to write of their experiences. Nor has such material, once committed to paper, been likely to find its way to an archive or historical library. A researcher can spend many days with autobiographies, diaries, and correspondence without encountering a violent husband.

The history of violence against wives in Oregon is thickly documented in its county courthouses: in a basement in Coquille, in a closet in Fossil, and on microfilm rolls in Portland. Without these archives I could not have written this book. Oregon had relatively liberal divorce laws from the beginning of its widespread Euro-American settlement in the 1840s, with cruelty, not just adultery or desertion, well established as acceptable grounds for dissolving a marriage. Just as important, most of its courts kept detailed records of divorce proceedings into the twentieth century. These records typically include not only the plaintiff's complaint (an attorney's summation of the grounds for divorce) but also transcripts of testimony from wives or husbands and at least one or two other witnesses. There is also the occasional letter introduced as evidence of a husband's brutality. I examined about 3,500 cases describing wife abuse for this study. They constitute the backbone of this book.

These documents, like all descriptions of family violence, are flawed. They generally served as a means to procure a divorce, so a fraction were no doubt false or distorted. But the breadth of the sources mitigates this drawback. Many cases featured a half dozen or more witnesses: parents, children, siblings, friends, neighbors, and law-enforcement officers described husbands, wives, violent episodes, and attitudes toward spousal violence from various perspectives. Of course, the couples who appeared in the suits were not a random sample of Oregon marriages, violent or otherwise. Until recent decades, divorce remained exceptional, even in the western United States. But not all of these wives had assertively escaped an abusive husband; many sought divorces only after their husbands had deserted them, or they appeared in divorce actions initiated by their husbands. The strategies these wives employed to control male violence were no doubt similar to those used by women who never sought a divorce and whose husbands never left them, women whose sufferings will never be revealed.

The Oregon divorce records possess a depth not common to grass-

roots social history. Unlike most rich primary sources on marital intimacy, they describe a broad range of people: the literate and the illit-
erate; husbands who farmed, ranched, logged, or worked in factories;
wives who took in washing in the nineteenth century, worked as waitresses during the Depression, or labored in Portland's shipyards during World War II. These materials provide a rare and broad window
into the largely private act of wife abuse.

Oregon has more than strong court records to recommend it as a
case study for the history of violence toward wives. The state has always
had something of a moderate social and political reputation. Percep-
tions of the Euro-American West are filled with the images of cow-
boys, miners, and volatile townfolk. But Oregon's development, which
began before that of most parts of the West, proceeded gradually. The
state, long dominated by the fertile and temperate Willamette Valley,
offered prospective settlers and residents not get-rich-quick bonanzas
but an unhurried, comfortable, family-centered way of life, a mild climate, and a moderate society. Its population, from the mid-nineteenth
century to today, has been overwhelmingly Euro-American, native
born, and middle class. Oregon has had few labor or race riots, lynch-
ings, or vigilante movements. It has, for its non-Native Americans,
been relatively free from major social disruptions. Popular Oregon historian Terrence O'Donnell remarks that aside from Indian wars, "ours
has been a tranquil past," a "summer's afternoon spent on the banks
of a pretty river."[3] The caveat is a very large one, and Oregon's Edenic
image is overdrawn. But the state experienced less public violence than
most in the U.S. West.

Oregon, then, is not the first place that the historian would explore
in search of wife beaters. Indeed, the nascent historical literature on
violence against wives in the United States has thus far treated more
contentious peoples: the working class of Boston and New York and
the hard-pressed settlers of the Great Plains.[4] Yet Oregon's history
proves not to be so tranquil when one steps away from the banks of
its pretty rivers and into its homes. Many thousands of Oregon wives
have suffered from violence over the past two centuries beneath the
state's veneer of public civility and moderation. Oregon therefore suggests, in a way that a case study of a more tumultuous place cannot,
the stubborn persistence of wife beating in U.S. history.

The history of Oregon is not simply the history of the United States writ small. Euro-Americans did not settle in the state in large numbers until the 1840s, several decades after the nation's founding. Settlement-era Oregon, treated in Chapter 1, by definition lagged behind the rest of the nation. By the 1890s, as detailed in Chapter 2, rural Oregonians approximated the social and cultural patterns prevalent in many parts of the United States much earlier in the century. Portland, Oregon's only large city, came of age in the decade and a half just before World War I; Chapter 3 focuses on that period in Portland. Finally, during the twentieth century, as explained in Chapters 4 and 5, the history of Oregon became increasingly indistinguishable from that of the United States as a whole.

Although social scientists seldom consider history, it has much to contribute to our understanding of why wife beating so commonly occurs in the United States today. For some scholars, male violence is essentially biological. "We are creatures who are by nature easily aroused to violence, we easily learn it, and we are wired to create situations . . . in which violence becomes a necessity," assert Lionel Tiger and Robin Fox.[5] Male violence, including presumably violence against women, is explained by male physiology and by millennia of ingrained experiences. Yet, as anthropologist David Levinson points out, wife beating is by no means an universal practice. It varies over place and culture. Sociologists have identified particular social causes for contemporary domestic violence. The influential "family violence" school of thought led by Murray Straus and Richard Gelles contends that husbands employ violence because it is socially acceptable to do so, because violence is so commonly used to settle disputes in the United States. Feminist theorists locate the roots of male violence more specifically in male dominance; in their view, violence serves as a tool to keep wives subjected to husbands' authority.[6] My own study of violence against wives substantiates the family violence and feminist schools of interpretation in many respects. Violence against wives has tended to be high when other forms of violence have been high, and a husband's violence often served to compel his wife's obedience. But social theories uninformed by history suffer from a certain flatness. To account for violence against wives simply or even primarily by citing a general culture of violence or male dominance is to overlook the details, subtleties, and paradoxes that history often brings to the fore.

This book's central thesis is that the history of violence against wives in the United States over the past two centuries has been profoundly influenced by two broad cultural transformations. The popularization of a production-oriented ethos emphasizing disciplined self-control in late-nineteenth-century Oregon made wife beating less acceptable and, apparently, less common than it had been during the state's settlement era. During the twentieth century, however, a culture of consumption undercut the practice of self-restraint, and violence toward wives became more widespread and severe. Women's ability to resist explicitly and vigorously their husbands' brutality also varied over time and for similar reasons, decreasing in the late nineteenth century and then increasing during the course of the twentieth century. Such broad historical developments also explain variations in other factors surrounding wife beating, such as the goals of husbands' violence and the reactions of others, such as police, family, and neighbors.

This book essentially offers an interpretation of violence against wives from the perspective of the *Annales* school. Particular events, such as the Great Depression, and even social structures, such as class, are not at its center. Long-term cultural transformations are the core causal agents. The history of violence against wives in Oregon, then, is inseparable from the larger history of Oregon and the United States. This is not to say that Oregonians have not commonly asserted otherwise. The state's whipping post law for wife beaters, in force from 1905 to 1911, vividly expressed Oregonians' belief that the wife beater was a highly idiosyncratic type, a man beyond society's pale. But, as we shall see, a broad range of Oregon men have assaulted their wives. More important still are the manifold and subtle links between men who have hit their wives and men who have not. The extent and context of wife beating in Oregon changed because of cultural and social shifts that all the state's citizens experienced, and the wife beater expressed, albeit often in exaggerated form, anxieties over women shared by his nonviolent counterparts. For these reasons, this book is a history of all Oregon men.

I attach particular meanings to certain terms that are often used more broadly. I define "violence" as the intentional infliction of immediate and physical pain on another person or a direct threat with a firearm or edged weapon. I use the term "patriarchy" to refer to gender relations characterized by explicit male dominance in all aspects of the household and family. By this definition, patriarchy has dwindled in the nineteenth and twentieth centuries, having been replaced by less extreme and less pervasive forms of male dominance. The term "instrumental violence" refers to violence used as a patently coercive tool, to force another person to behave in a certain way. The purpose of "affective violence" is less specific: it is to relieve pent-up emotions or to express anger or anxieties not directly related to the victim.

Because this book deals with highly personal and sensitive matters, I have obscured the identity of individuals who may still be alive. I have not used the actual names of any people in divorce suits from 1920 to the present, and all the case numbers for restraining orders filed in the 1980s and 1990s are coded. The names used in cases from the Boys and Girls Aid Society, a private organization, are pseudonyms.

I have avoided the use of "[sic]" unless the meaning of a passage would be obscured without it. It seems to me less important to identify misspellings than to let the subjects speak unencumbered by editorial asides.

I have tried to strike a balance between documentation and brevity in the notes. For the most part, only primary sources quoted or referred to in the text are included, although I have made some exceptions when further references seemed warranted. Those desiring more detail in text and notes may wish to examine my dissertation.[7]

Though not a quantitative study, this book occasionally presents some quantitative evidence and some chi-square tests of significance. The key part of these tests is the P measurement. $P < .05$, for example, means that the difference between two variables could have occurred randomly, by chance, less than .05 times out of 1.0, or less than 5 percent of the time. A level of .05 or less is typically considered necessary for statistical significance.

This book's most original conclusion, I suspect, is its assertion that wife beating varied over time, that it became less common over the course of the nineteenth century and more common during the twentieth century. Given the fact that this conclusion is based on an extensive reading of qualitative primary sources, I should discuss briefly how I read those sources. First of all, the divorce cases and other evidence often describe how a variety of people perceived wife beating. During the settlement period, for example, husbands more commonly claimed a right to hit their wives than they did late in the nineteenth century. Women's descriptions of husbands' abuse also varied over time. Twentieth-century wives depicted more frequent and more forceful violent acts than did their earlier counterparts. Late-nineteenth-century wives commonly described abusive husbands who exercised self-control more resolutely than at earlier or later times. Taken together, these types of evidence point to significant historical shifts in husbands' propensity toward violence.[8]

I have explored the relationship between historical and contemporary social problems more personally than most academics. My research for this book included working as a counselor for a year with groups of indigent men who had been found by the courts to have assaulted their women partners. That experience underscored what my historical research had indicated: that violent husbands were not highly deviant or unusual, that their beliefs about women did not much differ from the beliefs of nonviolent husbands, and that therefore the problem of wife beating could not be solved without assessing the characteristics of U.S. culture and masculinity generally.

One frequently posed question remains to be addressed before proceeding: Why is this a history of violence against wives rather than a history of violence against husbands and wives?[9] To some degree, this book does treat wives' violence, though largely as a means of resisting male authority and male violence. The moral texture of a violent act is contingent on its context. Larger patterns of dominance and abuse must always be considered. A slave's blow to a master is different from a master's blow to a slave, just as a young child's blow to an adult is different from an adult's blow to a young child. Whether a blow is abusive or not depends on such circumstances.

This is not to say that there are not or have not been abused or even battered husbands. These victims and survivors deserve our empathy and support. But their presence should not distract us from the larger issues of gender violence and domination. The social, economic, and physical advantages that society has disproportionately awarded to men has made husband abuse rare and wife abuse commonplace.

This book hazards some generalizations on the relationship between husbands' dominance and their violence, between wife abuse and wife beating. It aspires to help answer the tragic question of why husbands so often hit their wives. Just as important, it aspires to bring lives long hidden in the folds of court documents to the light of history. These lives deserve our attention. It is long past time for us to listen to the trouble that Sarah Moses and countless other women have seen.

— 1 —

"To Maintain His Authority": The Settlement Era

A sustained Euro-American presence in the territory that would become known as Oregon began in the 1790s, when ships from Europe and the United States began regularly trading at the mouth of the Columbia River. Settlement by Native Americans had of course started several millennia before. But these people's marital relations before European contact are extremely difficult to discern. Hence this study addresses only the last two centuries of violence against wives.

By the time sustained overland migration to Oregon began in the 1840s the United States was completing its transition from a traditional, localistic society to one based on bourgeois norms of self-control and other behaviors that would encourage the production of goods for far-flung and highly competitive markets. Oregon's physical and social geography buffered it from these national developments. Some parts of the area developed more quickly than others, to be sure. Much of the Willamette Valley had stabilized by the Civil War, while coastal and particularly eastern Oregon remained highly dynamic and volatile. But even the Willamette Valley and Portland, Oregon's only city, bore the stamp of newness and isolation. Indeed, the treacherous Columbia River bar remained Oregon's primary link to the outside world into the 1880s.

Oregon's distance from leading economic, social, and cultural developments had profound implications for violence against wives. Bourgeois values birthed masculine self-restraint along with increasingly bifurcated and, in some respects, equal gender roles in the eastern United States. Wives in mid-nineteenth-century Oregon lived in a more traditional milieu. Here male violence commonly served as a tool to enforce male authority, an authority that wives often resisted.

The United States was well along in a profound transformation when Robert Gray crossed the Columbia River bar in 1792. Geographic expansion was something of a metaphor for this lengthy revolution, as production and trade for growing and distant markets replaced local subsistence and barter systems. These economic changes had social consequences: communities became more open and dynamic, governed less by a sort of moral economy that stressed reciprocal rights and duties between static classes and more by a competitive individualism in which one's status could rise or fall suddenly.

Familial relations changed with social ones. Seventeenth-century households had tended to be patriarchal in the more literal sense of the word, with husbands recognized as powerful heads who controlled and directed the labor of wives and children. But by the late seventeenth century, young men began to defy paternal authority and to leave their close-knit communities on the East Coast. Urban and economic growth spurted in the North during the three decades before the American Revolution, further weakening the obligations between father and son. Children acted more independently of parents and, in at least some areas, divorce for women became more common. The Revolution discredited the idea of absolute rule and abetted the deterioration of patriarchal authority. Victory over the British also drew many settlers across the Appalachian Mountains, further undercutting social stability and deference.

The rise of industrialism quickened the movement to bourgeois values. By the 1830s the U.S. economy had begun to catch up to the growing nation's size; substantial northeastern factories displaced many independent artisans, and cash crops increasingly elbowed aside subsistence farming. As before, cultural changes accompanied economic ones. Success depended on disciplined production; hence such values as competitiveness, hard work, sobriety, punctuality, self-control, and deferred gratification came to the fore.[1]

The popularization of bourgeois values together with husbands' exodus from the home created new gender roles, including more separate and equal spheres for wives and husbands. Men who spent most of each waking day away from their families could not head them in the same way that their fathers and grandfathers had. In any event, the very idea of hierarchy had become suspect. Prescriptive literature emphasized the different roles of husband and wife more commonly than their different levels of status or power. Men labored outside the home, women within it. Men made money, women made a home. Men competed hard and ruthlessly in the outside world, women provided them with a secluded haven of warmth and nurture. Men used high character to succeed in the world, women created and sustained high character within the home. This new arrangement was much more pronounced in theory than in fact, even among the middle class. Most wives continued to work very hard, men maintained much of their domestic authority, and a substantial gap in status and power still separated the sexes. Yet the roles of husband and wife had became both more disparate and more egalitarian.[2]

This transition to more egalitarian sex roles occurred first in the industrializing and urbanizing Northeast. Most of Oregon's early immigrants, however, hailed from more recently settled parts of the country, particularly Missouri, and their roots more often than not reached back to the upper South. These areas, as historians John Mack Faragher and Suzanne Lebsock point out, were characterized by pronounced male dominance well into the nineteenth century.[3]

Missouri men earned a reputation for hard drinking and brawling long after the ascendance of gentility in the Northeast. Peter H. Burnett, who traveled to Oregon in 1843 before becoming governor of California, described in detail the fights that commonly followed Missouri militia exercises. The contests began when "some bully would mount a stump, imitate the clapping and crowing of a cock, and declare aloud that he could whip any man in that crowd except his friends." He characterized the fights as "a very severe trial of manhood, perseverance, and skill," noting that combatants might "lose part of the ear or nose, and sometimes an eye." The motive behind such bloodletting was not so much "hatred or animosity," but rather "pride and love of fame."[4]

A belief in absolute male authority within the home lingered in Missouri and central Illinois. Wives from those areas often emphasized their dutifulness and obedience in divorce petitions from the first half

of the nineteenth century. Such women commonly described themselves as moving to and fro between the authority of a father and the
authority of a husband. Laura Miner's 1848 complaint recalled that
she had "forsook . . . paternal roof" in Vermont shortly after her 1836
marriage to follow her husband west to Illinois.[5] Sally Harrison, daughter of the eminent Methodist minister Peter Cartwright, claimed in
her 1839 answer to Simeon Harrison's divorce suit that her husband
had seduced her "away from her paternal protection" so that he could
gain a portion of her noted father's property. Sally, barely thirteen,
soon became convinced of Simeon's "sordid and cruel" motives and
"returned as a disobedient but repentant child to her father's house,"
where she successfully "begged his forgiveness and protection."[6] Seeking a divorce, then, did not necessarily mean seeking independence.
Betsey Armstrong, also of central Illinois, claimed in her 1834 complaint that she desired a divorce so that she could be restored to the
"rights and privileges of single women," particularly "the right to procure her self a companion and protector for life."[7] These documents
are not a trustworthy guide to what divorce-seeking women truly
desired; but they indicate a general belief that such wives should be
moving not toward autonomy, but toward submission to another,
hopefully more benevolent, male authority.

Respectable Missouri men defended violence as an acceptable tool
for disciplining wives who disputed a husband's authority. In the 1830s
a group of petitioners from the St. Louis area asked the governor to
pardon a young slave named Matt who had stabbed another African
American male. The petitioners noted that the fight had begun with
some "rough fun" between Matt and a slave that he claimed "as his
wife." Matt, "in the exercise of the connubial rights told her to hush,"
and when she "persevered in her discourse" he "undertook to enforce
his authority with a slap."[8] Even a slave enjoyed the right to use a certain amount of violence to "enforce his authority" over his spouse.

Evidence from two Missouri divorce cases involving Euro-Americans reveals similar assumptions regarding male authority and violence.
The first, between Sally and John Adams, occurred near St. Louis
around 1809. John justified his blows by noting that Sally had called
him "a dirty Puppy" and told him that "she should do as she pleased"
when he ordered her to stop drawing vinegar. An onlooker noted that
the second blow occurred after Sally had "raised up & took a piece of

the broken bowl" in challenge to her husband's first blow.[9] The second episode occurred nearly four decades later and involved a well-to-do couple in western Missouri. The altercation began when Sarah Duncan demanded that her husband, William, pay a debt that she claimed against him. When William refused, Sarah "rushed at him and seized him by his privates in a violent manner," and he, in his words, "whipped the old Lady" with a cane. This particular event was part of a larger, ongoing struggle over family resources. William's answer to Sarah's divorce petition complained that "in utter disregard and contempt of her marital duties" she had "appropriated to her separate use" the earnings of slaves she had brought to the marriage.[10] William Duncan and John Adams used violence to underscore their claim to headship, a claim that their wives actively resisted.

This is not to say that midwesterners uniformly beat their wives, or that neighbors consistently sanctioned such violence. Even in the Duncan case, William claimed that he beat his wife only after she had attacked him, that he had acted in self-defense. In the early 1840s some 350 Missouri men petitioned the governor to pardon Rebecca Hawkins for poisoning her husband. According to one letter, the husband had been a *"brute"* who had "exercised his cruelty by kicking and beating and other outrageous indignities," leaving large gashes on her head.[11] Missouri men accepted violence against wives in some, but not all, contexts.

Violence by husbands and wives alike appeared to be growing less acceptable by mid-century. This trend seemed more pronounced in central Illinois than in Missouri, particularly among those from well-to-do northeastern families. Polly Alger, from a wealthy family in New York state, married Addison Alger in 1825 against her parents' wishes. In 1843 her divorce complaint cited twelve years of cruelty by Addison, including violent language, accusations of adultery, threats to kill, and, after their separation, breaking into her house. But the lengthy petition did not claim that Addison had hit or bruised Polly. Polly reacted to her husband's many abuses not by fighting back, but by withdrawing. Her sister reported that Addison's "improper language" and "rude conduct" had left Polly "very much excited, her nervous system deranged and her mind confused & bewildered." Polly's despondency culminated in an unsuccessful suicide attempt, not in a verbal or physical assault on her tormenter. New marital norms decreased both husbands' propensity to use violence and wives' capacity to resist.[12]

Oregon's settlers hailed largely from areas where the new norms had not made much headway. Missouri contributed far more immigrants to Oregon than did any other state, and the transplanted midwesterners were much more likely to trace their cultural roots through Kentucky than Massachusetts. Unlike many recently settled parts of the United States, Oregon was highly rural. Portland, its only major urban center, had about 8,300 residents in 1870, not even one-tenth of the state's population. Well-to-do Yankee immigrants tended to settle there, but the Yankees tended to be single men, not families. Eastern Oregon, dominated by mining, and coastal Oregon, dominated by lumber and fishing, also had highly heterogeneous, volatile, and male-dominated settlements. Only the fertile and temperate Willamette Valley had large numbers of stable families, and these families came, in the words of Ruth Barnes Moynihan, from "a man's world of camaraderie, horse trading, cattle raising, wild game hunting, unquestioning hospitality, and subordinate women."[13]

The move west to Oregon enhanced the male world of adventure and risk while rending female society. "When women wrote of the decision to leave their homes," notes Lillian Schlissel, "it was almost always with anguish, a note conspicuously absent from the diaries of men."[14] Even the strongest wives commonly opposed the decision. E. W. Conyers, on his way to Oregon in an 1852 wagon train, described how "a large-sized woman, weighing something over 250 pounds, with sleeves rolled up above her elbows, stepped out in front of . . . three men, smacking her fists and shaking them under the nose of the little man seated in the center," her husband. "She berated him for everything that was good, bad, or indifferent," Conyers continued, "charging him with bringing his wife and children out into this God-forsaken country to starve and die."[15] Picking up and moving to the edge of the continent profoundly disrupted women's lives by separating them from friends and kin.

Once in Oregon, women's relative scarcity both helped and harmed them. It brought a wide choice of husbands. Oregon white men in their twenties outnumbered their female counterparts by a ratio of about 2.5 to 1 in 1850, when the Donation Land Claim Act provided 320 acres for wives. Young women did not necessarily follow their parents' dictates in marrying. "The girls of that day liked to pick out their own husbands," recalled Catherine Thomas Morris, who had come to the Willamette Valley from Missouri in 1851.[16] The marriage bond often proved to be less permanent than in most parts of the United States. A male witness for Lucy Lynch, who sought a divorce in 1859 in eastern Oregon, recalled her saying that "she would only live with him [her husband] til good weather came," and that "she solicitted me to take care of her."[17] Such behavior was by no means typical, let alone acceptable. Yet Oregon's scarcity of marriageable women before the Civil War meant that wives were more apt to get away with leaving their husbands than were those in more settled parts of the United States. At the same time, Oregon's skewed sex ratios commonly led women to marry at a very young age. Abigail Scott Duniway, editor of the state's first women's rights newspaper, asserted that "when a man of forty, thirty, or even twenty-five, marries a child of fourteen, . . . the result is subjugation on one hand and despotism upon the other."[18] Bethenia Owens-Adair, who eventually became a friend of Duniway and the state's first college-educated woman physician, married at age fourteen in 1854 to a man who "was five feet eleven inches in height, and I could stand under his outstretched arm."[19] The man soon physically abused her. George Bennett reportedly remarked to an eastern Oregon neighbor that his wife, Lureana, "gave herself to him when she was but a child" and that he "had had her under his thumb ever since—he could use her just as he pleased."[20] "What could a girl of 14 do to protect herself from a man of 44," asked Elvina Apperson Fellows, whose husband "used to beat me until I thought I couldn't stand it."[21]

Wives of all ages often found themselves far from other women. Early in Duniway's marriage she and her husband lived on the margins of the Willamette Valley, where she "did not see the face of a woman" during four consecutive winters. She later wrote movingly of the farmer wife who "for months and months remains at home, not seeing the face of a single lady friend."[22] Women in rural eastern Oregon were particularly isolated. A man whose family moved there in 1851 recalled that more than a year passed "before my mother saw another white woman."[23] To be sure, most wives lived close to friends or kin after the earliest years of settlement in a given area. But women's communities arose in spite of, not because of, women's scarcity, and that scarcity pushed many of them into marriages to older men long before they had the emotional or physical resources to assert themselves.

The rugged nature of early settlement had its trade-offs for women. On the one hand, wives performed a variety of crucial and productive economic roles. Susan P. Angell came to Oregon in 1852, at age twenty. She later recalled that housework meant "making bread, doing the washing, making soap, and doing a score of other things." She also cared for eight children and "made all their dresses."[24] Many divorce-seeking women described themselves as their families' primary breadwinners. Victoria Brown, married in the southern Willamette Valley in 1855, gave a not unusual account of a woman's labors: "It [her family] was supported by my work in making butter, socks, selling eggs, and I also worked in the harvest field. I worked at Mr. Jenkins' binding oats to pay for cloth for a pair of pants for deft. [her husband]. The family was mostly supported by my work and care."[25] Women whose husbands went off to fight in Indian wars or to mine for gold had similar experiences. G. W. Kennedy recalled that his father left the family for about six months during the Cayuse War. Kennedy's mother "could have stood off quite a band of Indians," however, for "she could shoot the head off of a squirrel." "We felt quite safe," he concluded.[26] In some respects, then, the rigors of settlement facilitated women's independence.

Oregon offered economic opportunities to women as well as to men. "Their is but few" places, noted a north-coast woman in 1863, "wher womans work is more in demand and brings better pay than in Oregon."[27] Modest amounts of money could be had from teaching, selling poultry and dairy products, making and selling a variety of textiles, and running boarding houses. At some times and places, women's products brought high returns. W. F. Rigdon said that his mother quickly transformed a $50 sack of flour into $200 of bread in the southern Oregon mining town of Jacksonville in 1852. Agnes Ruth Sengstacken said that she made $300 in two months from selling her pies and cakes at about the same time in another part of the territory.[28]

Yet this sort of financial return was exceptional. Most wives who sought divorces described work that brought little remuneration, particularly cleaning, laundering, and sewing. Fully one-half of the 379 Portland wage-earning women listed in the 1870 census were domestics. Those listed simply as housewives by the census also engaged in a great deal of productive labor, but that labor tended to be hard and monotonous. Duniway, who spoke from years of tedious and tiring firsthand experience, granted that man's physical strength exceeded women's, and she lampooned them for trying to monopolize light and mental work "while women, equal to himself in mental capacity and scholarly attainment, *are washing and sawing stove wood*, and doing other hard and menial labor for which they are not fitted, at starvation prices, to earn a livelihood."[29] Women such as Duniway, who took up journalism and speaking, or Owens-Adair, who became a doctor, faced extensive opposition from Oregon men, as did far less prominent women who stepped beyond the domestic sphere. Margaret Jewett Bailey in 1844 noted that a young clerk referred to a woman as a "hag," apparently because "she is a great business character, and takes the lead, in preference to her husband, in buying and selling, collecting debts, going to mill, &c." Bailey herself felt the sting of public disapprobation, particularly in 1854 when *The Grains*, a book she wrote that criticized several Willamette Valley men, was published. The Portland *Oregonian's* acrid review of *The Grains* asserted that women's proper province was "darning stockings, pap and gruel, children, cookstoves, and the sundry little affairs that make life comparatively comfortable and makes them, what Providence designed them 'Helpmates.' "[30] The great majority of Oregon's settler women performed a wide range of essential and difficult tasks, and this work gave them a physical and probably psychological strength that less active women lacked. But this work offered few chances for economic autonomy outside the family or for much status in the larger community.[31]

Mid-nineteenth-century Oregon women enjoyed a high level of political and social rights only compared to their counterparts in most of the rest of the United States. The Donation Land Claim Act of 1850, a major event in the history of women's property rights, made it possible for Oregon wives to hold 320 acres, and many of them succeeded in retaining legal title to that land. Oregon's 1857 constitution stipulated that women could keep as their separate property resources that they brought to a marriage, and in 1872 the state legislature passed a law protecting the money a wife earned from seizure by her husband's creditors. Oregon also ranked high in marital dissolutions, with nearly triple the national rate by 1870. Duniway, for many years the

Pacific Northwest's most vocal and prominent advocate of sexual equality, repeatedly pointed out the inadequacies of these measures. In an 1871 article she described widows' difficulties in getting access to their deceased husbands' estates and noted that husbands could create wills that did not recognize their wives' role in amassing property. She called for men to "remove from your wives and mothers the reproach of being classed with idiots, criminals and minor children."[32] Duniway asserted that women had a right to full access to the professions, greater control over sexual relations and reproduction, less onerous work loads on farms, and the vote. But most Oregon men were not convinced. When Ada Weed, a practitioner of hydropathic medicine, lectured in 1858 on the need to improve the conditions of Oregon's women a Salem editor asserted that females belonged in the home. When Susan B. Anthony visited the Pacific Northwest in 1871, drawn in large part by Duniway's efforts, twenty out of thirty-three newspapers that reported on her speeches criticized them. Editors, ministers, and other Oregon men who expressed themselves on women's rights typically asserted that women belonged under men's authority and protection and were not equipped for the public sphere. Indeed, Frances Fuller Victor's account of Portland women's aggressive anti-saloon movement in the early 1870s noted that "very few of these women had ever prayed aloud in their own churches" and that only one "had spoken in public."[33]

Oregon settlers emphasized that a good wife was an obedient wife. John Irvine of eastern Oregon spoke highly of the character of a woman whose husband had deserted her in 1866: "I think she did her duty as a wife, whatever she was told to do by him she obeyed with pleasure."[34] Another eastern Oregonian, Sarah Thomas, similarly praised her mother, who "always treated him [her father] kindly, and did not answer back when abused."[35] Ellen Hobach of the Willamette Valley said of a wife whose husband had driven her away: "She was a good woman She was quiet like a child & never would fight back or tell much."[36] Nancy Palmateer, who sought a divorce in the northern Willamette Valley in 1866, recalled her "faithful and kind" treatment to her husband of eighteen years: "I never annoyed him but when he would come home drunk I would undress him and get him to bed and cry over him."[37] This sort of court testimony was of course calculated to prove that the petitioning women were innocent victims of a husband's abuse, and one should not assume that these women were in fact as meek as they represented themselves. But such evidence illustrates that the ideal, if not the practice, of woman's submissiveness to her husband was widely disseminated among Oregon's settlers.

Submissiveness was no guarantee against abuse and tyranny. An eastern Oregon woman recounted her futile attempts to satisfy her domineering husband: "When I would ask him if I did not do every thing in my power to make my home happy and comfortable he said yes that I was just as good a Negro as ever he had in Tennessee."[38] Little wonder that some Oregon women sought divorces so that, as Margaret Rondot's complaint put it, their spouses "may no longer have the authority of a husband and compel her by his orders."[39]

Purity was to accompany obedience. Some men interpreted even a married woman's desire for her husband as a sign of immorality. John Savage, a Willamette Valley laborer, reportedly believed that his wife "was a virtuous woman" because "she had never asked him [Savage] to 'screw her'."[40] Another witness in a divorce suit described a husband who felt the opposite about his wife, a man who claimed "that he picked up the d—d bitch— . . . on the plains with one petticoat on her a—s, a fiddle in her hand and a bastard by her side."[41] This image conveyed the exact converse of what a woman was supposed to be like.

Women's purity bequeathed to them a transforming power that men could not find within themselves. In 1851 the Willamette Valley's D. R. Williams registered his pleasure at the arrival of many members "of the fairer portion of the world." He explained that even refined gentlemen, left to themselves, "will invariably become harsh, uncouth, unsocial and immoral." Hence "the refining and elevating influence of virtuous female society cannot be too highly appreciated," for woman "regulated, chastens, and ornaments human society."[42] Orange Jacobs, who arrived in Jacksonville in 1852, recalled that large numbers of young men in the tumultuous, male-dominated mining town regularly visited a local family simply "to see someone who had the form, the purity and the affection of a mother."[43]

The idealization of the maternal and feminine did not lead Oregon's Euro-American men to embrace the concept of idle womanhood, which was gaining currency in more settled parts of the nation. Oregon wives were to be active and productive as well as submissive and chaste. An early newspaper article praised "the buxom, bright-eyed, rosy-cheeked, full-breasted, bouncing lass, who can darn a stocking, mend trowsers, make her own frocks, command a regiment of pots and kettles, feed the pigs, milk the cows, and be a lady withall in 'company'" and scorned "ye pining, moping lolling screwed-up, waspwaisted, doll-dressed, putty-faced, consumption-mortgaged, musicmurdering, novel-devouring daughters of fashion and idleness."[44] Being a good wife entailed hard physical work, not just abstract moral qualities. Vanburen Towner, for example, threatened to whip his wife because she could not steer a canoe. The next day he "asked me what God Damned woman was fit for" and refused to let her change out of her rain-drenched clothes until she cooked his supper.[45] The rough, demanding conditions of the settlers' lives necessarily blurred the sexual division of labor and therefore tempered or delayed the elaboration of separate sexual spheres.

A cluster of unflattering stereotypes also undercut men's idealization of women. Newspaper humor commonly portrayed women as vain, selfish, improvident, and extremely eager to marry. Much of this humor suggested that marriage, for men, was not all that it was cracked up to be. Since lightning never struck twice in the same place, "let a man whose first wife was a good one never marry again," read one maxim.[46] Other aphorisms expressed men's desire for authority: "Many a man who is proud to be a quartermaster, has a wife at home who is a whole-master."[47] Such humor identified women as the cause of domestic conflicts. "When a man is saddled with a bad wife, there is sure to be 'stir ups' in the family," read another newspaper aphorism.[48] A Willamette Valley newspaper recounted the story of a woman who was troubled by her husband's scolding. She went to a male soothsayer, who gave her a bottle of liquid to put in her mouth while her husband "was in a passion."[49] The bottle stopped the couple's arguments because, as the soothsayer explained, a husband would not scold a woman who kept her mouth shut. Stories such as these are not irrefutable evidence of intense misogyny, but wives were much more often the butt of newspaper humor than husbands were. This common lampooning of women suggests a general, if often covert, resentment of women and marriage.

Woman as selfless mother and pure goodness resided on the same pages with woman as flirtatious spendthrift and domineering scold. Man's view of woman was not of one piece, and the pieces diverged sharply from each other. Oregon's male settlers, like men in other places, simultaneously revered and feared women, idealized and debased them.[50]

A husband's right to control his wife rested largely on his ability to provide for her. George Bangasser, testifying in a divorce suit for a man he had known for fourteen years, recalled the days when his friend had been "a man . . . when on his farm . . . every body about him had to obey orders."[51] Frances Fernahan of the lower Columbia criticized David Graham by noting that he had frequently seen Graham's wife chopping wood and that she cleared and burned brush while Graham "was sitting by the door of his house smoking his pipe."[52] Likewise, a mill owner criticized one of his employees by saying that "his wife was out chopping wood," and he noted that "the boys at the mill grumbled at seeing the woman cutting wood."[53] A good husband was a good provider. W. C. Nevil of Portland recounted that he reproved his neighbor, Vincent Davis, for gambling away his last cow. Davis admitted that he knew better, "that he was not 'fit' to have a wife" and "would rather be around among the boys."[54] The ability and willingness to support a family separated a boy from a man and constituted the foundation for male authority in the home.

A good husband protected his wife rather than abusing her. "Insted of being a protector . . . and supporter of her and family," observed an eastern Oregon man of a husband, "his presents has been an injury a [unclear] and expence to her."[55] Men were to use violence to safeguard women. This assumption became graphically clear on the overland journey when wagon trains faced attack. A man who crossed in 1863 described how "the women and children were placed inside the inner circle" while "the men were posted in the outer circle of wagons to shoot at the Indians."[56] Reversals of this gendered arrangement struck the immigrants as ridiculous. A participant in an earlier crossing remarked on a woman who sat in a wagon during a disagreement with Native Americans with "a pistol in her lap" while telling a man hiding from the difficulty to "get on the other side of the wagon; be a man!"[57]

Masculinity in settlement-era Oregon required an intimate knowledge of violence. Homesteading entailed the repeated killing at close quarters of domestic and wild animals. Louis Albert Banks's account of growing up in the Willamette Valley during the 1860s dwelled with particular fondness and detail on his initiation into hunting, and he remembered that shooting his first deer left him "wild with excitement and delight."[58] Euro-American males were also socialized to use violence against other humans. Native Americans did not always submit peaceably to conquest, particularly in southern and eastern Oregon. Several large-scale conflicts stretched between the Cayuse War of 1848 and the well-publicized Nez Percé War of 1877. Individual acts of violence were commonplace. Joseph Williams reported that by the early 1840s Willamette Valley native peoples "almost starve for something to eat, which causes them to steal, and then they often get whipped for it."[59] Euro-American men also commonly assaulted each other. Sarah Morris, who arrived in the southern Willamette Valley in 1865, recalled that "the young fellows would fight over politics, over who had the best deer hounds, over their girls, and over anything else, so blue eyes and broken noses were pretty common in those days."[60] Such conflicts occurred frequently in mining-oriented eastern Oregon. In 1863 a newspaper referred to the commencement of "the Fall fights" at Canyon City.[61]

Boys were initiated into violence at an early age. Banks recalled how his mother taught him to read by age seven "by dint of her devotion, and a generous use of plum and cherry switches and various other orchard growths."[62] Teachers often employed such methods. A. J. McNemee began attending Portland schools in the late 1840s and recalled that each of his first four teachers commonly beat their pupils, usually with switches. One gave him such a blow with a ruler that he was bedridden for six weeks. When he went back to school the teacher "reached for the ruler to finish the whipping that had been interrupted some weeks before."[63] Even so, McNemee's mother asked him to return again, admonishing him to answer politely and sit quietly. Classroom violence cut both ways; older boys could end a teacher's tenure by putting him out the school window. School directors therefore "wanted someone who could subdue the big boys and control the school," in George Burnett's words. Burnett established order in his Willamette Valley school when he caught an older student making faces at him and "cuffed his head till it seemed it would snap off." "I never had the least trouble after that," he concluded, and "the students seemed anxious to please me and to learn."[64]

In theory, at least, the movement from girlhood to adulthood exempted women from violence. George E. Cole, on his way to a political convention in Salem in 1853, had an altercation with a woman that

"in case of a man would have called for a thumping."[65] In public, especially, Oregonians suggested that men who beat their wives were not
fit husbands, were not worthy men. A Republican newspaper damned
a Confederate leader by asserting that he was "a jail-bird and wife-
beater."[66] John Campbell, a hotel keeper on the southern coast,
remarked that the defendant in a divorce case was "not any man at all,"
for one morning Campbell found him kicking the plaintiff in the stom-
ach.[67] "Mr Jack's treatment of his wife was anything but manly, it was
brutal," asserted a witness in another suit.[68] Joseph Bachman, brother
of a woman who suffered physical violence, said that his sister's husband "beged me to say nothing about" his striking her, and "that the
like should never occur again." When Bachman learned that his
brother-in-law had broken the promise, he went to him "and on the
side walk in front of his store told him that he was a coundfounded
woman whip[p]er."[69]

Children, too, generally disapproved of wife beating. Edward C.
Blanchard recalled stopping his father from hitting his mother at age
fourteen: "He turned toward me & said 'you take it up then, do you?'—
I told him I did not want to see him strike her."[70] A thirteen-year-old
Willamette Valley girl likewise said she had recently pushed her father
off her mother. A south coast witness in a third divorce suit remembered how one day while tending bar a "little boy told me that his
father was whipping his mother and wanted me to stop it."[71]

Yet prescriptions against wife beating often proved to be brittle when
husbands so commonly viewed wives as their subordinates and so frequently used violence to settle disputes. The violence used to protect
a woman could also be used against her. Ferd Patterson claimed as his
defense for killing a man that the victim had spoken ill of his, Patterson's, fiance. But he also justified his threats to stab his sweetheart—
perhaps the same woman whose good name he had recently defended—
because he suspected her of infidelity.[72]

It is not possible to calculate with any degree of accuracy the actual
level of violence against Oregon's settlement-era wives. It is clear that
men seldom killed women. Only 6 of the 111 victims of Oregon homicides listed in a Salem paper from 1850 to 1866 were women, and only
3 were killed by their husbands. (These figures do not include Native
Americans.) The mortality schedules for 1850, 1860, and 1870 listed
no women among 20 adult murder victims for the previous one-year

periods. Yet divorce records reveal that Oregon husbands commonly used physical force on their wives. Some wives described frequent beatings. Fannie Barman indicated that her husband had slapped her three days after their 1866 marriage and that he thereafter hit or threw furniture at her weekly. "There was hardly a week passed without his striking or kicking me," recalled Sarah Steele of her husband, Samuel.[73] Most wives described more sporadic violence, but they also described husbands who used violence without much apparent reluctance.

Several distinguished Oregon settlers used violence on their wives. This was particularly so in lightly populated Clatsop County, in the state's northwest corner. Prominent figures whose divorce-seeking wives accused them of physical brutality included William Raymond, an early missionary and Indian sub-agent; Lewis Judson, an early Methodist missionary; D. C. Ireland, Astoria's first newspaper editor and later its mayor; and Michael Meyer, Astoria's first brewer. Susan Shively filed for a divorce in 1856, nine years after her husband John had become Astoria's first postmaster. Her complaint cited "almost every conceivable indignity" inflicted on her by her wealthy husband, including throwing water on her, spitting on her, hitting her with a book, kicking her, trampling some of her clothing, and taking her property and their children.[74] Clearly, economic and social standing was no safeguard from a husband's brutality.

Like their antecedents in Missouri, Oregon husbands commonly defended violence as a legitimate tool to enforce their authority. Pontius Howard had married Sarah in Illinois in 1843 and, according to one of their sons, asserted in 1865 that he had struck Sarah for committing adultery "and he would strike her again if she committed it again."[75] A witness in another suit quoted Henry Fleming as saying that he had kicked his wife "to maintain his authority as the head of the Family."[76] Elizabeth Dixon Smith Geer described a similar incident on the Oregon Trail in 1847. A woman refused to go farther west, and when her husband left her, taking their children, she caught up to one of his wagons and set it on fire. The husband, according to Geer, then "mustered spunk enough to give her a good flogging."[77] Geer's phrasing suggested that the husband would have been remiss if he had not beaten his recalcitrant wife.

Indeed, some accounts of wife beating read as if the husband were disciplining a child. Samuel Parker, the elected captain of a wagon train from Iowa, noted in 1845 that two women in the train had engaged in "a Small puling of hair" over some provisions. Parker ordered a settlement to the argument and "told them for each man to give . . . his wife A good licking that nite not over the Back But not far from the ass and all wod bee well."[78] Melissa Garrett recalled that in the early 1860s her husband had accused her of lying and that when she retorted that he had lied he dared her to repeat it. When she did, he "went out and returned with a stick, and after saying to me that I should now be punished, he struck me several times."[79] Other husbands admitted, apparently without reluctance, to hitting their wives with "a hickory" or "a small switch."[80] The choice to select deliberately a stick with which to administer a beating indicated an assumption that husbands had a right and even a duty to so punish their wives and that such beatings were calculated, even dispassionate.

This is not to say that wife beating was widely sanctioned. As noted above, most settlers appeared to view marital violence as an aberration from the desired norm. Not a few husbands blamed their violent acts on intoxication or an uncontrollable temper. An Oregon City man was heard to admit to pounding and kicking his wife almost unconscious, but explained that he "was drunk at the time."[81] Another husband reportedly tried to excuse his abuse by saying it "was *done in the height of passion.*"[82]

Oregonians' beliefs about violence toward wives were not of one piece. An attorney selected by the state in an 1864 eastern Oregon divorce case presented the traditional understanding. He asserted that the defendant had used only such violence "as was necessary and reasonable to enforce the rightful obedience of pl[ainti]ff to the rightful authority of Def[endan]t as her lawful husband." Violence was seen as a legitimate tool to enforce a husband's "rightful authority." Indeed, the husband in this case reportedly said that he would strike his wife again "if she did not do to suit him."[83] Amanda Leabo's 1870 complaint articulated a different viewpoint. It attributed her husband's violence to his temper and "his bad education, that a man's wife is only his Slave and has no right to say or do any thing or have any rights of her own . . . But must submit to the tyrannical will of her husband as to a lord and master & that he had a right to use threts & force to compel such slavery & submission."[84] Here violence was associated with tyranny, defeated in the Revolutionary War, and slavery, recently destroyed in the Civil War. As in antebellum Missouri and central Illinois, violence toward wives seemed to be undergoing increasing scrutiny as the nineteenth century progressed, as ideals of masculine self-control and a separate and in some respects equal feminine sphere spread westward.

Oregon's Native American women found it very difficult to qualify for protection under this developing norm. A Coos County judge argued in the mid-1870s that a woman's social standing had to be taken into account when deciding what constituted wife abuse: "Language and conduct that would cruelly wound the feelings of one person might often fail to affect in the slightest degree those of another. The amount of suffering depends in great measure upon the education, temperament, manners and social position of the party."[85] Oregonians closely equated dark skin with immorality and savagery. Hence Laura Coggan of the northern Willamette Valley told her husband in the late 1860s that "you abuse me like a slave & talk to me just like I was, some old squaw."[86]

The actual level of violence toward wives among Native Americans before sustained contact with Euro-Americans is difficult to ascertain. Captain Bishop, an English trader wintering on the lower Columbia from 1795 to 1796, hardly three years after contact with the native population had begun, noted that the local Chinookan women "are kept in great Subjection by the men who sometimes beat them unmerciffully."[87] Several observers indicated that Native American husbands harmed their wives over suspected sexual infidelity. A Native American informant from the Willamette Valley recalled that a husband "would whip his wife continually" to extract confessions of adultery.[88] A miner in southern Oregon in the early 1850s noted that the punishment for a woman's adultery was the loss of an eye.[89] Although the evidence is highly biased and fragmentary, it appears likely that violence toward wives preceded the arrival of whites.

The wide-ranging effects of the Euro-Americans' arrival led to an increase of violence and oppression within the Native American community generally. A missionary, writing of the early 1840s, noted that an Indian woman told his wife that poverty and lack of slaves meant that "the drudgery all fell upon the [free] women; . . . so that when their husbands came home weary and hungry, and found no fire and no roots to eat, they were angry, called them lazy, and beat and otherwise abused them." The woman said that she had lessened her work load and hence her beatings by killing her infants, although she had allowed her most recently born child to live, since "her husband had assured her that if she destroyed it he would kill her."[90] This story, if true, is a strong example of how disease, death, poverty, and cultural disintegration could reinforce each other, creating profound marital stresses for Indian women.

Yet Native Americans also opposed violence against wives. In some instances they linked prescriptions against wife beating with Euro-American norms. An 1875 letter from Allen David, an acculturation-minded Klamath leader, asserted that whipping one's wife, like gambling, had to be given up when one decided to "live like a white man."[91] A mother's questions to a prospective son-in-law on western Oregon's Grand Ronde reservation associated the practice with behaviors commonly ascribed to Indians: "Do you ever drink whiskey? Do you gamble? Will you whip Lucy when you are mad?"[92] Such pronouncements may simply have constituted an obeisance to white stereotypes, for native peoples clearly had prescriptions of their own against wife beating. A Wishram tale related how a woman "interfered" when her son-in-law "abused" her daughter.[93] A Klamath born around 1875 recalled that once as a young boy he saw his father "beat my mother with a stick" and that their "neighbors came and stopped it."[94] Even under the extreme pressures of the nineteenth century, it is not clear that wife beating became widely accepted among Native Americans.

There is no doubt that Native American women married to Euro-Americans commonly suffered extensive violence. Missionary Henry Spalding's 1840 whipping of a Nez Percé woman who had run away from her abusive white husband, the mission's blacksmith, vividly underscored the substantial power that white husbands held over their aboriginal wives. The Nez Percé tried to whip the blacksmith, whom they blamed for the marriage's problems, but Spalding stymied them. Divorce petitions from the 1850s and later described other instances of violence by white husbands against Indian wives. Antoine Servant noted in his 1863 answer to his wife's suit that he had warned her prior to their 1857 marriage "that he might at times get drunk and whip her," an admission that men married to Euro-American women seldom if ever made in court.[95] Caroline Evans, a Native American on the south-central coast, testified in 1871 that her husband of some thirteen years had drawn a knife on her and "always kicked me & brused me every body knows that he done it every week or two swearing & cussing."[96] Charlotte Smith, a half-Indian who lived in Clatsop County, testified that her first husband had abused her verbally and that her second, Charles Dodge, pushed and beat her with his hands.[97]

Violence against Native American wives by Euro-American husbands was part of a larger pattern of general physical and sexual assaults against Native American women by Euro-American men. General George Crook, stationed on the California-Oregon border in the mid-1850s, recalled in his autobiography that "it was no unfrequent occurrence for an Indian to be shot down in cold blood, or a squaw to be raped by some brute." Punishment for such offenses was, according to Crook, "unheard of."[98] These outrages occurred most commonly in mining areas, but they happened elsewhere, too. In 1857 a leader of the lower Rogue Indians at the coastal Siletz agency complained that an agent "troubles our women; he beats them."[99] A few years later an agent from Siletz reported that its residents hesitated to send their children, "especially the older girls," to school because its white employees seemed "only here to gratify their lusts."[100] Around the same time and place a William Choate recounted that he and two companions had passed three Native American women on the beach and that his two friends soon returned to them, swearing "they were going to *screw the squaws.*" Choate "heard the squaws halloo like blazes," apparently while his friends raped them.[101] Racism compounded sexism.

Indeed, racism tinctured sexism even when the woman in question was white. Some husbands employed invectives implying that sexual infidelity transformed a Euro-American woman into a woman of color: "lower than a Chinese whore"; "damned Cayuse bitch and squaw"; "damned old black bitch."[102] Husbands commonly linked female and animal sexuality. Robert Gate of eastern Oregon called his wife a whore and a "Coyote-bitch."[103] Henry Fleming, according to his wife's divorce complaint, called her "a damned whoring bitch" and "a dirty slut with all the neighboring dogs after her."[104] Violent husbands' easy and sexually pejorative conflation of femininity, race, and animality describes a violently misogynistic culture that put women of all cultures and stations at risk of physical abuse.

Yet the goals of husbands' violence tended to be directed not at womanhood in general, but at a particular woman's particular acts. Many hit their wives for showing signs of independence or assertiveness. Sarah Ann Hersey said her husband had struck her when she did not obey his order to take a kettle off the fire and had beat her for trying to keep him from severely whipping their young boy. Ella Phillips of the south coast said that when her husband, William, came home late and wanted a meal, "I told him I did not expect him home, then but if he would build a fire I would get him supper." William then called her "a god damed whore," dragged her out of bed two or three times, hit her, and threw a burning lamp at her.[105] Sarah Blanchard, of eastern Oregon, said that her husband first became angry with her in 1849, when "I wanted him to change his shirt": "I took hold of his arm to call his attention to the smell & [he] struck me & cursed me—& said he would put on his clothes when he was a mind to." She went on to describe the problems she had in 1869 getting her husband to work for a man they had hired out to: "I told him Mr. Colvin told me he would have to turn us both off—if he didn't go to work & he said he wouldn't work unless he had a mind to—then I told him I guessed I might go for myself & he might go for himself. He got mad & swore—& I tried to coax him. I went towards him—he told me if I came towards him he would knock me down. I did not think he would do it. I went towards him—he struck me . . ."[106]

Other husbands attacked their wives for hiding their liquor or for asking them why they had stayed out so late.[107] Such violence served to underscore the husband's autonomy and his aloofness from feminine sensibilities.

Husbands often responded violently to wives who persisted in disputing their word. Catherine Johnson said that when her husband "called me a d——d whore" she "told him he should not speak so before the children, that he was a liar. He said if I called him a liar again he'd knock me down. I told him he was telling lies and he knew it. Then he struck me."[108] Simon and Thulia Girty reportedly had a similar altercation on their way from California to Oregon in 1869. A witness recalled that Thulia had been very sick, and that when Simon cursed her and called her lazy she responded, "O Simon you know better than that you know I have been sick." "Don't you dispute my word," Simon retorted, and then rushed at her with a hatchet.[109] "When a quarrel was begun," said a witness of a Portland husband, "the first thing he would do would be to go and get his gun."[110]

Husbands used violence to try to silence their wives. Cecelia Liggett of eastern Oregon said her spouse hit her with a loaf of bread and swore at her for "always growling about something" when she objected to him making her get a stool when she was lame.[111] The son of Sarah and Chauncy Blanchard recounted an argument in which Sarah tried to get Chauncy to fix a stovepipe, "and he told her then he wanted her to hush up—he had heard enough already. She told him she would talk—he jumped up then & said 'you G—d— 'bitch'—'I'll knock you into hell'" and tried to strike her.[112] A witness quoted another eastern Oregon man as telling his wife that "by the humping Jesus if she did not go in the House and stop her noise he would take a club & knock her down."[113] Violence or the threat of violence could be used to stop a woman's voice.

Violence often served to maintain the isolation that many Oregon women suffered from. Martha Taylor of the northern Willamette Valley said that her husband, George, commonly locked her in the house. On one occasion, when she persisted in heading to her mother's, he "caught me around the neck and choked me until I was almost senseless until I was black in the face." Another day, when seven months pregnant, "I was hungry and sick and started to my Fathers to get something to eat." But her husband "overtook me when I got 50 yards from the house, and took me by the hand and dragged me to the house, on the ground and locked me in the house and kept me there that day and night, without any thing to Eat."[114] An eastern Oregon woman asserted that her husband, not long before hitting her, chopped up her saddle: "He said that would keep me at home so I wouldnt get to go and see mother any more."[115] Women's families of origin constituted alternative systems of support and even authority that abusive husbands tried to keep their wives from.

Violence also served to separate a wife from her friends and neighbors. Emeline Goodwin said that her husband fired a gun after she had started to church and at another time threatened to burn up her possessions and lock her out if she attended. Emily Rose, who also lived in eastern Oregon, said that her husband, Ira, became angry while they were going to church because she waited for another woman for a few minutes: "he swore I never was satisfied—unless some body was going along with us . . . he began to curse me swore by the Holy Jesus Christ I should not go to meeting and caught hold of me and slaped me."[116] Other husbands struck wives for trying to seek the protection of neighbors. Mary Davis complained that her husband put his hand on his pistol and said he would kill her if she spoke to a neighboring couple. James and Julia Birnie represented an extreme case of isolation, for they and their child were the only non–Native Americans on a lower Columbia River island. Her father reported that James had "beaten and Shamefully abused" Julia and had threatened to shoot her if she tried to leave the island.[117] Few violent husbands enjoyed as much privacy as James Birnie, but they commonly did what they could to make their home an island of unmonitored male authority.

Violent husbands' thirst for authority runs through settlement-era divorce records like a scarlet thread. A soldier reportedly beat his wife because he wanted her "to obey him as a dog would his master."[118] Paulina Meyer said that her husband had asserted that "he would not be bossed by any woman" as he smashed a chair in front of her.[119] Michael Menges of the Portland area told a third party that his wife "did not do as I wanted her to and damn her if she don't I'll whale her."[120] A minister on the lower Columbia quoted another violent husband as asserting that "there was a rebellion in his house & he had to put it down."[121]

These husbands often expressed a highly traditional understanding of women's place. Stephen Cornett, explaining why he had struck his wife, reportedly asserted that "a man should rule over his wife in every thing except religion— . . . in the kitchen as well as elsewhere."[122] Other husbands struck or otherwise abused their wives for not wanting to perform tasks the women may have considered masculine: hitching up horses, for example, or removing a dead skunk from a well. A man who lived with Henley and Margaret Jackson quoted Henley's outburst when Margaret said she did not feel well enough to plant potatoes: "that is always the way . . . I never can get the Gd D——nd Bitch to do anything."[123] Such men believed that men's traditional prerogatives called for them to control all aspects of the household and that their sex entitled them to use violence when women said otherwise.

Violence often flared in Oregon settlers' homes, then, not simply because men used it to buttress their authority, but because women resisted that authority. Hannah Smith, according to one of her witnesses, did not hesitate to tell her husband that he had picked the wrong location for a well at their south-coast home, asserting that "it was a fool that would want to dig it a way over there." As Hannah went to light her pipe, her husband retaliated by kicking and cursing her, whereupon she raised a stick of wood "and said she dared him to struck her again." Remarked another witness of her: "When she has her head set for any thing & thinks it right she tries to keep it so."[124] Resistance could assume less patent forms. A witness in Mary Hall's divorce suit asserted that "Mrs. Hall would never say any thing in retaliation" to Joseph Hall's abuse. Yet she also described how Joseph ordered Mary to start dinner and got a revolver when she "did not obey him immediately."[125] When Mary persisted in ignoring him he picked up a stick and threatened to strike her. Mary then ran out of the house. Margaret Brack, a settler in the southern Willamette Valley, left her husband, supported herself and her children, and faced down her husband, Philip, to keep them. She recalled how one day at the schoolhouse Philip met her "and refused to let me pass." She pushed him aside, but he persisted, attempting to take their child from her. Margaret then "told him to get out of the door, to go home and attend to his own business, that I was schooling the child . . . that I had supported those children and clothed them well since I left him and he should not take them from me." She took up a stick and threatened to "mash his head . . . If he attempted to take her away I would beat him to death."[126] These women were no respecters of men's alleged right to control their families.

Women with previous marital experience were particularly prone to resist husbands' violence. A daughter of Nancy Fleming by her first marriage recalled that when her step-father kicked Nancy, "mother took up a piece of stove wood and struck him on the shins."[127] A neighbor of Calaphinia Perkins in the northern Willamette Valley recounted a conversation in which she had described a recent fight with her husband, Edward. The quarrel began with a disagreement over whether Calaphinia could leave for an extended visit and heated up when she cursed and threatened Edward for hitting his daughter. He then struck her, and she fought back. Calaphinia informed the neighbor that "she should go where she pleased. She said she wasn't going to be tied to the damned old son of a bitch nor any other man." Calaphinia's age and experience clearly emboldened her. According to the neighbor's report, she reminisced about a former husband who was a "worthless drunken fellow and she shipped him off."[128]

Even spouses who did not use violence indicated that being a woman did not preclude using physical force against a husband. Sarah Ward's strength apparently gave her husband pause. He asserted to a court that "I cannot Strike a woman" for "it is againt my principles." But he also volunteered that "she is very strong & I could not conquer her without nearly killing her."[129] One woman frankly admitted that her husband's strength played a role in whether she decided to use force, remarking that "I scold him some times but I never fought him, he was a very large man and could beat me . . . If I had been a little stronger I might have fought him."[130]

Wives of violent husbands who did not resist physically often did so verbally. A daughter of Mary and Elias Keas said that when her father called her mother "mean names" her mother "would call him names back again. She was good to him when he was to her."[131] Anne McCarty asserted that she was not cross or scolding to her husband "any more than an angel would have been in my place. Any body that could have lived with him and not said anything could not have had a tongue."[132] Such women openly admitted that they did not patiently submit to verbal or physical abuse. A witness in Laura Coggan's divorce suit who said that Laura was "generally Kind" testified that when her husband was angry Laura would ask sarcastically, " 'What can I do for my little boy or my little baby, perhaps I should make a Sugar tit for him.' "[133]

Oregon's Native American women often resisted with particular vigor. Drawing on a tradition of female agency, if not equality, they employed force more readily than most of their Euro-American counterparts. Sarah Winnemucca, a prominent Paiute woman, asserted she would not easily succumb to rape: "If such an outrageous thing is to happen to me, it will not be done by one man or two, while there are two women with knives, for I know what an Indian woman can do . . . for there is no man living that can do anything to a woman if she does not wish him to. My dear reader, I have not lived in this world for over thirty or forty years for nothing, and I know what I am talking about." Indeed, Winnemucca used her knife or hands to protect herself on several occasions, including when a lascivious cowboy touched her while she was sleeping and "I jumped up with fright and gave him such a blow right in the face. I said, 'Go away, or I will cut you to pieces, you mean man!' "[134] The bleeding man fled. Jacob Evans, a white man on the Oregon coast, said that his Native American wife, "like the rest of Indian women," was "high tempered," and a witness remarked that she had a temper "like the rest of the squaws."[135] This ability to fight men was a precious resource. That John Owens, a white man living near The Dalles, reportedly tied up his Indian wife to whip her illustrated not only his brutality, but also her determined resistance. "He could not whip her if she were not tied," recalled an acquaintance.[136]

A pair of divorces involving women who were at least half Native American and their French Canadian husbands illustrates several ways in which abused Native American wives asserted themselves. In 1856, after but two months of marriage, Margarett Dagneau complained that her husband, Edward, had kicked and beaten her and dragged her by the hair. Edward's petition countered that Margarett had been "pulling his hair and wounding by mouth, & repeatedly driving him from the house, and throwing his clothes out after him."[137] Documents in the 1863 divorce suit between Elizabeth and Antoine Servant also described a marriage marked by frequent conflict. Indeed, Antoine's legal answer made no attempt to disguise his violence, which he attributed to "improper and unbecoming conduct in a wife." The document described her as being "peevish, fretful and continually scolding and finding fault with her said husband." Elizabeth asserted that Antoine had slapped and struck her frequently and that "I told him I would not live with him unless he would promise not to abuse me and do better."[138] Margarett Dagneau and Elizabeth Servant apparently resisted their husbands' abuse not only by seeking divorces, but by verbal upbraidings or even, if Edward Dagneau can be believed, by driving a husband from the house.

Native American women also appeared prone to separate from and divorce husbands. Samuel Parker, a minister who visited Fort Vancouver in the 1830s, noted that employees said that they hesitated to marry their partners in part because "these Indian women do not understand the obligations of the marriage covenant" and "might through caprice leave them."[139] Walter G. West, superintendent of the Klamath Indian Agency in the 1920s, remarked that during the nineteenth century the Klamath had been "rather loose in their marital practices."[140] Indeed, a half-Klamath woman named Minnie Corbell recalled successfully escaping her Euro-American husband the day after their wedding, when she was only thirteen.[141] A legacy of feminine independence and relative marital flexibility made desertion and divorce more workable options for Native American women than for their Euro-American counterparts.

German-American women constituted one of the few significant groups of foreign-born Oregonians. Like Native American women, they seemed prone to resist actively their abusive husbands. Michael Meyer, Astoria's first brewer, said that during one quarrel his wife "told me to kiss her ——."[142] Other German-American wives used force. An eastern Oregon attorney said that Simon and Mary Schubnell came to his office to make a settlement and that after some angry words she struck at Simon with a chair and a stick of wood and tried to scratch his face. Julius Lange said that during an argument his wife threw a hot iron at his head, put her nails in his face, and threatened him with a knife. Rosalie Wirtz admitted that when her husband, Jacob, came into a crowded Salem hotel "and called me a whore I picked up a stick of wood and hit him with it."[143]

Margaret Hodes, also a German-American woman, waged an ongoing and explicit struggle against her husband, Gustav. Margaret testified that "when he was sober I talked back to him," and she admitted to throwing a pitcher at her spouse. Gustav chalked their troubles up to a disagreement over a boarder whom she wanted him to fire and whip, asserting that "she has raised hell ever since." A woman witness attributed "the whole difficulty" to "crossways" dispositions: "he is too overbearing rough, and she is too overbearing fine. She is a very nice woman except her overbearing ways." An old farmer described Margaret as "a dreadful scold of a woman" and compared her to a "smoking chimney."[144]

In sum, German-American and particularly Native American women seemed most capable of taking to heart Duniway's assertion that "we'd like to see the man who'd undertake to abuse and browbeat a woman, who sets her head that she won't stand it."[145] The rugged nature of the settlement experience encouraged in even many native-born white wives a spirit of strength and independence that stood them in good stead when facing physically abusive spouses. The elaboration of genteel feminine norms still had a long way to go in Oregon by the time of the Civil War. To the extent that such an ideology did take root, however, it was most influential among the native-born middle class. Wives with a background of Native American or German traditions seldom felt its constraints.

All Euro-American women who left even highly abusive husbands courted social shame. As Duniway put it: "Let the subtle poison of falsehood touch her ever so lightly, and her social damnation is assured."[146] William Thompson, who came to Oregon in 1853, recalled the settlers' "stern code of morals," a point he illustrated by citing a social gathering at which women shunned a divorcee.[147] Dr. Owens-Adair referred to her divorce as a "stigma . . . which would cling to me all my future life."[148] Women's vulnerability to such criticism explained why a woman like Maria Shriver felt compelled to remarry her husband, though he had cursed her, failed to support her, accused her of adultery, and finally left her before their first divorce: "He said he would do any thing that was possible if I would take him again. I considered it my duty to try to forgive for the past."[149]

A woman's duty as a wife dovetailed with her duty as a mother. Children of divorced parents faced substantial difficulties. Ed Carr recalled that "in 1859, when my father and mother were divorced, not only the divorced couples were looked at askance but the children of divorced parents were pariahs and were treated as if they themselves were responsible, and were held up as terrible examples."[150] One wife remarked that "I have not Mutch Com Fourt" with her husband, "but he is the father of All My Children And so it is and I have to Beare it."[151] A series of letters between Annie Vririni, a young woman whose mother had separated from Annie's father, and Joseph Vririni, that father, illustrates the sort of strains that mothers who left their husbands faced. In 1874 Annie, then about ten years old, wrote that her mother "dont Want to live With no man no more if She Would Die." But Annie added that "to please us mama Said you come and keep peice and live With us as our father." Four years later, after sporadic contact with the family, Joseph wrote Annie and her brother that "one day, . . . you will see how much wrong" their mother had done to them "to deprive me, and keep me separeted from you."[152] Mary Vririni had originally applied for a divorce in 1869, citing an instance in which her husband had driven a fork far into her breast, several other acts of violence and abuse, and lack of support. Yet Mary, mindful of her children's desires, had not received a divorce by 1883 and had apparently tried to live with the father of her children at least occasionally.

Women who left violent husbands commonly courted poverty as well as notoriety. One witness remarked of an eastern Oregon wife that she "was a neat and tidy woman and industrious & I often remarked that if she had a husband half as good as she was they would be rich."[153] The compliment underscored women's economic vulnerability: even the most industrious wife had to depend largely on her spouse for support. To be sure, some settler women did much better on their own than with a husband. But the great majority of wives who worked outside the home ended up cleaning other people's houses, taking in washing, or sewing. These jobs paid but a fraction of what even a laboring man could make, and the circuit courts seldom awarded alimony or child support. Even wives who had suffered physical violence cited nonsupport as the key reason for leaving their husband. Theresa Cagle of the Willamette Valley complained that when her husband beat her in bed, "I told him I could stand it no longer, and would not live with him any more. He never has provided anything for me."[154] A witness in a different case testified that she had heard another wife say of her husband "that she was willing to put up with almost anything and live with him if he would only provide for her, and not drink so much."[155] Duniway, in arguing for women's full access to the professions, asserted that "women are mistreated by brutal husbands because of their pecuniary helplessness."[156] Women often stayed with these brutal husbands for that same reason.

Isabella Rude faced a particularly difficult struggle in keeping and supporting her child. She married Thompson Rude in Iowa in 1861, and they crossed the Plains after he had served for two years in the Civil War. Thompson hit Isabella in the face and several times accused her of unchastity before driving her away in March 1866. But the people she fled to "advised me to go back and said that he might get my child on the plea that I had left him. Rather than to leave my child I returned home the same day." The next morning her husband cursed her "and said If I would not leave he would." He deserted the family, although Isabella "talked kindly to him and tried to get him to stay at home." She then had to hire out at several places to support herself and her eight-month-old child. One of the women she worked for later recalled telling her that "it was wicked for a woman in her [weak] condition to work." Isabella replied that "if it was not for her child she would sooner die than live." Several months later Thompson returned, promising to do better. But he was soon cursing her again, and Isabella continued to be the family's main support by taking in washing.

Thompson slapped her and in April 1868 "left me in a rented house and one months rent due without a dollars worth of provision."[157] Isabella continued to eke out a living by taking in washing. Within a year, and despite all her sacrifices, her only child died.

Oregon's legal system sometimes benefited abused wives such as Isabella Rude. Some women used the threat of divorce against their husbands. Mary Ann Keas explained that she had told her husband "several times before he left that I would apply for a Divorce if he did not do better."[158] Peace officers occasionally fined or jailed husbands on assault charges. An 1876 article in a Clatsop County newspaper noted that a local judge had just sentenced a wife beater to a $25 fine plus costs or thirty days in jail, and that "the justice threatens that he has his eye on two or three more in the city whom he soon expects to enlighten upon 'domestic administration.' "[159] Some wives took the initiative in securing such services. Mary Etta Hall said that when her husband threatened to kill her if she visited her mother "I told him I thought there was a law that would take care of a man that would make such threats as that." When he then struck her and expelled her from the house she "went to see a Justice of the Peace," and her husband left.[160] Some husbands realized that wife beating could lead to jail. Catherine Varney testified that after her husband hit her with a fire shovel he showed her how it had cut her "but says he[,] mind you if you go into court it will have to be a bruise."[161] Jennette Bloway testified that when her husband began abusing her after beating her the day before "I then went out and got an officer . . . to arrest him—he took him to jail—The next morning I left the house— . . . Since then I have not lived with him."[162] Even a brief incarceration could offer wives enough time to escape from a violent home.

But wife beaters seldom went to jail. During a fourteen-month period from 1867 to 1868 only three husbands faced charges in the city of Portland for assaulting their wives.[163] Most women married to violent husbands depended on less formal assistance.

Mid-nineteenth-century Oregonians commonly identified a woman's family of origin, particularly her father, as her natural protector. Royal Bensell, a corporal in the Willamette Valley, remarked of a young woman widowed in 1864 that she "is now defenceless as her relatives are all dead."[164] Abusive husbands seemed well aware of the protective role that a wife's family might play. The divorce complaint of a woman who came to Oregon in 1852 noted that "as soon as they left the place where her relatives lived in Illinois he, defendant, commenced a course of [ill] treatment."[165] Melinda Jane Riggs likewise indicated in her complaint that her husband had taken her to California "where she had no friends or relatives to look to for care or support if she left him." Her husband later abandoned her in eastern Oregon where "I was amongst strangers and had no relations there and no means to come home with."[166] A woman's family could provide an alternative source of authority and support.

Yet a reflexive and pervasive fear of divorce commonly conditioned the sort of aid that parents proffered their abused daughters. S. S. Brown, the defendant in a southern Willamette Valley divorce case, claimed that his wife's parents "told her she had to go home" when she left him and went to their house.[167] Likewise, Anna Gamble returned to her violent husband "on the advice of my brother."[168] Dr. Bethenia Owens-Adair recalled her parents' reactions when she told them "I did not think I could stand it much longer." "Mother was indignant, and told me to come home," that "with his temper, he is liable to kill you at any time." But Bethenia's father wept, lamenting that "there has never been a divorce in my family" and telling her "to go back, and try again." Only if Bethenia found that she "*cannot possibly* get along" was she to "come home."[169]

Abused wives' return to paternal protection became particularly problematic when they had defied paternal authority in marrying. An early Oregon newspaper carried an apparently fictional story in which a young woman against her father's orders wed a dissipated suitor who deserted her after a year's abuse. The young woman at last returned home, but had become so weak that she collapsed on her parents' doorstep and lived only long enough to seek and receive their forgiveness. Melinda Jane Riggs, an actual woman who had flouted parental authority, pursued a similar, though less tragic, course. Samuel Parker, her stepfather, noted that in 1860 she had "married Def[endan]t against mine and her mothers will." About two years later Melinda came to their house, soon followed by her husband, Roland, who "acknowledged that he had abused and mistreated her and promised to do better" if she would return, which she did. In 1868 an eastern Oregon man wrote Parker that Melinda had been living at his house for about one year after being deserted and that her husband had taken some of her children from her. Melinda had told him "that She had almost as soon dye as to have to write home for help for she had disobeyed her parents in marrying this rogue and that she did not feel herself at liberty to ask for help."[170] Melinda eventually received her parents' assistance, but only after years of suffering.

Parents and other family members intervened more readily against violent acts than to help end marriages. Malissa Miller's mother said that she ran to her daughter's rescue when she saw Malissa's husband trying to throw her over a fence. The sister of Mary Etta Hall testified that when her sister's husband started after Mary Etta with a sharp stick "I caught hold of him and stopped him as well as I could."[171] But these sorts of interventions were not common during the settlement period, in part because many women lived far from their family of origin.[172]

Children often represented a more reliable source of aid for abused wives than parents did. George Kandle, whose father had threatened to kill him, said that he and his mother slept behind doors that "are barred with boards at night for fear of father" and that he, George, "would not stay at all except to protect my mother."[173] Even young children sometimes prevented attacks. Mary Wilkinson said that when her husband approached her with a razor while she slept "the little girl seen him and screamed out and told him that he should not kill her ma." The husband reportedly told a third party that he intended to cut Mary's throat, but that "the child would scream" and that he therefore "could not have the heart to do it."[174] Irvin Sanburn recalled that he came home to find his mother crying, with her face in her hands, and that when he asked her what the matter was she showed him "where Mullins had struck her." Sanburn then went to Mullins, his stepfather: "I says Billy whats the matter with Ma. he mad no reply I said do you not know better than to strike a woman."[175] Mature children from previous marriages offered wives particularly strong protection.

Wives more often relied on neighbors than family to intervene against violent husbands. Catherine Varney said that when her husband of nearly thirty years pushed her into a corner she asked their daughter "to go and tell the neighbors how her father was abusing me."[176] Joseph Vririni, the defendant in a divorce suit, claimed that he had never struck his wife, and "if I would have done it she would have told it to the world."[177] A witness in an eastern Oregon divorce suit remarked that the husband had left because "in beating her he was afraid the affair would be investigated . . . I do not think any thing else would have driven him away from his family."[178]

The concept of familial privacy was not well-developed in mid-nineteenth-century Oregon, and people commonly took an interest in their neighbors' marriages. J. B. Sams, for example, recalled chatting with William Purceil and remarking that "I never had any thing come over me and strike me so as your conduct to your wife in election day," when Purceil had spoken rudely to his spouse.[179] Violent husbands who lived with boarders or landlords were particularly apt to face opposition from third parties. A Portland boarder testified that one day "I came into the House" and found Joseph Bloway choking and trying to strike Jennette Bloway: "I immedetly took hold of him and took him away . . . This was the day before they separated."[180] Likewise, John Campbell, a south coast hotel keeper, said that he "often kept" a boarder, Patrick Monaghan, "from whipping" Margarite Monaghan.[181] Even strangers might step into a home to stop a violent husband. Catherine O'Donald recounted how a man who had heard her husband swear at her came to the door of their Salem residence and told him that he had come "to prevent him from beating me."[182]

The domestic architecture of mid-nineteenth-century Oregon facilitated this sort of intervention. In 1867 a resident of rapidly growing and densely built Portland remarked of a couple that "I live next door so that I can hear most every thing they say," including the husband's threat to kill his wife.[183] Eastern Oregon's dynamic and thickly populated gold-rush towns of the early 1860s afforded particularly scant privacy. George Lewis recalled that in 1862 he lived next to a couple "in adjoining rooms without board partitions between us" and that the husband would come home "drunk and whip his wife."[184] Joseph Brown remembered that an abusive husband had "lived in a canvass house, within a few feet of where I did" in The Dalles and that he saw the man's wife "come out of the house with her face all bruised up and bloody, just after they had a row in the house."[185] Other witnesses in this and other early eastern Oregon divorce suits testified that they viewed or intervened against wife abuse in the region's highly public towns.[186]

Men appeared to be more apt to interfere directly with a violent husband, but women often offered more sustained support. Their assistance could include physical intervention. Bell Hulsey of eastern Oregon said that George See came into her house with a whip while his wife, Amanda, was visiting her. When he "raised the whip to strike her, . . . I steped in between them and said he should not horse whip her in my house." Amanda recalled Hulsey telling her that "I should not go home unless he . . . would promise that he would not whip me."[187] Women more commonly offered shelter to abused wives. Lizzie Baughman of Portland testified that one such woman "has come into my house some two or three times, crying" after her husband had abused her.[188] Another Portland woman, Clara Friendley, said that a neighbor who lived two blocks away "always came over to my house" when the woman "had difficulty" with her husband.[189] Wives in smaller towns also went to their neighbors. Agnes Labriere, of Empire City on the south coast, said that Catharine Clark "has come to my house asking for protection" from her husband, who followed and threatened to kill Catharine, "upon one occasion breaking the window lights."[190] This sort of crucial, high-risk assistance, conducted by women for women's benefit, is reminiscent of patterns discerned among New York City's nineteenth-century working class by Christine Stansell and Pamela Haag.[191]

Lack of privacy could deter violence. The wife of Willamette Valley farmer Joseph Hall said that he hit her, but that "when other people were present he was more careful."[192] Eastern Oregon's Georgina McKinzie said that her husband was still more discreet. He had struck her, but "even while abusing me if any person would come in he would stop talking and appear as if all was pleasant between us."[193] A good many settler husbands who harmed their wives did not seem greatly concerned with who witnessed the abuse. But such husbands lived in a society in which community members frequently viewed abuse and not infrequently took steps to end it.

Not all women had access to this sort of support. Julie Birnie, the woman who lived on an island inhabited only by Native Americans, her child, and her violent husband, was an extreme example. Almira Raymond, whose spouse was first a missionary and then an Indian subagent, seldom enjoyed the company of other settlers. In 1840, while still in the Willamette Valley, she wrote to her parents that "I am without female society."[194] Later, on the coast, she lived nearly one mile's distance from white neighbors at one post, two miles at another. Almira and her husband, William Raymond, received radically different sorts of support during their divorce. William had testimony from several leading citizens of Clatsop County, the fruits of his long public life. One of his friends even wrote to say that while at Oregon City he had "headed off an application for a division of the claim" by Almira "that would not have suited you" and "had a talk with Judge Olney about it."[195] Almira's witnesses, on the other hand, consisted almost entirely of her children and their spouses.[196]

A growing sense of familial privacy or simply apathy could also undercut community intervention against violent husbands. E. G. Dodge, a northern Willamette Valley farmer, said that when a husband began to verbally abuse his wife "I saw how things were going & I got up & left."[197] Mary Corcoran, who lived with a couple in Portland, recalled that when she walked into an argument the wife "did not want me to see how he behaved toward her & told me to go into my room."[198] Neighbors sometimes hesitated to intervene, even when a woman seemed at great risk. A witness in one divorce suit noted that "the community generally believed that the pl[ainti]ff was in danger of her life," but he and other witnesses indicated that they helped the plaintiff only when she requested it.[199] Duniway complained that men too often ignored battered wives even when the women did seek help, citing a newspaper article that remarked that a woman's assault charges against her husband made no headway because "no one feels enough interest in the matter to find out which story is true."[200]

Community members seemed particularly lax in coming to the aid of abused wives who appeared strong or independent. This was particularly so of Native American wives, whom Euro-Americans commonly perceived as inherently lascivious. Sarah Winnemucca, the Paiute woman who actively fought off male attackers, faced numerous charges of immorality throughout her very public adult life. In 1879, after she had apparently been divorced but once, the *San Francisco Chronicle* accused her of having "an extensive and diversified matrimonial experience, the number of her white husbands being variously estimated at from three to seven." An Indian agent she charged with defrauding and abusing her people retaliated by gathering affidavits that described her as "a Harlot and drunkard."[201] Abused Euro-American women also found that the sort of explicit resistance that served them well in their homes could work against them in the broader community. The courts discriminated against overtly strong wives, and determined attorneys for husbands or the state commonly put them on the defensive in court, sometimes costing them a divorce, custody of their children, or property. Strong women risked forfeiting the sense of paternalism that might elicit sympathy or assistance. Maria Besserer of eastern Oregon said that her husband "always struck me several times before I ever [even?] attempted to defend myself." But Emil Meyer testified that when the couple got in a dispute one day at his home he "rushed into the house" when "the dispute grew violent" and saw "both parties striking and kicking each other." Meyer tried to stop the fight but "saw that I could not stop them and so I went into the Brewery about my business."[202] Meyer did not feel obligated to defend a woman who was defending herself.

The churches' treatment of wife beating underscored the benefits and costs of paternalism. Preachers and laypeople alike typically urged wives to stay with their husbands unless the husbands had committed adultery. Bethenia Owens-Adair recalled that an old family friend advised her to go back to her husband "and beg him on your knees to receive you," even after she explained that he had "whipped my baby unmercifully, and struck and choked me." The friend (who years later reversed her position when one of her own daughters suffered at the hands of a violent husband) asserted that "the scriptures forbid the separation of man and wife for any other cause than adultery."[203] Churches typically tried hard to keep couples together, and some of them disciplined members who sought separation or divorce on grounds other than adultery. In 1847, for example, a northern Willamette Valley Baptist church expelled John Holman for refusing to live with his wife. But churches also became involved with abusive husbands. In 1875 B. Dorris of Eugene's First Baptist Church charged William Parker of being "guilty of conduct unbecoming a christian" toward Parker's wife because some twelve days before "he *struck* her one or more Blows on the face or side of the head with his fist or open hand."[204] Parker at first denied the charge, then asked to have his name dropped from the church's membership rolls, a request the congregation unanimously acceded to. Church records are too thin and incomplete to support detailed generalizations about how religion affected violence against settler wives. In general, however, churches opposed both violence against wives and women's flight from that violence.

Margaret Bailey, a former Methodist missionary, paid a particularly dear price for her highly visible resistance to her husband's violence. She noted that one of the Methodist mission workers told her that the mission family, with whom she had fallen out, predicted trouble for her when she married Dr. Bailey: "you'll not live together long—they know his character and temper, and think that *you* are too independent to bear with him."[205] Margaret did indeed manifest independence in her marriage to her abusive husband. She fled from him, remonstrated with him, shut him out of a room, and took from him money she considered her own. She also presented her views of the marriage in a very thinly disguised 1854 novel that outraged many Oregon settlers and brought the heavy weight of male censure down on her. In 1882 a retired Hudson's Bay Company employee, who had taken Margaret horseback riding on her first day in Oregon some forty-five years before, noted that she was living in destitution in Seattle at age seventy. Dr. Bailey, in contrast, had continued his career as a physician and stood as the Democratic gubernatorial candidate in 1855, only one year after Margaret had divorced him.[206] Oregon's leading men could more easily forgive a wife beater than a woman who had publicly criticized her husband and other prominent citizens.

The lives of women like Margaret Bailey cannot be understood outside the context of larger social and cultural forces at work in the nation and in Oregon. Wives in mid-nineteenth-century Oregon, like their counterparts in Missouri and central Illinois before them, lived in a society characterized both by pronounced male dominance and by the general use of violence to establish and buttress various types of dominance. Most men who addressed the issue of wife beating condemned it. But these same men also typically assumed that a man had authority over his wife as he did over his children, and many believed that a woman could be hit for flouting that authority. Like a child, the ideal wife was obedient and submissive.

But women had ideas of their own about a wife's place. Linda Gordon argues in her history of impoverished twentieth-century Boston families that violence against wives is not simply the story of male brutality. It also arises from women's resistance to male domination, a domination much larger than wife beating.[207] Men's violence may escalate as women's resistance to male oppression grows more determined.

In settlement-era Oregon, violence toward wives commonly occurred around instances of women contesting male authority. This was especially true of Native American wives, women removed from the increasingly influential norms of middle-class domesticity.

Only a fraction of wives could count on outsiders to intercede against a brutal man. Some lived with boarders or relatives who might intervene to stop a husband's abuse. Yet these people did not uniformly come to the aid of wives, and those who did often counseled reconciliation over separation or divorce. Many women, furthermore, lived far from friends, neighbors, or their families of origin. These women had to depend on themselves. Not a few had wed in their mid-teens, to older and powerful men. But the balance of marital power became less skewed over time, as wives became stronger and more experienced, abetted in their strength and autonomy by the same social forces that isolated them from each other.

Social isolation, nascent and rudimentary economies, skewed gender ratios—all these factors served to move Oregon's settlers back in time as they moved westward in space. But the characteristics that set Oregon apart from larger national trends were evanescent. They receded as soon as they appeared, as durable towns and cities arose, markets and transportation spread, and families multiplied. Never again would Oregon's history be so conditioned by the local, the traditional, the idiosyncratic. Its future, in every respect, would be increasingly and inextricably bound up with the nation's.

National trends would condition the nature of Oregon's marriages no less than the nature of its particular demography or economy. Marital relations shifted in the United States during the first half of the nineteenth century. The spread of bourgeois social and family norms qualified husbands' household authority and made violence toward wives less acceptable. This trend was first apparent among the middle class of the Northeast. It had spread to parts of the Midwest by the 1830s and 1840s, and by the close of the Civil War it was increasingly evident in Oregon. Within a few decades, in the 1890s, this new understanding of marital roles would become the norm across the state, profoundly altering both the nature of violence toward wives and wives' reaction to it.

— 2 —

"When a Man Stoops to Strike a Woman": The 1890s

By the late nineteenth century bourgeois culture had become influential across the United States. There were, to be sure, holdouts, groups and individuals who continued to practice more traditional ways: farmers who favored subsistence crops, artisans who clung to hand-oriented craft skills, fathers who perceived themselves as absolute heads of their households. On the other extreme, small but growing numbers of urbanites looked forward to a new era dominated by a less moralistic ethos: disaffected writers, such as Frank Norris, who brought to their art a decidedly nongenteel, even amoral realism; and members of the upper class who pursued excesses in wealth and consumption as ends in themselves. The leading edge of urban culture foreshadowed a second great cultural transition, one that would ultimately repudiate the themes of self-discipline and self-control that had come to the fore during the nineteenth century.

Oregon, outside of Portland, showed few signs of anticipating the twentieth century at the end of the nineteenth. To be sure, the state's population had grown markedly since 1870, at a faster rate than the nation as a whole. By 1890 Oregon's population was 318,000, a more than threefold increase in only two decades. During the 1890s it gained another 96,000, the nation's severe depression notwithstanding. Local rail lines that began in the 1870s and the long-awaited national connection in 1887 quickened a movement toward market-oriented agriculture, general material progress, and a more cosmopolitan outlook. But Oregon remained largely rural. By 1900 Portland was the only city in the state whose population exceeded 10,000. Marshfield, the largest town on the south coast, did not even have 1,500. Canyon City and Prineville, county seats in eastern Oregon, had far fewer. Nor had manufacturing progressed very far. Only about 8,000 of the state's 310,000 non–Multnomah County residents worked in factories by 1900. Nearly half of Oregon's non-Portland male work force labored directly in agriculture, not counting lumber.[1]

Like the settlers before them, the Oregonians who lived outside Multnomah County in the 1890s were a homogeneous lot. Only about 14 percent had been born overseas. Only about 3 percent were people of color: Asian American, African American, or Native American. Most of them had roots in the Midwest and could be considered part of the middle class, broadly defined. Some 87 percent of farms, for example, were owner operated. These native-born, non–Multnomah County whites also had relatively even sex ratios: 1.21 men for each woman by 1890. The ratio was a bit higher in remote parts of eastern Oregon and on the coast, a bit lower in the Willamette Valley. Everywhere it was much more balanced than it had been in the 1850s, and everywhere women exercised more public influence than before. Rural and small-town Oregon had matured into the sort of society that had dominated the United States for most of the nineteenth century, one that emphasized economic progress, discipline, hard work, moral self-control, and separate spheres for women and men.[2]

The displacement of a masculine, often inchoate settlement society by a more orderly and feminized one had obvious ramifications for the history of violence against wives. The growing ideal of women's equality made it more difficult for husbands to claim violence as a legitimate tool for coercing wives' obedience; more important still, the general ethos of self-control meant that even many abusive husbands internalized the idea that hitting a woman was unmanly. Other developments were not as salutary. Romantic love altered the nature of violence against wives even as that violence declined, and wives generally resisted violence more cautiously than their settlement-era counterparts had. The florescence of bourgeois values in Oregon left wives more secure from violence in some respects, less secure in others.

*　　*　　*

Oregon women's roles had shifted by the 1890s. A witness in an eastern Oregon divorce suit remarked that Eliza Osborn "always had to keep up the fences and improvements" on a homestead "and did a mans work all the time ... I have seen her out in the field harrowing and putting in the grain."[3] A woman's work and a man's work were not to overlap much. A study of late-nineteenth-century gender roles on Willamette Valley farms found that although women commonly milked cows, tended poultry, and gardened, most farm work was sex segregated, with only young girls doing much fieldwork and only young boys doing much housework. Women in the United States worked in a growing number of occupations in the late nineteenth century. In Oregon, however, this trend affected relatively few rural women and few wives. The 1900 census listed less than 8 percent of non-Portland females as employed and only 15 percent of women employed throughout the state as being married. Rural and small-town women's work had, on the whole, become more distinguishable from their husbands'.[4]

Women's social influence rose as their economic influence declined. Baptist women began taking a more active part in church work after the Civil War, a trend that accelerated in the 1890s. The Oregon Grange, a social and political organization for farmers, utilized women in a variety of public roles by the 1880s, as did the Populists in the 1890s. Lydia Ann Buckman Carter arrived in the northern Willamette Valley in 1867 and later recalled that women at local grange meetings "were supposed to cook the meals and to be seen and not heard."[5] But Carter began debating male members and won election as her grange's master in 1879. Most settlement-era women had been too isolated or overworked to form the sorts of social, reform, or political organizations that men had quickly built. That changed dramatically in 1881 when the Woman's Christian Temperance Union appeared in Oregon. Only a decade later Oregon's W.C.T.U. had nearly 2,000 members in seventy-one chapters. This added up to a lot of women questioning men's behavior. In 1891 members of the chapter in Elgin, a small eastern Oregon town, reported that they had convinced one church to discontinue the use of fermented wine and were circulating a petition to prevent the licensing of a new saloon. Members of the Forest Grove chapter, in the northern Willamette Valley, noted that they had staged a successful boycott to halt a new saloon and had uncovered a gambling den, as well as three establishments selling liquor clandestinely. The 1898 state convention rejoiced upon hearing of a marker at one place that read:

Died,
A Saloon.
Nagged to death by Women[6]

Like so many of women's reform movements, Oregon's W.C.T.U. did not launch a frontal attack on the cult of domesticity, on women's exclusion from the public sphere. But it emphasized women's rights within the home, rights so dear that in their defense women might step beyond the boundaries of the home to reform men's habits and even politics. Formed in 1889, Oregon's Federation of Women's Clubs constituted another powerful vehicle for women reformers. By 1902 it had thirty-six chapters and nearly 1,500 members devoted to improving themselves and their society. Commenting on Oregon women's first temperance movement, in 1874, Frances Fuller Victor had noted that only one of their number had ever spoken in public.[7] By 1900 that act had become commonplace.

Oregon women's status and influence had also risen within the home by 1900. Court records from the 1890s occasionally referred to "wifely kindness[,] submission[,] and devotion," but this sort of language appeared more rarely than it had before.[8] Indeed, the legal complaint of Ida Brown, an eastern Oregon woman, identified such ideas as retrograde and uncivilized and blamed them for her husband's abusive behavior. The plaintiff, the complaint explained, had come from the North, where she "had been accustomed to being treated as man's equal, and not as a slave." But her husband, a southerner and ex-Confederate soldier, "acted towards her as though he was her master." He had informed her on their wedding day that "he was a man who believed that women were only made for men's convenience" and that he expected complete obedience from her. An amended complaint asserted that Frank Brown was "an ignorant, uneducated man, not being able to either read or write, and belonging to the class there [in the South] designated as 'poor whitetrash'" who had "acquired the style from living among slaves and slave beaters, of treating his wife as he saw the slaves treated."[9] For Ida Brown and her attorney, Frank

Brown's traditional beliefs regarding women's subservience and inferiority, his social background as an unlettered Confederate, and his
brutality toward his wife were all of a piece, each reinforcing the other.
Rural Oregon in the 1850s and 1860s had been a highly masculine
society, both in numbers and in general culture. By the 1890s, patriarchal attitudes like those imputed to Frank Brown had become more
suspect and less common.

Self-restraint was the handmaiden of feminization. E. Anthony
Rotundo notes that "above all, a boy learned from his mother to hold
back his aggressions and control his own 'male' energies." "When the
conscience of a nineteenth-century man spoke," he concludes, "it generally spoke in feminine tones."[10]

Yet women's capacity to act overtly on their own behalf diminished
even as their broader influence increased. Ann Douglas has explored
this paradox among well-to-do women who became marginalized in
their everyday life despite the "feminization of American culture."[11]
Oregon's settlement-era wives had often exercised a sort of rugged
aggressiveness with their husbands. Abigail Scott Duniway, one of a
handful of highly public women, had employed ridicule and invective
as readily as her male counterparts. By the century's turn, women tended
to be more circumspect. The magazine of the Oregon and Washington State Federations of Women's Clubs in 1903 published a "matrimonial creed" that closed with this advice: "Let him think how well you
understand him; but never let him know that you 'manage' him."[12]

In sum, by the 1890s women's roles in rural and small-town Oregon approximated patterns established earlier in the century in the
Northeast. Historians are far from agreed on the precise nature of this
movement to separate and more equal spheres for women and men,
or on how salutary its effects were for women. But it appears that nineteenth-century wives generally favored the creation of a more distinct
gender role. This sphere had some well-marked limits, and it surren-
dered the basis by which women could claim explicit political and economic equality. But by emphasizing women's moral authority, it created opportunities for political agitation by groups such as the
Woman's Christian Temperance Union. In the home, it gave women
a basis for requiring men to respect their ascribed strengths and weaknesses.[13]

This bourgeois gender system circumscribed male behavior. As before, being a man started with being a good provider. A south-coast logger who boarded with Matt and Sarah Anderson remarked that "Mrs. Anderson was the main support of the family" and that therefore if Matt "was any relative of mine I would kill him for the good of the family."[14] But by the late nineteenth century a good husband had to be more than a good breadwinner. Joseph Hanna, an Oregon minister, identified "character" as "so much more than wealth or knowledge, fame or power, that it is the *measure* of *the man*."[15] Good character manifested itself as self-control. A south-coast man castigated his son-in-law by describing him as a man who "loses complete control of himself on a small provocation . . . He is not fit to live with white folks at all."[16] "By the end of the century," observes Gail Bederman, "a discourse of manliness stressing self-mastery and restraint expressed and shaped middle-class identity."[17]

A growing emphasis on marital intimacy and mutuality also shaped the accepted limits of male authority and autonomy. Julia Couch, a Willamette Valley woman seeking a divorce, cited nonsupport as only one of several abuses her husband had inflicted upon her: "He has treated me bad. He did not provide for me, he has cursed me, and called me vile names, would go away from home and not come back untill one or two oclock at night, and leave me alone."[18] Couch's complaint began with her husband's failures as a provider and ended with his failures as a companion. "When the companionate ideal was emotionally charged with romantic love," explains Karen Lystra, "it was a powerful counterbalance to male dominance."[19]

Not all men acceded to these rising standards for husbands' behavior. A. W. Fellows wrote a friend in Coos County from California in 1897 to report on his poker winnings and to declare that "a man is a damb fool to work and try to be sober honest or upright." He closed by noting that he had just been asked out for a drink and that he would not refuse, "for you know the good book says Eat *drink* and be *merry* to day for tomorrow *you may die*." Fellows's wife complained that he had refused to provide for her, that he had ordered her to go out into deep snow to chop wood less than two weeks after she had given birth, and that he had threatened to put her in charge of a whore house so they could live in luxury. Fellows had clearly rejected the ideal of masculine industriousness and self-control. But he also realized that this rejection set him against established norms. Indeed, an anonymous group of community members in Washington state had reportedly threatened to "call upon" Fellows if he did not "get out, get to work and do something to support his wife and babies."[20] Historians of masculinity are beginning to explore the subtle ways in which late-nineteenth-century men chafed against their roles as responsible, disciplined breadwinners. But men such as Fellows, men who carried their dissatisfaction to the point of open irresponsibility, courted being expelled, perhaps literally, from respectable society.[21]

The belief that husbands should treat their wives respectfully and gently, as Christian gentlemen, crested in the nineteenth century's last years in rural and small-town Oregon. To the state's women, who had done so much to create and maintain it, this development offered a potent tool with which to condemn irresponsible and abusive husbands. For husbands, the ethic of inward self-restraint and outward deference toward women became part of how they defined themselves, of how they measured their success as head of the family.

It was difficult to reconcile self-control with wife beating. Violence against wives had excited inconsistent condemnation during Oregon's settlement era. Many regarded the practice as unmanly; but many others, certainly many violent husbands, perceived it as a legitimate means by which to reprimand a recalcitrant or scolding wife. The practice had fewer defenders by the 1890s.

Frederic Homer Balch's *Bridge of the Gods*, probably the decade's most popular Oregon novel, identifies wife beating as a savage practice. Set in the Pacific Northwest around 1700, the book features a young protagonist named Cecil who had traveled to the Columbia River to convert its Native Americans. Balch repeatedly describes the aborigines' cruelty and violence toward women. Cecil behaves much differently. In one instance, he confronts Snoqualmie, a particularly debased and powerful Cayuse leader, who had just struck Cecil's old Native American nurse. The normally self-restrained Cecil immediately "caught the chief's rein and lifted his own whip" to strike Snoqualmie, before remembering his godly mission and settling for a "withering" scornful glance. Cecil's "blood burned" over Snoqualmie's act, "and he half regretted that the blow had not been given."[22] Cecil's chivalry toward women set him apart from his uncivilized, dark-skinned counterparts.

Flesh-and-blood Oregonians also condemned wife beating in strong terms. Minnie May Wood's eastern Oregon complaint cited verbal cruelty, including cursing and accusations of infidelity, before remarking that her husband "has even resorted to Striking the Plaintiff."[23] J. J. Murphy, an eastern Oregon farmer and stock raiser, said that when William Worsham accused him of taking too much interest in protecting Worsham's wife, he replied, "I dont like to see a man strike a woman and I can whip any s—— of B—— who would whip a woman."[24] A witness in another case, testifying for the husband, said that the man had hit his wife only after she had knocked a pipe from her husband's mouth. Even so, asserted the witness, "I don't think anything justifies a man striking a woman."[25] Oregon's courts often agreed. The attorneys for an eastern Oregon husband appealed to the state Supreme Court in 1888, arguing that "an assault or slap of the hand in a single instance, occasional turbulence, rudeness of language, etc., [was] insufficient" grounds for a divorce.[26] But the court, citing two or three instances of violence and accusations of adultery, disagreed and upheld the lower court.

Even husbands who violated the ideal of masculine self-restraint paid their respects to it. Some tried to pass their violence off as a mistake. Miranda Karst said that her spouse had choked her late one night, then claimed that he had mistaken her for a burglar. Ella Felger of the Willamette Valley said that her husband had angrily thrown her head first out of a window, but "afterwards as an excuse for what he had done clai[m]ed he had the night-mare."[27] Isham Small, the defendant in another Willamette Valley divorce suit, admitted that he had slapped his wife, but only to stop her from handing a butcher knife to another man when Isham had come upon them in an embrace. Even under such conditions, under danger of death and upon discovering his wife's infidelity, Isham's complaint struggled to justify the slap, stating that the blow "was almost involuntary, in the excitement of the difficulty, and was done simply to protect himself from great bodily harm."[28] Estella Scott, also of the Willamette Valley, indicated that her husband of less than a year had struck her with his open hand and fist, then told her "that he had no love for her or respect for her, that he could not treat any woman with decent respect," that she could "go back to her home."[29] This man associated his violence, apparently the first he had inflicted on his bride, with an inability to treat women with respect, as a husband should.

Emma Hotchkiss of Eugene agreed. After her husband, M. E., had hit her, "I told him . . . that when a man stoops to strike a woman, he is not fit to live with."[30] Most husbands seemed to feel the same way.

Men more often attributed their violence to a lack of self-control than to a well-entrenched right. Witnesses described violent husbands as "headstrong, violent in temper and cannot control his own passions" and as having such a "high temper" that he "could not control himself."[31] One husband, trying to win back a wife who confronted him with a lengthy list of violent acts, replied, "I was mad when I done that."[32] W. W. Armstrong of eastern Oregon pursued this logic to its gruesome end. His wife testified that "he said that his temper had run on until it was a kind of insanity that he could not control; that if I displeased him, he might some time do me great bodily harm in a fit of insanity."[33] Likewise, Charles Lewis's spouse, Olive, remarked that he had told her mother that "I was a perfect wife, it was his violent temper, he could not help it, he could not control his temper" and that "if I wasn't careful not to anger him he would kill me sometime."[34] These men's remorse seems more than a little disingenuous. Yet their explanations suggest that violence occurred only when a man was not in his right mind and that it was therefore an unnatural and inappropriate act.

External and even internal constraints against hitting wives were of course not new in Oregon history. As described in the previous chapter, legal and social strictures against wife beaters existed in Oregon during the 1850s and 1860s, and some violent husbands of that era expressed remorse for their acts or attributed them to alcohol or anger. But disapproval of violence against wives had grown by the century's close.

This increased disapproval of violence against wives had strong practical ramifications. Unlike husbands during the settlement period, many highly abusive husbands of the 1890s stopped short of physically hurting their wives. Parilee Crow of the Willamette Valley indicated that her husband had angrily pushed his fist in her face and said "you nasty stinking Spanish bitch, you nasty hoaring bitch, if you were a man I would cut your liver out."[35] But she did not indicate that he had ever hit her or otherwise harmed her physically. Alice Yeats of the southern Willamette Valley characterized her husband, A. J., as "a man of violent temper and when he gets mad he is almost insane."[36] Yet he apparently did not hit her. Emma Smith, who had lived in eastern Oregon, said of her husband, Otto, "I heard him threaten to kill one or two of the neighbors, he threatened to kill every body on the river. I took it he would begin at home."[37] But she also stated that Otto had never struck her. Adelia Baird of the Willamette Valley said that her husband, Joseph, had "very frequently" called her "a damnd liar a damned fool a Bitch Whore," that he "has a very bad temper and never tried to control it."[38] But she, too, said that her husband had never struck her. Another eastern Oregon woman, Iva Miles, said that Charles had begun cursing her the day after their marriage and that he remarked that a "woman was like a dog. If you whipped her she thought more of you."[39] But she gave no indication that Charles had ever in fact whipped or otherwise inflicted physical harm on her.

Other abusive husbands struck their wives only rarely. John Shelton had reportedly hit his wife, Naomi, some fourteen years after their marriage but not in the seven years since then, though he had "threatened to strike me time and again" and "would overturn chairs and tables and break things up generally" when angry.[40] Many women cited long periods of abuse that led up to an act of violence. Ione Williams, married in Nebraska in 1882 and later a resident of the Willamette Valley, said that her husband began cursing her the first Sunday after their wedding. Later that year he accused her of infidelity. In 1896, after more than fourteen years of marriage, he laid violent hands on her. Another wife recalled that her husband "became cross, overbearing and abusive" soon after their marriage in 1871 "and grew worse and worse on up to the present time."[41] In 1895 he threatened to use force, and in the spring of 1896, after twenty-five years of marriage, he tried to hit her with a poker. A month later he struck her with his fist.

Even violent husbands, then, often tried to exercise self-control. The wife of J. W. Severs noted that he frequently sharpened his knife while muttering about letting out the paunch of one of his enemies. A neighbor asserted that Severs "could scarcely control his passion when angry and the least provocation would make him completely wild in his expression."[42] Yet, according to his wife, Severs hit her only once. The era's emphasis on self-control, particularly towards one's wife, existed not simply as an abstract cultural norm. It was a standard that men, including many abusive husbands, internalized.[43]

Scholars have identified a decline in general homicide and assault rates during the nineteenth century. High levels of violence and disorder, they argue, did not mesh with an economy that put a premium on productivity and discipline, with a culture that emphasized self-control.[44] These same trends brought a decline in wife beating.

Violence against children also appeared to decline in Oregon in the late nineteenth century. A Salem newspaper reporting on a reputed whipping in a local school took pains to point out that the teacher had used a switch, not a whip. Much more brutal schoolhouse beatings had excited little if any concern a few decades before.[45]

Oregonians more commonly defended violence toward children than violence toward wives. Divorce-seeking women who complained of relatively minor acts of abuse against themselves took issue only with extreme acts of child abuse. Susan Adams said that William had frequently cursed her and that he had beat her children until they were covered with putrid sores. Maggie Baldwin's complaint described only verbal abuse against herself but whippings that left their six-month-old child black and blue. Other acts of child abuse extreme enough to merit mention included cutting a boy's head to the skull with a rake, sticking pins into children "to make them mind," hitting them with blacksnake whips and rocks, and whipping an eight-year-old girl until "blood run from her arms and back."[46] Even the language used to condemn blows inflicted on children underscored that such violence was ordinarily acceptable. One woman remarked that her son-in-law had whipped her two-year-old grandchild "unreasonably."[47] An eastern Oregon woman complained that her husband had whipped their three young children "when there was no cause for it."[48] Other women objected to being hit for hitting their children. M. A. Kelley of the Willamette Valley said that her husband, T. J., "would strike me for correcting my oldest girl, I was whipping her with a whip and he took it from me and struck me over the head with it." Her spouse, she complained, "would strike me just as quick as he would one of the children."[49] Violence deemed acceptable when directed toward children became unacceptable when directed toward wives.

Like their counterparts from a few decades before, many husbands used violence as a coercive tool. Meda Morrison said her husband "did strike me for not complying with his wishes; and he threw me against the wall."[50] Other wives reported violence for a variety of commonplace acts: persisting in going to neighbors' homes; going to an attorney; milking the cows when a husband had said not to; failing to head off a cow; not coming quickly enough when called; buying a pair of shoes against a husband's orders; objecting to a husband's taking a newborn baby out in the cold; telling a husband that he did not need a watch; and forbidding a husband to sell a horse.[51] As before, husbands tried to silence women with threats of violence. Wives quoted them as saying, "God Dam you, if you won't keep your mouth shut, I will slap it shut"; "If you dont hush god-dam you I will kill you right here"; "Shut up your mouth God-damn you or I will stick this knife into you."[52]

Husbands commonly became abusive when their wives pointed out their failure to live up to the era's higher domestic standards. Flora Grange of Coos County recalled that when "I smelled whiskey on him and I told him I wished he would stop his drinking" her husband "flew into a rage and struck me on the face" and breast. He "picked up a club then and he just ran me from the house and told me to let him and his drinking alone."[53] John Northup of eastern Oregon may have also associated alcohol with his failures as a household head. His wife said that when she was about eight months pregnant he dragged her through the kitchen, swore at her, threatened to hit her, spit in her face, told her to leave, and, in the words of her complaint, "shook a whiskey bottle in her face telling her that it was his 'little Jesus Christ.' "[54] John Northup, like the women of the W.C.T.U., perceived drink as a sort of idolatry, one that unfitted men for the responsibilities of a husband and father.

Some husbands used violence to try to retain traditional male prerogatives. One woman said that her spouse cursed and struck her in part "because I wanted him to not hunt so much instead of working."[55] Another Willamette Valley wife testified that her husband hit her when she was sick and weak "because I would not get up in the morning and build the fire and allow him to remain in bed."[56] Rhoda Haley recalled that her husband had struck her for going out to an entertainment, saying "your place is at home" and on another occasion "whipped me" after "I told him I would not go out and work any more."[57] He had turned the cult of domesticity on its head. Even in turn-of-the-century Oregon, some men believed that their status as household heads conveyed seemingly unlimited privileges, not responsibilities.

Older husbands played the role of all-powerful patriarch more commonly than did younger men. Sarah Perkins, married to Joseph in Missouri in 1864, recounted a long history of widespread abuse in her 1890 divorce suit. His physical cruelty began in the late 1860s, a month before she gave birth, "because I did not want to go to town barefooted . . . he whipped me and made me go barefooted." Joseph also beat her for going to see her mother and for telling him "to burn two cows which died so as to keep flies away from the house." He made her bake bread for his hounds and "get up in the morning and make a fire and warm his pants for him before he would get up." She complained that he "never bought me [a] handkerchief in his life," and their son remembered her putting on his father's pants "to wash her only dress."[58] R. E. Johnson, married in the southern Willamette Valley in 1863, also described a husband who violated the tenets of paternalism with little or no remorse. James had begun habitually beating her within three years of their marriage, had been an indifferent breadwinner, and had compelled her and their daughters to gather wood for fires and tend their cows and horses. A farmer who had known the couple for many years recalled James telling him that "he had intended 'to Kill the damned old Bitch but the children beat him off.[']"[59]

Yet violent husbands played the part of the all-powerful patriarch less convincingly than they had a few decades before. Indeed, letters from several estranged husbands expressed a high degree of self-pity. W. M. James, formerly of eastern Oregon, accused by his wife of choking her, wrote her from Idaho to say "that I am rather Blue I am here doing nothing and have almost give up in dispar and I must say you ar the caus of all of it." W. M. wrote of his suspicions that she was seeing another man and then closed by noting that their home would soon "be a deserted spot" and that he might not live long.[60] Likewise, Millard Parker wrote from southern Oregon to his wife on the Oregon coast that "I shall not live long. The sweat just pours out of me all the time." He closed by mixing nostalgia with bravado: "We were fixed to live so nicely Look at us now then get on your knees & ask God to forgive. I've taken the buffet of the world for 20 years do you think I will falter now."[61] Wallace Wilson of eastern Oregon penned a similar letter to his wife, Nancy, after he had reportedly cut his arm breaking into a hotel room in search of her:

> I have only one word to say my arm is bad I think blood pois[on]ing is setting in if so and we meet no more until we meet in Hell—I hope my dear wife you may life for years—I do not think you can be happy after the ruin and desolation you have wrought in my life . . . if I go to Hell with this cut on my arm if there is any thing like the dead coming back remember you will see me
>
> may God forgive you I cannot[62]

Yet, according to Nancy, Wallace had been the one to insist on a separation, a step she had resisted for some time.

Violent men of the 1890s very frequently expressed feelings of jealousy over their wives, a development that underscored their sense of powerlessness. Minnie Vandervort recalled that her husband struck her on the way to town in eastern Oregon, telling her that "no woman but a 'damed whore' would wear a red dress."[63] Hattie Alexander said that her jealous husband tripped her and her partner during a dance. Fannie Gregory said that her spouse, Braxton, became so jealous of one of her relatives that he threatened to shoot him, that he constantly watched her and "would not leave the house even to attend to ordinary chores."[64] "Whenever any man speaks to Pl[ai]n[ti]ff," read another woman's complaint, "Def[endan]t accuses Plnff. of having impure thoughts of him and of having secret understandings with such person." This sort of jealousy, more commonly expressed during the 1890s than earlier, is another indication that the context and causes of husbands' violence had shifted.[65]

Violence also occurred more commonly around pregnancy and childbirth than it had before. Mary Stewart said that her husband pushed her out of her bedroom and made her lie on the sofa the night before she gave birth. John Tapp reportedly demanded intercourse from his wife only three days after she had given birth. When she refused he beat her black and blue and made her sit in a cold room for thirty minutes, which gave her a painful cold. William Naas allegedly struck his wife with his fist because she refused to have sexual intercourse four days after giving birth. Such abuse suggested jealousy of a fetus or infant, particularly when demands for sex accompanied the abuse.[66] It illustrated the increasingly noninstrumental aspects of husbands' violence, since it occurred when wives were pregnant and hence at their most vulnerable.

Violent husbands' increased use of suicide threats illustrated the movement to less explicit forms of abuse. M. A. Poill recalled that her Willamette Valley husband one day "laid the pistol on the table and said in the morning we will have a little fun we will die together & he also set a bottle of stricknine on the table & said he would take it."[67] Several husbands threatened murder and suicide if their wives tried to leave. Others threatened to kill only themselves. A. A. Witham, a Baptist minister for a number of Pacific Northwest churches, became agitated when his wife, Clara, discovered a letter from his lover. Clara described how he "pushed me in the bedroom and caught me by the throat, and made me promise him, that I mustn't ever speak about that or he would commit suicide."[68] Much more prosaic events could trigger a suicide threat. Jessie Seales recalled how her husband reacted when she neglected to call him to supper:

> he said he would leave the ranch and go off and be a tramp as he thought none of us cared for him. He asked me to pack his clothes up ... the children cried. I finally went and got his clothes and he held the sack and I put them in for him. He then sent the children to bed crying and he got a rope and said he would go to the barn and hang himself and I would find him in the morning hanging to the third beam. He shook hands with me and went out and I locked both doors and told him I dont think you ought to go and hang your self and go off in that shape.[69]

Albert Seales neither hung himself nor left his wife; he continued to hit her.

The threat of suicide, more prominent at the century's close than earlier, constituted more than another method of abusing and coercing one's wife. It indicated that greater numbers of men felt more self-pity and less self-assurance than before, that violent husbands increasingly saw themselves as powerless, not powerful.

Sexually pejorative expletives, common enough at midcentury, had become if anything more graphic and shrill by the 1890s. Jefferson Glenn reportedly referred to his wife as a "Dam'd heifer" and accused her of "fucking until midnight, in the McAtee barn" with another man. Another witness in the eastern Oregon divorce suit remembered Glenn telling him that if his wife did not "quit her dam'd Whoring around" he would "kick her God Damned Cunt onto the back of her neck."[70] "He calls me lots of bad things, beasts and things like that," said another wife of her spouse.[71] A Willamette Valley woman remarked that her husband called her names like "bitch, hog and rip and sow."[72] Edwin Spofford, a south-coast machinist or engineer, reportedly referred to a woman he was attracted to as "some damned old pelt."[73] Eastern Oregon's Hattie Masterson said that her husband, Joseph, had called her a "damned cunt-lapping little bitch" when he choked her.[74] This sort of language indicated that many men's feelings toward women were highly misogynistic, even as men's general behavior toward them had become more chivalrous.

Some violent men manifested a deep ambivalence over marriage and the home. Margaret Simpson of the Willamette Valley indicated that her husband, Allen, had once ordered her out of the house and threatened to kill her. The next day he went to her and stated, "I will just give you until tomorrow morning to come home."[75] B. A. Lilly recalled that her husband, B. F., literally threw her out of their house, left home himself, then "coaxed me to come back and live with him," all apparently in one day.[76] A few months later he again left, saying he would never come back. He returned the next day. She eventually resolved his indecision by leaving after a quarrel in which he asserted that she was not fit to live with. J. W. Severs, also a resident of the southern Willamette Valley, likewise struggled with contradictory feelings over home and marriage. His wife said that he referred to their house as "nothing but a penitentiary hall" and threatened to take an axe to it. But he also nailed up all its entrances save one and, while gardening, kept a close watch on that door. "As soon as he would see any one go in," observed a neighbor, "he would drop his work and go in and stay till they went away as if he was afra[id] to [l]eave her left there alone."[77] For Severs, house and marriage were a metaphorical prison that oppressed him and an actual prison in which he sought to contain his wife.

Violence had become not simply a patent instrument of coercion, not simply a tool with which to punish strong-willed wives. It often centered around women's pregnancy or accompanied expressions of extreme jealousy or threats of suicide. Some violent men also seemed highly ambivalent over marriage and the home, uncertain over whether to drive their wives away or compel them to stay. As we have seen, much violence toward wives still functioned simply or primarily to coerce or punish them. But wife beating had, for many men, become an expression of male anxieties that operated independently from a wife's actions.[78]

The wife beater was not alone in these anxieties. Historians of masculinity have identified the late nineteenth century as a crucial dividing line for U.S. men, a time when opportunities to be a pioneer, a skilled artisan, or an independent businessman seemed to be drying up, a time when men noticed—and exaggerated—the extent to which society and culture had become more feminine and less masculine. Violent men's increased ambivalence over women and the home very likely had something to do with an unease bestirring a great many men who did not strike their spouses. J. W. Severs, the Eugene man who hit his wife and called their home a penitentiary, expressed emotions that many husbands, violent and nonviolent alike, secretly shared.[79]

This trend toward more affective, noninstrumental forms of wife beating did not overwhelm the era's dominant theme of self-restraint. Violence against wives evidently declined markedly from the mid-nineteenth to the late nineteenth century in Oregon. But the same ethos of self-restraint behind this decline appeared to inhibit women's behavior, too.

Wives fought back less commonly than they had during the settlement period. There were, to be sure, exceptions. On the whole, though, women resisted with more persistence than aggression. Many simply tried to avoid husbands who were in a foul temper. When Mary Lowery's husband became abusive she occasionally "would talk with him and try to reason with him," but more commonly "I would leave the room."[80] Likewise, Vina McKalvey of eastern Oregon stated, "I never shoed out my madness very much I didnt dare."[81] These two women filed for divorce only after their husbands had left them. Wives who seemed highly accommodating could stand up for themselves. Miranda Karst advised her daughter to keep quiet about John Karst's attempts to rape the child, and she filed for divorce only after he had left. Yet Miranda's determination to see the marriage through did not keep her from physically intervening when her husband hit her daughter or from directly terminating at least one of his extramarital affairs. O. E. Lewis allowed her estranged husband, Hank, to continue to take meals at the house she owned and to sleep in a separate compartment. But when he came to her room one day and acted aggressively, "I left the room went to another bed and locked the door, for I was determined that he should not occupy the same bed I did."[82] Elizabeth Binge, of eastern Oregon, undertook a similar course of ongoing resistance before she and her husband separated. She said that when her husband, O. W., began to strike her as they rode home from town in their wagon she told him to "take care where you are going if you don't care anything for me remember we have our baby with us and you don't want to kill it." O. W. righted the team and continued to abuse her verbally, "but I talked to him and gradually got him quieted down before we reached home."[83]

This sort of ongoing, unobtrusive resistance offered late-nineteenth-century wives a way to assert themselves while avoiding the difficulties that more overt protests might have brought. A woman's violence could disqualify her from the court's protection. In 1899 the Oregon Supreme Court ruled that a woman was entitled to a divorce from her physically abusive husband in part because "she at no time, . . . resorted to personal violence, or visited upon him any personal chastisement."[84]

Oregon's rate of divorce, like the nation's, rose significantly after the Civil War, from 80 per 100,000 in 1870 to 134 per 100,000 in 1900, when it ranked behind only four other states. Qualitative evidence, too, underscored Oregonians' increased tolerance for divorce. Emma Hermann of the southwest coast said that a "great many of my friends and relatives advised me to leave" her husband.[85] Not all friends were so supportive of women who sought divorces in the 1890s, however, and scandal spread easily in Oregon's small communities. Mary Kerrigan of the south coast balked at testifying of her husband's cruelty: "I hate to tell. Every body will hear it."[86] Social pressure remained a strong incentive for staying with an abusive husband in rural and small-town Oregon. A witness in a south-coast suit recalled the defendant saying to the plaintiff that "if she would withdraw this suit and come back and live with him as his wife that it would be all right, if not that he would make scandal so that she could not live on Coos Bay."[87] Some women pursued a middle course, insisting on legal agreements before returning to violent husbands. Clayton Delaney reportedly promised to give his wife $500 and to forfeit custody of their children if he broke his promise to reform his treatment of her.[88] The persistence of communities whose residents still saw marriage as something of a public covenant no doubt served to deter many husbands who would have been violent if afforded more privacy. But those same communities could also judge harshly wives who terminated abusive marriages.

Divorce often brought poverty, sometimes danger. In 1900, over 2,500 women in Oregon were employed as teachers, and around 700 each in sales and stenography. But some 7,500 labored in domestic and personal service, most commonly as servants. Oregon's female manufacturing workers earned, on average, only about $250 per year, not even half of what their male counterparts made. Hence wives often stayed with violent husbands who supported their families. Nora Marcott, a Eugene waitress, said that her husband had struck her several times and cursed her frequently. But when asked why she had left him, she replied, "Well he would not try to make a living for us."[89] Divorce seldom improved the financial lot of such women, for courts rarely awarded them more than a few months' support. Highly jealous and possessive husbands, furthermore, might pursue a woman who fled them. Eastern Oregon's Henry Kizer reportedly told his wife "that if she ever left him he would follow her to the end of the earth to torment her."[90] Mary Britton of The Dalles said that her husband, John, had abused her for two years after she had left him, that he would "come around and curse and threaten to kill me and he called me chippy when he passed me on the street."[91] O. E. Lewis, a Corvallis woman, said that her estranged husband, Hank, had appeared at her gate almost nightly for several months, sometimes throwing "tin cans against the sides of the house to frighten us" or even breaking in.[92]

Oregon Police or other law-enforcement officials more commonly protected such women in the 1890s than they had before.[93] Some wives used the courts to put their husbands under bonds to keep the peace. Mary Britton of The Dalles took this step and said that the city police told her "that they were watching him closely."[94] Police sometimes intervened on the spot against violent husbands. Charles Williams, a marshal in a small eastern Oregon town, recalled a day when he heard loud talking in a couple's house. He "went to a bay window on the east side of the house and saw him standing over her, she sitting down, she having a small child standing in front of her, he was gnashing his teeth with his fist drawn threatening to kil her, I thought by his actions that he intended to do something of the kind . . . so I rushed into the door and put a stop to the trouble by threatening to lock him up if I heard any more threats or noise."[95] Likewise, Hermana Albright said that the Marshfield city marshal stopped her husband, Carl, from choking her when he heard her cries. But officers did not consistently act to protect women from violent husbands. A police judge in Dallas, a Willamette Valley town, said that he had fined a man convicted of assault and battery on his wife $5.00 plus court costs and "he was discharged upon payment of this fine and in less than an hour thereafter was again brought before me on a like charge . . . and was fined $10.00 & costs."[96] Protection from law-enforcement personnel remained unreliable.

Family members appeared to intervene more readily in violent marriages than they had during the settlement period. Ida Brown indicated that her parents had advised her to leave her violent husband, but that "I did not then want my father and mother to support me and my prospective child." After further abuse and neglect "my father and mother saw my condition" and "absolutely refused to allow me to return" to her spouse.[97] Other relatives provided ongoing protection. Andrew Emerick said that he had lived near his sister and her husband for twenty-seven years and that "many a night I have had to get up and go and settle him down and make him behave himself."[98] Maurice Allen, also of the Willamette Valley, said that his sister often went to his house to get away from her husband and that "I have frequently went there [to her house] and remained all night to protect her."[99] Live-in relations were particularly useful. Annie Brown of the south coast said that when she and her husband, John, went to bed "he began to strike me in the face and I had to . . . hollar for my mother to come and take me out."[100] As during Oregon's earlier history, older sons and daughters from previous marriages could offer crucial assistance. Emma Hotchkiss, a woman with several young adult daughters, described how they came to her aid when their stepfather assaulted her. Her oldest daughter "pitched into him and scratched his face" while another "run out of the porch crying, 'murder! murder! papa will kill mama,' and the neighbors came running into the yard."[101] Greater tolerance of divorce together with the more settled nature of Oregon society brought increased assistance from wives' families. There was, then, an element of braggadocio in John Tapp's assertion that he would hit his wife in front of her father, and her brothers, too, and in A. G. Ryan's boast that his wife did not have a relative who could stand up to him.[102]

Abused wives' reliance on rural and small-town neighbors had apparently declined by the 1890s, at least relative to their reliance on family members and police. This trend was most pronounced in western Oregon, the most densely settled part of the state, but also the region most influenced by norms of familial privacy. Many couples still lived with parents, boarders, domestic servants, or farm laborers, but such people had become more reluctant to interpose themselves in a couples' argument. Charlie Apperson, in his late twenties, testified that while he lived with Hattie and Joseph Masterson in eastern Oregon he heard a scream and "ran in to see what the trouble was." He arrived just as Joseph threw Hattie onto a lounge. "He turned to me then," Apperson remarked, "and said, 'You go right back to the kitchen where you belong.' I turned and went back to the kitchen, and I don't know what happened after that."[103] Likewise, Philip Maus, Harvey Lockhart's nephew, testified that when his uncle swore at his wife, Ida, "I never chipped in, it was none of my business." When Harvey knocked Ida against a seat in a wagon that Maus was driving and "hurt her back pretty bad," Maus recalled that "all that I done was to sit there and drive," that he made no protest of the abuse.[104] Many onlookers who witnessed violence against wives were not so passive. Florence Glenn of eastern Oregon said that when her husband "drew his pistol on me" she "ran out in the yard and hollered for help." Jefferson, still holding the pistol, ordered her back inside, but "a young man came to the house pretty soon, and I made him come in and stay until I was ready to leave the house."[105] But this sort of spontaneous, on-the-spot intervention had become less common, particularly in western Oregon.

Formal community interventions against cruel husbands, though still rare, appeared to increase late in the century. A south-coast witness in a divorce suit asserted that "the willful neglect of Mr. Markam's family at his hands were common Town talk."[106] Such talk could coalesce into collective action. Milton McMurry of the southern Willamette Valley received the following letter from a Eugene group signed "Many Citizens": "The Masons are after you hot and heavy . . . if you want to save yourself you had better leave here for a while. Your wife we understand is in good hands and will be well taken care of and if you want to save your head you had better *leave.* for we know *all* and intend to *set you* through if you dont go."[107] Just why the Masons and "Many Citizens" objected to McMurry is not clear, but it probably had to do with his wife's accusations of adultery, violence, lack of support, and attempted rape of her daughter by a previous marriage. A second Eugene husband reportedly stopped calling his stepdaughters vile names when his wife asked the Masons to intervene. A witness in another divorce suit said that those among the "best citizens" of Grass Valley in eastern Oregon threatened to give A. A. Witham "a coat of tar and feathers if he was not gone by a certain time" because he had spoken so scandalously of his wife.[108] Other vigilante-style groups objected to husbands who did not provide for their families. Nannie Fellows said that when she and her husband lived in Washington state he had received a letter signed "The Whitecaps," which threatened they "would call upon him" if he did not start supporting his family.[109] (The White Caps were an extralegal organization that operated in many parts of nineteenth-century North America against violators of community norms.)

Some community members took offense at husbands' violence, not just their nonsupport. One girl remarked that her stepfather had begun "to whip his wife and then the neighbors were so against him he had to get out."[110] A newspaper reported on another case in much more depth:

The practice of wife-whipping is becoming a little too prevalent in this locality. We have, on several occasions, heard rumors of offenses of this character, but until now have been unable to certainly fix the fact upon those said to be guilty of the crime. In the present instance, however, there is no doubt. On Monday afternoon last persons living at the north end of Front street were startled by the loud screams of a woman, and an investigation of the cause disclosed the fact that a man named John Hierly, . . . had beaten his wife into an insensible condition . . . Brutes such as this man Hierly has shown himself to be, ought to be triced up to a lamp-post and whipped until life was about extinct. The law is powerless to inflict adequate punishment for such offenses.[111]

Like the cases cited earlier, this one indicated that community pressure bore most heavily on violent men who failed to meet community standards. The newspaper noted that Hierly did not support his family and had but recently moved to the area from Portland. Wife beaters who faced public criticism and threats from editors and other leading citizens tended to be socially marginal men. Yet occasional public acts against wife beaters underscored the public's condemnation of the practice and its unwillingness to regard marriage as a purely private institution.

Unlike the settlement period, when Oregon wives relied largely on themselves in resisting violent husbands, women of the 1890s commonly looked to their families, to law-enforcement officials, and occasionally to quasi-formal community groups. They also looked to the church.

The church assisted women not so much by encouraging direct intervention against violent husbands as by establishing a moral tone that dovetailed with the broader cultural emphasis on self-control. Hence abused wives at least occasionally identified church as a place where abusive husbands might be reformed—a prospect that their spouses usually resisted. Ida Lockhart, explaining her decision to return to her physically abusive husband, remarked, "I thought if I could go back and get him to join the church, and lead a christian life that we could live happy, together, I told him after I went back that I would like to have reading and family prayer, and he swore at me, and wanted to know if I had gone crazy."[112] Other violent husbands took pains to keep their wives out of church. Nella Porter said that when she told her spouse, Isaac, that she wanted to join a church, he retorted, "If you do, you will have to leave here. They don't try to get anyone into the church but dummies,—people who haven't got any sense."[113] Josephine Hunt's husband reportedly objected to her attending church at Zena, a small Willamette Valley community, asserting that such "God Damned foolishness Had To Be Stopped."[114] F. P. Hermann, the postmaster of a south-coast town and nephew of Congressman Binger Hermann, reportedly told his wife "that all she went to church for was to get a screwing out of preacher Martin."[115] Church, for violent husbands and abused wives alike, represented an alternative social and moral community. Like many other social institutions of late-nineteenth-century Oregon, it discouraged both explicit acts of feminine independence and patent acts of male brutality.

The settlement-era husband who had used violence on his wife commonly presented the act as a confirmation of his role as household head, of his authority over his children and his wife. By late in the century, however, such an act represented instead a contradiction of the husband's role. This shift from paternal authority to paternal self-control was related closely to broad social and cultural changes: increasingly separate spheres for women and men and, most important, a general emphasis on self-restraint. These ideas had existed in Oregon during the 1850s and 1860s, but the nature of settlement had impeded them. Later in the century most rural Oregonians lived in towns or farming communities that had matured and stabilized and where women's influence—in sheer numbers and general cultural tone—had become more pronounced.

A decrease in violence against wives accompanied the establishment of more settled, feminized societies. Highly abusive husbands were often reluctant to use outright violence. Even many men who hit their wives paid obeisance to the ideal of male self-restraint by using physical force only after long periods of cruelty.

The law, women's families, and the general community offered some external restraints to complement these internal ones. Assistance by law-enforcement personnel and by women's families appeared to rise near the century's close. Neighbors were perhaps a bit less apt to intervene than during the settlement period; some indicated that they viewed a couple's private life, even if it included brutal treatment of the wife, as none of their business. More formal community intervention occurred more commonly than before, however, at least if violent husbands outraged community standards in other respects.

But the late nineteenth century was no golden age for Oregon women. Some husbands, not all of them of an older generation, hit their wives frequently and without compunction. This violence, moreover, had become less predictable than before, less related to a woman's specific actions. Other abusive husbands, who hit rarely or not at all, visited a wide range of cruelties upon their wives—curses, accusations of adultery, attempts to force them into prostitution, and threats to kill, sometimes while brandishing a firearm or knife. The late nineteenth century's lower tolerance for and incidence of violence against wives should not be dismissed. But wife beating, let alone the other expressions of wife abuse, was by no means eradicated.

Enhanced male self-restraint, moreover, was achieved at the cost of diminished female agency. Divorce suits less commonly described wives who fought their husbands physically. On the whole, wives married to violent husbands enjoyed more support from others, but they had less permission to act assertively on their own behalf.[116]

Turn-of-the-century Portland women enjoyed more agency and autonomy than their rural and small-town counterparts did. Indeed, Oregon's only major city had already begun to stir with social and cultural changes that still lay in the future for most of the state. From this dynamic and heterogeneous milieu sprang a highly distinctive measure: the whipping post law for wife beaters.

— 3 —

"His Face Is Weak and Sensual": Portland and the Whipping Post Law

The decade or so before the outbreak of World War I was Portland's greatest period of growth and expansion. The Lewis and Clark Centennial Exposition of 1905 drew over one and a half million visitors to Portland and helped establish it as a modern city. These years also saw a vigorous and often successful challenge to political corruption that brought Oregon national attention, a movement that culminated in a series of progressive laws, including legislation establishing the initiative, the referendum, and the direct election and possible recall of U.S. senators. The whipping post law for wife beaters was a much-discussed part of Oregon politics at this time, although it has attracted very little attention since.[1]

The whipping post law ostensibly protected women from brutal husbands. On closer examination, however, it is clear that it served a cluster of other, less worthy purposes. The law in large part constituted a reaction by well-to-do Portlanders to shifts in class, ethnicity, and gender that seemed to be transforming their city. It offered them an opportunity both to define the problem of wife beating and to identify its perpetrators.

By 1900 Portland was very different from the rest of Oregon. Sheer size accounted for much of that difference; by the century's turn the city at the mouth of the Willamette River had over 90,000 residents.

72

Astoria, the state's second largest city, did not have even 10,000. Salem, the state capital, had barely 4,000. Portland's population boomed in the next decade. In 1910 it had over 207,000 people, 31 percent of the state's total.[2]

Portland also had a much more varied population than the rest of Oregon. In 1910 about one-quarter of its residents originated from outside the United States—45 percent of the state's foreign born. This was a highly heterogeneous group, hailing predominantly from Germany, China, Great Britain, Canada, Sweden, Russia, Norway, and Italy. Well-to-do Portlanders had their misgivings over the new immigrants. The *Oregonian* observed that "most of the material at hand is partly Americanized, but with a steadily increasing number of foreign laboring people, particularly from Southern Europe."[3] Another editorial, addressing the need for "more competent physical inspection of aliens," made specific reference to "the Italian, Hebrew, Polish, Slavak and Magyar races."[4] Portland also had a different occupational mix from the rest of Oregon. Its number of factory workers even outpaced its sharp population increase, growing from over 5,000 in 1899 to more than 12,000 in 1909.[5]

Women participated in the city's social and cultural transformation. Portland's Abigail Scott Duniway, a longtime advocate of women's rights, recalled in a 1902 address to the Oregon Federation of Women's Clubs "the time, thirty years ago, when, of the many silver-haired women now present, few, if any, imagined that the time would come when any Oregon woman, save only my foolhardy self, would ever be guilty of such a supposed-to-be unwomanly act as to assist in forming, much less in addressing, a public assembly of this character."[6] Large numbers of Portland women participated in the Federation of Women's Clubs, the Woman's Christian Temperance Union, and other organizations dedicated to improving society and reforming men's habits. Suffrage was of course the most powerful symbol of women's growing power. Oregon advocates for a woman's right to vote waged a vigorous grass-roots campaign in 1906 and less public ones in 1908 and 1910. In 1912 they returned to an open campaign. Their victory gave Oregon women the vote nearly a decade before the passage of the nineteenth amendment to the U.S. Constitution.[7]

Portland women gained power and independence more rapidly than their rural and small-town counterparts. In 1900 they constituted about

15 percent of the city's wage earners, but just 9 percent for the rest of the state. Ten years later the census showed only 56.5 percent of Portland women age fifteen or over as married, this despite a sex ratio of 134.5 to one. Portland women also divorced more frequently, a trend that the *Oregonian* properly linked to women's "developing individuality."[8]

Increasing numbers of Portland women sought autonomy. One "working woman," attempting to explain why many of her peers shunned a boarding home run by the Portland Women's Union, asserted that "the very fact of having to live under restrictions makes it appear as if we are in need of surveillance and incapable of taking care of ourselves, and no girl likes to admit that." She identified "liberty" as "the fundamental principle underlying all successful American institutions."[9] Married women evinced similar desires for independence. John Illk's answer to his wife's divorce petition asserted that she often neglected to prepare his meals, wasted her money on theaters and other amusements, and went out drinking with men. Two times she had gotten abortions, saying that "if she was burdened with children she would be deprived of her good times and that children . . . were too much trouble."[10] "I like to go out; any lady will," asserted another divorce-seeking woman to a judge.[11] To be sure, the early twentieth century did not see a revolution in gender roles—not in Portland, not in the rest of the nation. But a broad if subtle shift was occurring, one that was already straining the nineteenth-century paradigm of separate spheres and the self-sacrificing wife.

Portland men noted and often criticized women's expanding roles. Some complained that their wives worked instead of, in the words of one legal reply, "remaining at home and caring for their home, as a wife should."[12] Woman suffrage elicited much less negative press than it had in the nineteenth century, but Oregon editors more often ignored the movement than supported it. Other men asked women to retain their traditional roles. Presbyterian minister Henry Marcotte, preaching in Portland in 1911, spoke against the city's fashionable dress, admonishing women that "the fight of the vast majority of men, to keep clean, to be worthy to ask some good woman to be our wife, is hard, harder than you good women know."[13]

Marcotte asked women to be touchstones of purity and selflessness in a society in great flux: "Our men are in danger of being materialized. You women can prevent it. You can be the idealists, priestesses of true culture, knowing the best of literature, art, music, and yet true home makers, realizing that your highest honor is to be the companions of great & good men, the mothers of the more glorious men of the future."[14] Another Portland-area Presbyterian cleric, Andrew Carrick, preached that *"The greatest heroine in the world is the self sacrificing mother"* and quoted a line that read "O, spotless woman in world of shame!"[15] "When the old-fashioned mother ceases to be in this land," preached Marcotte in 1911, "the end is not far off."[16] Carrick in 1909 praised the woman who "will endure more suffering and hardship uncomplainingly than any other person," the mother who "literally yielded her life to her worthless husband and her increasing family until before she was fifty," leaving nothing "but the shell of former beauty and attractiveness."[17] That fewer women seemed to be willing to undertake such sacrifices was of course cause for alarm. The ministers expected women to counterbalance modernity, not to spearhead it.

Several trends troubled well-to-do, native-born Portland men early in the twentieth century. Portland had always been more stable than most western cities. Now it was growing quickly, and its foreign born and working class seemed particularly salient. Women, too, were demanding and assuming a greater role in public affairs. These demographic and social shifts were accompanied by what James McGovern has described as "a vast dissolution of moral authority."[18] For prosperous Portland men, who had long enjoyed a highly disproportionate amount of power and authority, this erosion of authority probably seemed quite personal.[19] It was in this context that Oregon legislators considered a law that would punish wife beaters with a whipping.

Elizabeth Pleck characterizes Oregon's passage of the measure as "unusual," since the only other two states to make wife beating punishable by whipping, Maryland and Delaware, were located in the upper South and had passed the laws well before the turn of the century. T. J. Jackson Lears identifies the whipping post movement as part of a backward-looking shift to a more martial culture among the well-to-do, and Pleck asserts that "in Progressive era America, the whipping post was an anachronism."[20] Yet Oregon, certainly on the Progressive Movement's leading edge, became the third and last state to adopt the law. Portland-area legislators played a large role in its passage. The law, the debates over male violence and women's behavior that accompanied it, and the way in which Oregon judges enforced it reveal a great deal about how well-to-do Portland men understood wife beating.

Governor George Chamberlain, a progressive Democrat born and raised in Mississippi, recommended the whipping post for wife beaters in his January 12, 1905, message to the Oregon state legislature. Chamberlain opened his discussion of family legislation by arguing that husbands who had deserted their families should be extradited from other states and given a choice between supporting their wives and children or going to jail. "But criminal statutes will not reach the brute who strikes and beats a defenseless woman," the governor remarked. Imprisonment would simply punish "the helpless wife and children who are dependent upon him for their daily bread. For such inhuman creatures the public whipping-post has been proven to be the most effective punishment."[21] Although the conservative *Portland Oregonian*, no friend to Chamberlain, remarked that the governor's call for the whipping post "struck a popular chord," neither the governor's remarks nor subsequent debates of the bill identified it as the child of popular agitation.[22]

On the same day that Chamberlain addressed the legislature, Senator Sigmund Sichel, a freshman Republican from Portland, introduced a bill stipulating that wife beaters receive up to forty lashes within the walls of county prisons. Twelve years later one of Sichel's many obituaries explained that the gregarious Jewish merchant "had listened to so many pitiful stories about brute husbands who had beaten their wives that he determined to try and put a stop to this."[23] A member of Portland's police commission and many benevolent organizations, Sichel had a strong interest in both criminology and civic reform.

The Senate's judicial committee drew some of the teeth from Sichel's bill. It strongly opposed whipping as a mandatory punishment, and Sichel agreed to make the bill part of the existing statute on assault and battery, which imposed penalties of three to twelve months in jail or a $50 to $500 fine. The committee also changed the bill so that local justices of the peace could not sentence a wife beater to be whipped, and it reduced the maximum penalty to twenty lashes. As amended, the bill stipulated that a man must be tried and found guilty in circuit court before being flogged, and it gave judges the option of imposing jail terms or fines rather than a whipping. The amended bill won the judiciary committee's "hearty approval" and passed the Senate by a vote of twenty-three to zero on February 3, 1905.[24]

The legislation faced much stiffer opposition in Oregon's House of Representatives. Robert S. Smith, a southern Oregon progressive, objected to judges having discretion over whether to sentence a wife beater to flogging since, as one reporter paraphrased him, "a poor man would feel the whip, while a richer man would escape with a fine."[25] Smith also argued that twentieth-century Oregon was neither the time nor the place for corporal punishment: "They do not have such a law in England, they do not have it in Germany, and they do not have it in France, but they do have it in Maryland and Delaware, down close to the line where they burn niggers for [a] pasttime."[26] Representatives Linthicum and Mears of Portland's Multnomah County countered Smith's arguments. One asserted that Maryland's whipping post law had nearly eradicated wife beating; the other cited an instance in which a man had stamped upon his wife's face with spiked logging boots, a brutal act that, he argued, deserved a whipping. The whipping post law carried the day by a comfortable margin.[27]

Portland's editors were divided on the new law. The conservative *Oregonian* readily agreed that "the brutal creature miscalled a man who beats his wife deserves forty lashes well laid on," but it blamed wife beating largely on wives' reluctance to fight or prosecute violent husbands: "She is a moral coward—he a physical coward . . . The simple truth, tersely stated, is that if a woman won't be whipped she doesn't have to be."[28] No law could make good the moral defect of women who allowed themselves to be beaten. Portland's other major conservative newspaper, the *Evening Telegram*, was much more sanguine about the bill. It predicted that the whipping post "would eventually lead to" wife beating's "extirpation."[29] The progressive, Democratic *Oregon Daily Journal* agreed that the wife beater deserved the lash, but noted "a popular prejudice against this form of punishment." It instead recommended that a violent husband be forced to work and that "for a considerable time his wages shall be given to his wife."[30] This system, the editor concluded, made much more sense than simply jailing the wife beater and thereby depriving his family of his income.

Just a few years later the law faced determined legislative criticism, led by John Buchanon, a freshman representative from southern Oregon. Reporters identified the Roseburg attorney as a key leader of Oregon's conservative machine, a man who backed corporations at the expense of progressive legislation. Yet Buchanon, conservative credentials notwithstanding, cited progressive reasons for repealing the corporal punishment of wife beaters. He called the measure an "emblem of the Dark Ages" that did not belong in "enlightened Oregon."[31] He asserted, in the words of a reporter, "that the whipping-post was an institution of revenge rather than of punishment; that its use does not serve to reform the inhumanity of the man punished."[32]

Most representatives disagreed. Several Portland legislators asserted that the law had deterred wife beating, and most of their rural counterparts also stood by the whipping post. The repeal effort failed decisively.

The whipping post law proved to be much more vulnerable during the next legislative session, in 1911. In 1909 the *Oregon Daily Journal* had editorialized that "the whipping post law, good or bad, might as well be repealed; it is not enforced."[33] In 1911 Buchanon, again attempting to repeal the whipping post, claimed that it had been employed only twice, and not at all since 1909. He termed the law "a dead letter on our statutes" and remarked that "the officers in Multnomah county will not enforce this law."[34] Indeed, each of the nine Multnomah County representatives who voted on Buchanon's bill joined him in calling for its repeal, a strong reversal from 1905 and 1909.

Buchanon opposed the whipping post on both moral and practical grounds. "I remember the last time I saw a man whipped and when the process was over there were a dozen gaping wounds on his bare back," he asserted. "Is that civilization?"[35] Reading from a report by the Prison Reform League, he asserted that such treatment "deprives a man of self respect without reforming him."[36] The whipping post contradicted the Constitution's guarantee of freedom from cruel and unusual punishment. It was "a relic of slavery days retained only by Maryland and Delaware," a "blot on the good name of Oregon."[37] According to Buchanon, the whipping post law was an inefficient, inhumane, ineffective, and anachronistic embarrassment.

The opponents of the law's repeal apparently had difficulty countering Buchanon's arguments. An eastern Oregon representative argued that the whipping post, unlike prison, cured wife beaters. A

Clackamas County legislator from just outside Portland recalled a bloodied woman who had fled to his home for protection: "Gentlemen, I tell you that if that drunken brute had come to my house and attempted to take that woman away I would have committed murder. I believe in humiliating such men."[38] But Buchanon's bill passed easily. Five days later, on February 2, 1911, it passed the Senate, apparently with little or no debate.

But newly elected Governor Oswald West vetoed Buchanon's bill to repeal the whipping post. His official veto letter allowed that whipping criminals might be "a barbarous practice," but asserted that "the wife-beater is also a relic of barbarism." It was only fitting, then, to "retain upon our statute books at least one such barbarous punishment for these barbarians." Because West attributed his life's successes to "my mother, my wife, and other good women," he could not "see my way clear to give my approval to any measure framed in favor of their common enemy."[39] West also argued for the law's efficacy, contending that men who had been lashed stopped battering their wives.[40]

Governor West's veto changed few votes. The Democrat had just won a hotly contested election from conservative Republicans, who had hoped to gain back some of the power that the reformers had distributed to the electorate. He remained at loggerheads with old-guard politicians such as Buchanon throughout the legislative session and vetoed many bills. Buchanon tried to exploit this issue: "I don't believe that the members of this Legislature are going to let the Governor do their thinking, that every time he coughs, they will cough, that every time he speaks they will applaud."[41] The governor, he continued, had apparently not given the question much thought and did not realize that one could oppose both wife beating and the whipping post. Most of Buchanon's colleagues apparently concurred; only three members changed their votes, and two of these went against the governor. The House overrode West's veto, and the Senate did so without debate. "We have no more whipping post for the cowardly brutes who beat their wives," lamented an *Evening Telegram* editorial.[42]

Buchanon's arguments suggest why Oregon's whipping post lasted for only six years. He asserted that corporal punishment was inhumane and that he had decided to oppose the bill after reading a firsthand account of a flogging. Even the conservative *Evening Telegram* allowed that "the whipping of a human being . . . excites involuntary repulsion in the average person, however vigorously we may tell and repeat to ourselves that it is right, proper, meet and expedient that cowardly, brutish wifebeaters should be so treated."[43] By 1911, furthermore, Buchanon could describe the law as "a dead letter."[44] For legislators, the law's efficacy was something of a moot point if judges refused to use it. In late 1906 a Portland judge had remarked that "two years is not enough for a proper test" of the law.[45] By 1911, though, Buchanon could make a strong case that six years had shown the law to be unworkable.

Indeed, Oregon's whipping post had not made much of an impact. It did not last long, and at the time of its repeal the *Oregonian* could recall its being employed only four times, three in Portland and once in isolated Baker County. Oregon's short-lived whipping post law directly affected only a handful of men.[46]

Yet many influential Oregonians clearly felt strongly about the whipping post law. Most of the state's major newspapers wrote editorials on the bill's passage in 1905 and repeal in 1911, and they devoted more space to it than most bills received. The legislators themselves often warmed to the topic. A reporter wrote that the 1909 debate over the bill "was the most animated discussion of the present session."[47]

A desire for social control united many of the whipping post's supporters. Portland legislators, living among the state's major working-class and ethnic populations, supported the bill in disproportionate numbers in 1905 and 1909. Indeed, they so vocally backed the law during the 1909 debate that a coastal legislator quipped that "it appears from this discussion that all of the wifebeaters come from Multnomah County."[48] Sichel, the bill's author, was a Portland merchant and police commissioner. Others hinted strongly at links between violence and class. Two legislators who cited personal experiences with wife beaters indicated that the violent husband had been a logger or a drunk. "The trouble for this wife-beating is whisky," asserted another.[49] The superintendent of Portland's Boys and Girls Aid Society, addressing a related issue, called for stringent immigration restriction, asserting that "the manner in which foreigners, especially those of Russia, Italy and other European countries have raised their children is not permissable in this country, as we do not allow them to cruelly beat or punish their children."[50] Such comments represented violent husbands or fathers as men who had not achieved a white, native-born Protestant level of civilization and self-control.

The three Portland husbands who felt the lash were precisely the sort of men for whom middle- and upper-class Oregonians had little use. Portland arrest books for the six years that the whipping post law existed reveal little if any bias in the sentencing of men who assaulted their wives—with the exception of the three men who were whipped. Charles McGinty, the first, was an unemployed waiter at the time of his trial in June 1905. McGinty's wife, a waitress, testified that "I wouldn't give him money that I had earned and he blackened my eye and bruised my body."[51] A few weeks later Clem Bieker, an immigrant blacksmith from Russia, received ten lashes for beating his spouse. He reportedly drank up much of his own earnings and then "would demand coin from his wife, who took in washing to provide clothes for herself and the children." "When this money was refused," the article continued, "he would beat his wife."[52] Some two years later the *Oregonian* reported on a third whipping, this time of Henry Schaefer, a laborer. The story identified Schaefer as a "Slavonian" in its first line, and it included quotations from him that underlined his poor command of English. Another reporter referred to him as "the gigantic Russian wife-beater."[53] These men drank, took money from their spouses instead of supporting them, or could barely speak English. They not only hit their wives, they were failures as men, failures as Americans.

The identification of wife beaters as anti-American was most intense with Shaefer. One newspaper quoted his remarks after being whipped: "For seven years I break my back for my womens, in the old countries black bread an plow enough for woman, here you make a Saint Maria of 'em and de black whip hits my back for woman."[54] The whipping post's proponents could hardly have scripted a more edifying testimonial, the lesson of which was not lost on Portland women. One who identified herself as foreign born castigated Shaefer for perceiving a wife as "the husband's property, his chattel and his slave." "What mercy can a woman expect from a man with such ideas or from a [foreign] government that makes it possible for these men to have such ideas?" she asked rhetorically.[55] A year before, another woman had declared her "pardonable feeling of pride . . . that it is generally men of mixed nationality, and generally, too, drunken or otherwise morally degraded" men who beat their wives.[56] Strongly identifying the wife beater as a debased foreigner served to affirm his counterpart, the upright, native-born husband.

Wife beaters were not truly men. A reporter described McGinty as "the type of man one might have looked for in a search for wife-beaters. His face is weak and sensual."[57] Corporal punishment was a suitable punishment for this monstrosity, this "brutal creature miscalled a man" who beat his wife, for the act of whipping served to reveal these husbands' unmanliness.[58] A reporter happily noted that Shaefer, though determined not to flinch while being beaten, in fact cried out. Robert Cecil of eastern Oregon, apparently the only non-Portlander to be whipped, reportedly spent the night before his punishment "crying and blubbering in a disgusting manner." While being whipped he "blubbered like a baby."[59]

At best, the whipping post law reflected Oregon men's paternalism. Several legislators or editors emphasized battered women's helplessness, as did newspaper accounts of the three Portland cases. The same writer who referred to Shaefer as "the gigantic Russian wife-beater" described his wife as "a little, frail woman."[60] Governor West accompanied his veto of the law's repeal with a tribute to his mother and wife. In a much later reminiscence, he dated his support of woman suffrage to a summer day in 1883 when he heard Abigail Scott Duniway speak on women's rights. The words that "struck home and never left me all down through the years" were "Don't you consider your mother as good, if not better, than an ordinary Salem saloon bum?"[61] In locating women's antagonists among boozy loafers rather than the male sex as a whole, progressives like West could favor women's suffrage and temperance without forfeiting masculinity's more substantial prerogatives. Historians have pointed out that much of progressivism was shot through with masculinist rhetoric, that a more muscular type of reform seemed to be shouldering aside the feminine variety of the late nineteenth century. The whipping post well fitted this model. Legislated, imposed, and enforced completely by men for women's benefit, it reached back beyond the nineteenth century's sentimentalism to a time when justice was more retributive, bloody, and manly. Hence a male reader of the *Oregonian* referred to it as "that good old whipping post law."[62]

Oregon's legislators and judges seldom exhibited much respect for women as they argued over a measure ostensibly for women's benefit. Accounts of legislative debates did not indicate that the participants had consulted women. Judges, too, drew their own conclusions on what wives needed. Judge H. L. Benson of southern Oregon asserted that wives who accused their husbands of physical brutality changed their stories once the case reached court and might even refuse to testify. "Such women need beating," argued the judge: "They have got to have it in order to respect and admire the man they swore to love, honor and obey."[63] If battered women truly wished to escape their husbands, argued Benson, they should get a divorce. Two Portland-area judges also pointed to divorce as a better recourse than the whipping post for battered women, though they expressed much more empathy for such wives than Benson did. Portland district attorney John Manning, however, identified "loose ideas of marriage and divorce" as wife beating's "primal cause."[64] Only one of the judges interviewed by the *Oregonian* pointed out that the law's effects were hard to gauge because wives might "remain silent, as she hesitates at having her husband lashed."[65]

Oregon newspapers often assumed a lighthearted, highly misogynistic tone while speaking of the whipping post law. The reporter who asserted that twenty lashes was too few for McGinty, that the man "should have been made to scream and plead for mercy" closed his article by assuring readers that he would not "interfere with the ancient and honorable custom of wifebeating if practiced privately and in moderation."[66] Likewise, a rambling editorial in the *Oregonian* entitled "Women and Dogs" remarked that woman, "while refusing to be licked by any stranger that comes along, recognizes the prescriptive right of her husband to administer a thrashing." With the cost of marrying a wife going up "and Sichel flogging a man for beating one after he has got her, who is going to marry in Multnomah County?" wondered the editor. Several other newspapers also offered editorials making light of the law.[67] Indeed, spousal violence was something of a staple of newspaper humor. Just before the law's repeal, the conservative *Oregonian* published a mock conversation between a judge and a woman who wanted her husband arrested for assaulting her. When the judge expressed surprise that the wife would not need the warrant for a month, she explained that her husband would be incapacitated for that long because after he "slapped my face I took my rolling pin and hit him on the head, so that he had to be removed to the hospital."[68] A few weeks later another conservative Portland paper printed a cartoon showing a prissy young wife thrashing her drunken husband before calling her mother to complain that "I just can't stand this abuse!"[69]

Cartoons of women favoring suffrage pictured them hitting or threatening to hit men with umbrellas or rolling pins.[70] Many of the whipping post's supporters, as well as its opponents, no doubt felt a strong and sincere opposition to wife beating. But men on both sides of the issue not uncommonly found it difficult to take the problem seriously.

Women, for their part, expressed much less interest in the whipping post law than did men. An account of the state suffrage association's February 1905 meeting noted a discussion on forming a Travelers' Protective Association to safeguard women visiting Portland during the Lewis and Clark Exposition but made no mention of the whipping post law then being passed. Perhaps these women agreed with a suffragist in California who attributed violence against women to political and legal inequality and asserted that once women received a "square deal" they could "manage the wife-beater without the whipping-post."[71] Oregon's Woman's Christian Temperance Union also apparently ignored the law. In 1909, the year of Buchanon's unsuccessful repeal attempt, the W.C.T.U.'s legislative report indicated that it had worked for bills to establish a Sunday law, discourage cigarettes, suppress the sale of liquor in dry counties, and prohibit liquor from being shipped into dry states. It had also lobbied to get a bill introduced to establish a girls' reform school. In 1911, the year that the legislature overturned the whipping post, the legislative report of Oregon's W.C.T.U. expressed concern over prostitution, and its resolutions praised Governor West's prison reforms. But, as in 1909, it was silent on the whipping post, the law West had identified so strongly with women's interests. The measure captured the attention and support of some of Oregon's leading male progressives, but not their female counterparts.[72]

Oregon's women reformers may well have expressed so little interest in the whipping post because it was of so little utility. In the first place, the law could only be employed against husbands who had been charged with and convicted of assault and battery against their wives in circuit court. The court for the city of Portland referred only about seventeen wife beaters to the circuit court during the law's six years on the books, three of whom were then sentenced to a whipping. Only one man faced assault and battery charges for hitting his wife in the circuit court of Marion County, the second largest county in the state. Moreover, the few women whose husbands were whipped may well have regretted it. Such men could return straight home after being flogged rather than spending some months in jail, a fact that perhaps accounted for why McGinty's wife was reportedly "nearly overcome" when the judge announced that her husband would be whipped.[73] A columnist who followed the case no doubt compounded her difficulties when he wrote that only "bad women" would fall in love with a man like her husband, who "looks as if he had lived comfortably off the earnings of those whose ways take hold on hell."[74] Henry Shaefer's wife apparently suffered less calumny for being beaten, though the *Oregonian* quoted her husband at some length on her alleged behavior: "She spit in me face, and called me names of a vileness; she go places no womens should go."[75] Wives who read or heard of such accounts could not have been much encouraged to avail themselves of Oregon's new law.

Clem Bieker's whipping and subsequent behavior vividly illustrated the law's problems. An editorial quoted or paraphrased him as saying that "the punishment did him good."[76] Katherine Bieker's attorney noted that Clem then "went to one of the clergymen here and was very penitent and whined around being sorry . . . and there was some sort of a compromise between them, and they went back to live together." Three months later Katherine returned to her lawyer and related that "as soon as he got to drinking he seemed to feel that she was responsible for him being whipped," that he was "mad all the time . . . and strike me all the time." "We hoped the whipping post would have been a blessing in his particular case," her attorney noted, "but after a while he went back to the old life again." Indeed, Katherine's complaint described Clem as being "a frenzied monomaniac on the subject of the whipping post" who, when drunk, "has sought vengeance on plaintiff for being publicly disgraced by being whipped at the whipping post."[77]

Oregon's whipping post law probably better served Oregon's men than its women. The focus on brutal, barbaric husbands may have reassured politicians beleaguered by women's repeated demands for suffrage and other reforms that they were looking out for women's best interests. The law passed only a few months before the National American Woman Suffrage Association held its annual convention in Portland. In welcoming delegates from across the United States, Governor Chamberlain asserted that although Oregon had not passed suffrage, "it had given women more rights in other public matters than any other State" and cited the newly passed whipping post law.[78] A 1906 pamphlet from Oregon's anti-suffrage organization offered the whipping post law as evidence that Oregon men could be trusted to protect disenfranchised women.[79]

Respectable Oregon men used the whipping post law to define themselves as women's proper guardians at a time when women's demands for equality and autonomy were becoming increasingly determined. Discussions of wife beating and the whipping post commonly stressed women's helplessness and the need for men's paternalism, topics that reassured men who regretted women's growing independence. Even the reporter who implied that McGinty's wife was a prostitute referred to her as "a frail little woman."[80] The conservative *Oregonian* happily paired women's vulnerability and inferiority in a 1908 editorial on the Supreme Court's decision on *Muller v. Oregon*, the landmark case affirming protective laws for women wage earners. It praised the Court's observation that women and men differed "in the amount of physical strength, in the capacity for long-continued labor" and noted that such differences justified laws "designed to compensate her for some of the burdens that rest upon her." The editorial then quickly moved on to Milton on sexual inequality: "He for God only, she for God in him."[81] This was quite a leap, from acknowledging women's vulnerability to asserting their subservience, but the editorialist made it look easy. Men who began a discussion of women's issues with seeming empathy often closed with a reassertion of male dominance.

The public discourse around the whipping post law was a male discourse, with men assessing the law's purpose and efficacy. Women had no seats in the state legislature. They wrote no editorials for major Portland newspapers. The powerful men in these positions assured the public that the law had served women well. A representative from Pennsylvania asserted in Congressional debate that by 1906 wife beating had "almost disappeared" in Oregon due to the whipping post.[82] The *Oregonian* editorialized in early 1911 that since the law's passage "there has been very little wife-beating."[83] Sichel, shortly before his death, stated that his law had reduced the frequency of wife beating by 75 percent.[84] Such assertions reflected a remarkable confidence in men's ability to solve quickly such an intractable and widespread women's dilemma.

Despite Sichel's assertion, wife beating remained common in early-twentieth-century Portland, and it rested on a set of broadly shared masculine ideas that the men who debated the whipping post law often articulated themselves. Oregon newspapers attributed wife beating to wives' cowardice, repeatedly treated the practice as funny or improbable, and implied that the wife of a man punished at the whipping post was a loose woman.

The whipping post law did not prompt men to search their own souls. The reporter who noted that Charles McGinty "slunk out of sight, a thing ashamed" after his whipping wrote from the perspective of a guiltless bystander.[85] When the managers of the Southern Pacific shops greeted Clem Bieker on the day after his whipping with the news that "wifebeaters were not wanted, and that he would have to look elsewhere for work," they could watch him leave feeling better about themselves as men and as husbands. Bieker carried on his shoulders the guilt of many men as he "hung his head and left the shops."[86]

The whipping post law offered men troubled by the discomforting relationship between wife abuse, male dominance, and misogyny a simple and painless solution. The handful of wife beaters who suffered a flogging were classic scapegoats, marginal men selected by community leaders to bear the larger group's largely unacknowledged flaws. McGinty was ideal for this role, a contemptible, grotesquely abusive man whose bloodied back served to cleanse the consciences of more powerful and respectable husbands. He distracted attention from the more stubborn and widely shared causes of wife beating.[87]

In actuality, of course, many different sorts of men hit their wives. Evidence from nearly 500 Multnomah County divorce petitions indicates that husbands' propensity toward violence varied little by class. Wives in divorce suits described 70 percent of abusive working-class husbands as violent compared to 74 percent of proprietors, white-collar workers, and professionals. The frequency of violence for the two categories was nearly identical.[88] Qualitative evidence underscores this quantitative evidence. Bertha Sproat, married to Dr. James Sproat, a surgeon, asserted that he subjected her to personal violence on her slightest remonstrance to his ungovernable temper when he was intoxicated. Edwin Mayor, a manager in an investment company, reportedly gave his wife an extensive beating with his fists.[89]

Immigrant status was somewhat more likely to predict physical cruelty. The proportion of abusive spouses who used violence stood at 83 percent for first-generation immigrants, 73 percent for second-gener-ation immigrants, and 72 percent for those with native-born parents. The frequency of violence for the foreign-born versus the other two groups was virtually the same, however. Measuring use of wife beat-ing by particular social groups is notoriously difficult, even among con-temporary populations. But the evidence offers scant support for whip-ping post proponents' connecting foreign birth and low socioeconomic status with wife beating.[90]

Proponents of Oregon's whipping post law identified and punished a handful of wife beaters and claimed great success in assisting abused wives. Yet such women more often looked to neighbors and friends for help than to the law.

The city court tended to handle assaults against wives differently from other assaults. Only 21 percent of men arrested for assaulting their wives received a fine or jail sentence compared to 45 percent for the other assaults. The wife beaters who were fined tended to get stiffer penalties. They were much more likely to receive a continued or sus-pended sentence, presumably so the police and the court could keep an eye on them, and to be sent on to the circuit court, where they might receive a harsher penalty than the lower court could impose. The court, then, punished wife assault less commonly than other types of assault, but the punishments for wife assault it did mete out were relatively stiff.[91]

Only small numbers of Portland wife beaters encountered the police. Out of nearly 500 divorce cases describing wife abuse, only 34 depicted intervention by the police. Intervention did not necessarily result in arrest. The city's arrest books indicated only 157 arrests of husbands for assaulting their wives during the whipping post law's six-year life, or barely 2 per month. African American, foreign born, and working-class husbands were arrested in disproportionate numbers. But the police commonly hesitated to arrest all types of husbands. Mary Glaze, who had just recently left Russia with her husband, asked them to arrest Minon for threatening her life. They chose not to, for he assured them that no further disturbances would occur. Later that day Minon was dead from a gunshot wound, apparently inflicted by his wife in self-defense.[92]

Neighbors were often more helpful than police were. Portland wives apparently enjoyed more assistance from third parties early in the twentieth century than had their more rural counterparts late in the nineteenth. The boarders or servants with whom so many Portland couples lived could be particularly useful. G. W. Phelps resided at Zerrildea Pershin's boarding house and on at least two occasions "interfered" when her husband tried to assault her.[93] A boarder at the Clifton House, kept by Eliza and Thomas Dodson, said that when Thomas shook his fist at Eliza "I thought he was going to slap her and I stepped between them."[94] Charles and Harriet Carlson's housekeeper acted similarly:

> At one time I was in the kitchen doing something and I knew when he went into the other room that he was angry and I heard her scream I did not want to go near them at all but I had to I did not want to interfere I heard Mrs. Carlson scream, I went in and he had a great long butcher knife he had it in one hand and the other hand he had raised as if he was going to strike her, he was using hard words. I said "Mr Carlson what do you mean by this["] and I separated them and Mrs. Carlson went over and laid on the lounge and fainted.[95]

Even a servant, employed for less than a month, felt obligated to interfere with a knife-wielding husband.

Neighbors in densely packed neighborhoods often felt a similar obligation. Mrs. Slatton, neighbor of Ada and Frederick Diez, literally rescued Ada from the upstairs window that she had climbed through as the drunken and threatening Frederick searched the home's interior: "I got the ladder and took her down into my room in her night clothes; in the pouring rain and she was wet and hanging with her finger tips."[96] Male neighbors ran similar risks. S. C. Hilton recalled an evening when he and a friend were sitting out on his front porch:

> We saw quite a gathering over in front of Mr. Pederson's place, and I sat there and didn't pay much attention to it, but directly the crowd got a little larger, so I proposed to the other fellow we go over and see what the trouble is; so we came down and he was out there on the sidewalk talking very loud, and she was standing there with her clothes bursted open down as low as my vest or a little lower, and he asked some one to go and get a doctor; he tried to leave the impression on the crowd that she was out of her head. I could tell that the man had been drinking some which I had heard that he had right along before; and then he wanted her to go back in the house with

him and she says, "No, I will never go back in the house again with you for you to beat me and tear my clothes off.["] Shortly afterwards he seemed to get ashamed and he goes back into the house by himself. I asked the plaintiff to go over to the house with me, my wife and I were living in the next block, and she asked me to go in and get her child, but I refused to go in and get the child, but I told her I would go into the door with her, and she could go in and get the child, which she did, and she went in and went over to my place, and stayed probably a couple of days; something like that.

Hilton asserted that "I didn't know them at the time . . . my wife had never been over there," though he had heard from "the general talk of the neighbors" that Pedersen was a poor provider. He concluded his testimony by remarking that "I would have done the same with any one as I did that evening. I thought it was every man's duty."[97]

Portland men often exercised this duty cautiously, however. C. W. Peckham recalled being awakened by "some hollowing" one night and looking out his window to see a couple arguing and struggling. Peckham then "opened my front door and stood in the door and watched them" and "waited until I was called" rather than rushing to the woman's assistance.[98] Likewise, Fred Bauer recalled a day when "I mistrusted something" about his neighbor, Peter Sitta. Hence "in the evening when I saw him going down to the saloon, thinks I, I better kind of look after him and see what he does." Bauer watched Sitta "fill up pretty well on beer," and noted that when Sitta returned home "he didn't blow out the light but he walked back and forth, storming around" and kicking chairs.[99] Bauer eventually left his post at the window and went to bed. At about 1:00 a.m. a noise from the Sittas' home awakened Bauer, and as it grew louder he dressed himself. But the tumult then ceased, and Bauer again retired. Some two hours later Rose Sitta, an invalid, sent her foster daughter to the Bauers' for help, and Fred Bauer awoke to see his son carrying the bloodied Rose to safety. Fred Bauer took considerable pains to monitor Peter Sitta's behavior, but he hesitated to intervene without strong evidence of a physical assault.

Not all neighbors were so attentive. Maud Logan recalled becoming "so angry that I had to go away" from her neighbors. "He was striking her," she explained, "and I didn't want to get into the fight myself."[100] Some Portland wives found themselves expelled from their homes along with their violent spouses. Docia Stevens noted that a landlady told her and her husband to move: "she could not stand it; she was afraid he would do something to me."[101] T. Hammersly, a landlord and police officer, recalled hearing a quarrel between his tenants late at night: "I says, 'What is this trouble about?' And she says, 'This man is trying to kill me, and I want to show you where he has beat me,' and I says, 'No, I want you folks to get on your clothes and get out of here as soon as you can.'"[102] Yet Hammersly testified that he had believed the woman's claim of physical abuse.

Violent husbands fiercely contested the rights of others to interfere in their domestic affairs. H. F. Cuthill recalled awaking to the sound of his sister, Marjorie Coles, screaming as her husband James tried to wrench some money from her. Cuthill separated the couple, an action that prompted James to threaten "trouble" if Cuthill went "between me and my wife." "I don't care for law, heaven, hell, nor God," he explained, for "I will kill the first man that interferes between me and my family."[103] B. Phelps witnessed an especially explicit assertion of absolute patriarchy when she heard a gunshot and ran to her daughter's apartment to find her prostrate and the son-in-law in the act of fatally shooting their fleeing child. "Get out of here," he told her: "Everything here belongs to me."[104]

Homicidal Portland husbands might refuse to draw a distinction between their wives and their wives' families. In 1902 A. Lester Belding shot and killed his wife and mother-in-law and seriously wounded his father-in-law. After the shootings he reportedly rejoiced that "I have got three of them" and asserted that "I would have liked to kill everybody by the name of McCroskey." E. P. McCroskey, the slain wife's brother, explained that another sister "often urged Mrs. Belding to leave her brutal husband, and for this reason the fiend wished to slay the whole family."[105] In 1907 Portland's Fred Martin, formerly a salesman for the Pacific Biscuit Company, fatally shot himself after wounding his wife and murdering her sister, whom he held responsible for the end of his marriage. In a letter written just before the shootings he explained to his wife that his sister-in-law "stands between us" and "has put us both where we will soon be."[106] Martha Dickerson's 1907 divorce complaint noted that her husband had said, "I mean to kill you, your child and your father and wipe out the whole race."[107] In early-twentieth-century Portland, a time and place poised between the traditional public family and the emergent private one, a wife and her family could appear to be one.

A sense of shame could inhibit how wives reacted to violence. Minnie Tweed recalled telling a sister who inquired about her swollen face that "I bruised it on the sewing machine" since "I was ashamed" of her husband's blow.[108] Clara Young remarked that "I ought to be ashamed to tell it" before describing to the court how her husband, A. G., had threatened her with a revolver and slapped her.[109] Portland's large size did not keep divorce cases from being something of a public spectacle. Newspapers routinely summarized the most lurid cases, and curiosity seekers attended in person. In one instance a judge "cleared the courtroom of a curious crowd of men" before a divorce-seeking wife testified.[110]

Yet divorce became increasingly attractive to Portland's wives. Even the *Oregonian*, one of the state's most conservative papers, editorialized in 1910 that divorces, though "doubtless regrettable," were "not so deplorable as they are depicted sometimes."[111] The court apparently agreed. In a sample of over 240 wives who cited abuse in suits filed from 1905 to 1907 it awarded 82 divorces for every suit it dismissed.[112] Oregon courts also ordered long-term payments to divorced wives more commonly than they had during the nineteenth century. In 1905 the Oregon Supreme Court established that a man owed his former wife child support, even though he had been the one to obtain the divorce.[113] Such decisions, though by no means common, combined with Portland's growing economic opportunities to take some of the economic sting out of divorce.

Nonetheless, the decision to leave a violent husband still brought many financial risks and hardships, particularly for wives with children. A 1913 survey of Oregon's women workers found that three-fifths of the women employed in Portland industries made under $10.00 per week. "A large majority of self-supporting women in the state are earning less than it costs them to live decently," the report concluded.[114] Pauline Gray left her husband and had to board her six-year-old boy out while she earned a living. "After I worked myself down," she recalled, "I could not keep the boy and I sent him back to his father . . . My health would not permit me to support myself and the boy any longer."[115] Carrie Rees said that her husband, Park, had left her and that she gave up her custody of their two children to him because "he would not support them and have them with me."[116] Portland's separated or single mothers might also lose their children to institutions like the Boys and Girls Aid Society, which grew increasingly common and powerful around the turn of the century. In one case the court ordered that organization to turn over the children to their father, who had recently won a divorce from his wife on grounds of adultery. A couple of years later the woman learned from a newspaper report that her ex-husband had been accused of sexually abusing their oldest daughter, not yet a teenager: "I cant express my feeling when I heard . . . and must say that it is why I fought so hard for my children and I think that peeple will began to realize what I have had to contend with but it seems as it mite be to late."[117] Leslie Tentler, in her survey of wage-earning women, concludes that "regardless of how unsatisfactory she felt her marriage to be—no matter how genuinely she resented the restrictions of her life—the working-class wife could not help but learn . . . that, in the real world, women needed men."[118] Working-class women on the West Coast, less apt to belong to conservative ethnic groups and living in states with more liberal divorce laws, probably felt these restrictions less keenly than those in the East did. But in Portland, too, divorce continued to bring many risks and hardships.

Much of that hardship consisted of threats, assaults, and even murders by estranged or former husbands. O. C. Ogden reportedly tricked his way into the home that his wife had fled to by saying that their infant daughter was dying. He then beat his wife unconscious. Bertha Highfield said that her estranged husband waited outside her place of employment "and when the girls would start out from work he would stand out and abuse me." She consequently had to quit the job, since "the firm wouldn't stand anything like that."[119] A witness in another suit recalled a conversation between Eliza and Thomas Dodson: "They would have difficulty some time and he would seem to be very angry and mean to her and she says to him 'If you don't treat me better I will leave you, I will leave you and get a divorce from you and won't live with you', he says, 'If you do . . . I will kill you and every one that helps you.'"[120] Such threats were not always empty. From 1900 to 1910 at least five Multnomah County wives died at their husband's hands.[121]

Class and immigrant status, apparently of little import in predicting husbands' violence, more strongly conditioned how wives reacted to it. Fifty-one divorce cases citing physical violence that described one of the spouses as leaving could be traced to the 1900 manuscript census. Foreign-born women left in only 38 percent of the cases, second-generation women in 54 percent, and women born to native-born parents in 77 percent.[122] Class also influenced whether or not a woman left a violent husband, although less dramatically. Only 50 percent of women married to white-collar men left, compared to 62 percent for women married to working-class husbands. This same pattern emerged from accounts of third-party interventions. Some 38 percent of the wives with working-class husbands described such interventions, while only 28 percent of women wed to proprietors or white-collar men did.[123] Women married to men with high-status occupations and immigrant women left violent husbands more rarely than did other women, and well-to-do women benefited from direct interventions more rarely than other women did.

As during the settlement period, staying with a violent husband did not necessarily mean submitting to him. Portland women seemed to resist their violent husbands more directly than their rural and small-town counterparts of the 1890s had. Zerrildea Pershin testified that her husband had "choked me so many times that I learned the habit of standing perfectly still, allowing my body to relax." In another instance she resisted more overtly: "I grabbed him by the whiskers, he kept trying to get nearer and kept gnawing at my hand with his teeth, I kept close to his face so he could not eat me, he kept kicking me, I thought he was trying to kill me."[124] Other women successfully fought their husbands off. Jennie Fine recalled how her husband returned home at 3:00 a.m. one morning, hit her, and declared: "Now, God damn you, I am going to kill you." "But he did not amount to anything anyhow," remarked Jennie, "and I finally got loose from him," went to a friend's house, and "have not lived with him since."[125] Eva Hazel described how her husband, Edwin, attempted in vain to terrorize and intimidate her:

> I had dinner waiting for two or three hours, and there was words about dinner being cold, and I said, "I have waited since 12 o'clock for you, and now it is nearly three," and we had some words, and he says, "I will fix you" and he made a dive at me and tore my waist off, and then he says, "I know a better way," so he went right to my canary

bird and tore its head off of it and threw it out into the yard and then he made another dive at me, and I told him I wasn't afraid of him, and then he said he would skin my dog, and I got the dog away.[126]

Another women reportedly hit her husband over the head with a shoe to repulse forcible attempts at sex; another knocked her spouse downstairs with a broomstick to keep him out of the house.[127]

Elsie Siedow recounted a particularly harrowing struggle with her ex-husband, Fred, when he accosted her on the street with a revolver. She later recalled that she "looked him in the eye, like you would an animal . . . and I got up close and jumped at him." Fred fired and missed, then tried to shoot her again, "but I threw all my strength on him, caught his wrist and began tearing at it to make him let go of the revolver." The weapon eventually fell from Fred's hand, and Elsie picked it up and ran to a neighbor's home. "This is the third time he has tried to kill me," she concluded, "and I think he ought to get about six years this time."[128]

Ida Carlisle's ex-husband, John, accosted her on the street, fired into her head from only four feet away and then, believing her dead, shot and killed himself. The bullet, deflected by Ida's teeth, passed through her cheek, leaving her only slightly wounded. "I could not make up with him," Ida explained to a reporter. "I had suffered for 30 years through him and I did not intend to go back to that terrible life."[129] Increasing numbers of wives married to violent men exhibited that resolution in early-twentieth-century Portland, even at the risk of horrible cruelties, even at the risk of death.

The resources that women such as Ida Carlisle actually used against their violent husbands contrasted sharply with the images painted of them by proponents of Oregon's whipping post law. Rather than acknowledging and abetting women's power, the law was a unilateral male solution. It was also an attempt by prominent men to define and ultimately to minimize this problem by representing the wife beater as a highly deviant and unusual type.

In Portland's homes and streets wife beating assumed a much different form than it did in debates carried on at the state capital or in the columns of leading newspapers. Physical violence occurred commonly among all types of Portlanders, including the well-to-do and the native born. A wife's best defense against a violent spouse was not the threat of twenty lashes, but the help of neighbors, together with her own courage and skill.

More than six decades would pass between the repeal of the whipping post law in 1911 and renewed public and legislative concern for the safety of Oregon wives. Yet those six decades were hardly safe ones for these women. Sigmund Sichel died in 1917, apparently believing that his law had brought a dramatic decrease in wife beating. He was mistaken. Violence against wives would in fact grow during the twentieth century, abetted by a cultural transformation that had already begun in Portland and that would soon spread even to the state's most remote hamlets.

4

"To Use His Muscle on Her": 1920–1945

As Oregon legislators debated the whipping post law in the early twentieth century, deep social and cultural changes were taking place. By the 1920s the transformation was evident even in Oregon's small towns. Cars had largely supplanted horses, movies had shouldered aside many traditional, home-centered modes of entertainment, and young women increasingly looked and acted like young men. Oregon, like the nation as a whole, became modern after World War I.

An abundance of consumer goods accounted for much of this change. The basis of prosperity was shifting from a production-oriented economy to a service-oriented one. Machines displaced workers in both field and factory, and a growing proportion of people worked for large corporations as clerks or managers. Neither set of employees enjoyed much occupational autonomy. Workers therefore often defined themselves by what they did off the job, as consumers. Indeed, the nation's well-being seemed based more on the number of consumer goods that people purchased than on the tons of steel they produced or bushels of wheat they harvested. Technology had unlocked the secret of production, and prosperity depended on people's ability to absorb the cornucopia of goods. This revolution in technology and economy fathered a revolution in values. Warren Susman points out that in the 1920s the leading cause of death shifted from tuberculosis, a sign of deprivation, to heart attacks, a sign of affluence, as befitting a nation that had become more oriented to consuming than producing, to spending than to saving.[1]

This orientation persisted through the 1930s, its severe depression notwithstanding. Winifred Wandersee notes that early in the Depression, especially, consumption remained remarkably high. Radio and movies retained their popularity, and people continued to find money for cigarettes, alcohol, and gasoline. To be sure, the 1930s had a more somber tone than the 1920s. But the years saw a reversal in people's economic fortunes, not their core beliefs or aspirations. World War II offered a respite of sorts from the hardships of the Depression, since it restored people's earning power, if not the widespread availability of consumer goods. Hence the key values of the 1920s—consumption, freedom of expression, and independence of action—remained relatively unscathed by depression and war.[2]

These values profoundly influenced the nature of violence against wives. A consumption-oriented culture, in Daniel Bell's words, entailed "a shift from the hold of restraint to the acceptance of impulse."[3] Self-restraint, the prime virtue of the late nineteenth century, was going out of style. Modernity also brought a blurring of husbands' and wives' spheres and an increased intimacy between them. These developments raised marital expectations and conflict and isolated wives from traditional sources of support. But this movement toward self-realization and privacy expanded the limits of acceptable behavior for wives and husbands alike. The modern wife would become increasingly vulnerable to violence, but she would be increasingly able to resist and escape it.

Oregon came of age between 1900 and 1945. In many ways, the state's historic homogeneity became even more pronounced. Ethnic distinctions softened over time, as the percentage of foreign born dropped from 17 percent in 1910 to 8 percent in 1940. People of color became even more scarce after 1900, until World War II brought an influx of African Americans. Nonwhites constituted 4.6 percent of Oregon's population in 1900, and only 1.3 percent in 1940. Oregon retained its middle-class orientation. In 1920, 55 percent of its household heads owned their homes, compared to 46 percent for the nation as a whole. Homesteading continued in parts of eastern Oregon well into the 1920s. But other demographic trends dwarfed the homesteaders' largely futile efforts to wring a livelihood from the state's most arid and isolated lands. The percentage of urban residents in Oregon rose from 32 percent in 1900 to just under 50 percent in 1920, where it varied little until spurting again during World War II. The state's population grew from approximately 673,000 in 1920 to 954,000 in 1930, expanded more modestly in the 1930s, then shot up during the war.[4]

Urban and rural Oregon remained divided in many ways. Some 58 percent of Portland households had radios in 1930 compared to 34 percent of rural farm families, for example. Sex ratios varied by place. Portland, where men had always predominated, had a male-to-female ratio of 0.954 to one in 1940, as women in search of jobs and autonomy moved there. The figure for Wheeler County, one of the least populous in eastern Oregon, then stood at 1.34 to one. The genders tended toward parity in small towns. Eastern Oregon's Prineville, with only 2,356 residents, had a ratio of 1.16 men for each woman in 1940, markedly lower than the 1.42 to one ratio for the rest of sparsely populated Crook County. On the whole, eastern Oregon languished during the twentieth century's first decades while Portland and the Willamette Valley continued to grow. Portland remained the state's only metropolis. A woman explained in 1923 her husband's reasons for moving to Portland: he "hates Bend," she said, "because it is a small town and he can't jazz around enough."[5] A writer for a Bend newspaper described the hubbub in a local restaurant when a woman from out of town lit up a cigarette one day in 1924: "The row of heads from one end of the counter to the other bobbed back and forth in an effort to see the performance."[6] Yet Nard Jones's *Oregon Detour*, a realistic novel of life in a small eastern Oregon town, showed clearly that the Jazz Age affected even rural families. "The farm people weren't like they had been," he wrote. "Etta could have hummed the latest tune" of New York composers "just as quickly as any city girl. She heard them every night over the radio."[7] In Oregon's only major city the twenties roared the loudest, the Depression hit the hardest, and the wartime boom went the farthest. But every nook of Oregon had entered the modern era by the time Japanese bombs fell on Pearl Harbor.[8]

A broad and profound shift, a sea change, was at work beneath the Jazz Age's tumult. Presbyterian Andrew Carrick, preaching near Portland in 1934, reported that local high school students went "*joy-riding* to dances in Portland and other places, usually *unknown* to parents, and the *affairs end* in a drunken carousal." Carrick attributed such practices to a pervasive "unrest" and "lawlessness." "There is," he asserted, "a chafing under the constraint of society."[9] The Reverend Goodsell, preaching in Portland in 1937, recalled the negative impact that World War I had made on the nation and that "an orgy of materialism, hectic finance, pleasure seeking and what was—and still is sometimes called—sex freedom" had followed.[10] Robert Charlton Lee, who served churches in both Portland and eastern Oregon, best summed up the era's mood when he remarked that "the so called search for happiness is an amazing contrast to the old time search for character."[11] To be sure, more than a few Oregonians continued to value character over a good time, just as many late-nineteenth-century residents had made the opposite choice. But the quarter-century between the end of the two world wars saw a significant and widespread shift in culture and values in Oregon and across the United States.

The most fundamental way to trace major changes in the U.S. family during the twentieth century is to examine its shifting functions. Simply stated, the family dropped many of its roles while intensifying those it retained. Public education, including high schools, had spread throughout Oregon, and growing numbers of institutions cared for the elderly, the sick, the infirm, and the motherless. Few people, aside from farmers, performed remunerative work in the home. Housewives increasingly purchased food, clothing, and other materials rather than making or even processing them. The Reverend Goodsell, in a 1939 sermon delivered in Portland, contrasted modern life with the nineteenth century, when "all life . . . centered in the home": nowadays "we buy our soap ready-made. The factory can make it cheaper and better. We buy canned goods; we buy most of our clothing ready-made or tailor made. We send our soiled linen to the laundry; we buy our bread from the baker; we do considerable of our eating at restaur[a]nts and hotels. We are born at the hospital; we are taken there again when we are sick. When the end comes we die there; and we are buried from a mortuary."[12] The days of home manufacturing and home nursing had largely disappeared.

The home's role as a source of nurture and intense emotional interaction grew as its more prosaic functions withered. Familial privacy rose as servants, other employees, boarders, elderly parents, and even children became less numerous. Oregon's average dwelling shrank from 5.07 people in 1890 to 3.85 in 1930, from 7.43 to 4.05 for Portland. The family's psychological functions became more salient as its membership diminished. Indeed, John Demos calls the twentieth-century family an "encounter group," a place of intense emotional interaction.[13]

Marital satisfaction increasingly rested on the mutual provision of emotional fulfillment, not simply on complementary work and social roles. A husband illustrated his love for his estranged wife not by recounting his faithfulness as a breadwinner, but by remembering how "I give you coffe on the bed every morning and I kised good buy when I whent to work."[14] Historian Elaine Tyler May has argued that rising material expectations wreaked havoc on early-twentieth-century marriages. The modern woman demanded more love, as well. A Willamette Valley wife complained in 1923 that "I never have any good time since I married" and told the man that she hoped to wed after leaving her husband that "you said you made enough to keep us but I am sure I could live on love the rest of my days with you Honey."[15] Another dissatisfied wife, writing from a tiny eastern Oregon town a decade later, told her beau to "write and tell me if you love me and want me. I don't care if you haven't got a penny and I have to live in a tent. I'd love you just the same." "Darling," she remarked, "its sure hell living with a man you don't love."[16]

Shifting the foundations of marriage from duty and obligation to love and happiness made for frequent divorce. Marital dissolutions in the United States rose gradually from 1920 to 1940, then sharply during World War II. Oregon's rate continued to exceed the nation's, and Portland had a national reputation for divorce. Divorce flourished because it offered a chance for happiness. "Why live with some one that takes all the joy out of life when theres another that makes life worth liveing," remarked one woman.[17] "We're both young enough to enjoy a great deal of our lives," wrote a husband in 1935 to the wife he had left: "Life is just too darned short for us to 'amble along', being dissatisfied or miserable most of the time."[18] Romance could assume such an intoxicating, ennobling form that it overrode and transcended conventional commitments and morality. A Willamette Valley woman, unhappily married to one preacher and deeply in love with another, spoke movingly of the latter as "my own Godgiven husband," and asserted that they must "meet to part no more . . . on this earth. God must let us live and work together. *Yes he must.*" "I know," she remarked, "we are not doing anything that any other natural human creature would not do."[19] Following one's heart, even at the expense of sundering a marriage, had come to be seen as a natural and therefore healthy act. The typical wife or husband seeking to escape a marriage devoted much less energy to moral, theological, or scientific justifications and simply asserted a right to happiness and independence. A divorce-seeking war bride in 1944, for example, informed her husband that "I'm young and have a lot of life ahead of me—too much to be tied down to a cold self centered prude like you." "You have often said you wanted me to be happy above all," she concluded. "Please, Charles, set me free."[20]

Higher expectations of one's spouse encouraged more intimacy as well as more divorce. Even the sexes' appearances, so starkly different during the nineteenth century, converged as women shortened their hair and flattened their figures. The terms that spouses and lovers employed while writing to each other signified the shift: "dearest Daddy"; "sweet Daddie"; "Sis"; "papa"; "kiddo"; "sweetheart mine"; "Billie Boy mine"; and "dear little baby."[21] The common use of diminutive and highly familial terms indicated a relationship between the sexes that had become at once more intense and more casual, an erosion of the gap that had separated woman from man during the nineteenth century. One man, confessing his love for another woman, wrote his wife that she should have been "more of a sweet heart & less of a mother," that "if a man hasnt a sweet heart at home he'll have one some place else."[22] By the same token, an estranged woman wrote that her marriage would have gone better if her husband "would have been loving & gentle toward me I mean a lover instead of just a husband."[23] Marriage was supposed to be fun. In 1923 a Bend area woman left her husband a farewell note in which she told him, "You are to old in your ways for me. All you do is stick around camp don't want to go no where."[24] The flapper, seeking and enjoying the company of men, had replaced the home-centered lady as the leading image of womanhood.

This image, and the social reality it reflected, brought many advantages to twentieth-century women. Most obviously, it undercut the double standard for sexual and general pleasure, thus making available to them a range of gratifying and exciting experiences that had been off-limits to respectable women. Opportunities for freedom probably peaked during World War II, certainly for Portland women. One young wife recalled how at "the last of my school life—I decided to get some of the attention the other girls did" and "started to go around with the Naval Air Cadets." Her "dates took me to all the best places— no movie-cake dates!" She eventually decided to woo a shy sailor, someone "not even the most glamourous gals I knew could get a rise out of." He soon fell for her, but after wearing his ring for two weeks she "told him to jump in the lake." "Cold blooded you say?" she asked rhetorically: "Nope—just smart!"[25] The quintessential wise nineteenth-century woman had guarded her virtue carefully and had waited for the suitor most likely to offer a lifetime of respectful treatment and financial security. Twentieth-century women, including many from the middle class, were much more apt and able to pursue aggressively their own pleasures and opportunities.

Increased intimacy between the sexes also brought advantages to women within marriage. Wives seeking divorces in the 1920s and 1930s evinced higher standards for marital reciprocity than had their nineteenth-century counterparts. One remarked that "just as soon as we got married he wouldn't pay any attention to my wishes at all. I don't think we ever went to one picture show that was of my choosing."[26] Another wife, asked if she had given her husband any reason to be cruel, replied: "Never that I know of, unless I have been too easy with him and given him his way too much."[27] Another divorce-seeking woman, responding to a similar question, retorted: "I was evidently too good to him, he was so over-bearing."[28] Nineteenth-century wives had emphasized to the courts their obedience and submissiveness, even if their actual behavior contradicted these norms. But these twentieth-century women criticized themselves before the court for being too agreeable, and they assumed a rough equality between the sexes. Hence one wife's complaint quoted her husband as saying that he wanted " 'to be his own boss' meaning that he wanted to be single again."[29] The increased emphasis on romance and intimacy meant that wives expected more of their husbands than they had before.

But increased intimacy had its costs. The erosion of the sexual double standard could be used by husbands to deny wives sexual safety or privacy. An eastern Oregon woman complained in 1924 that her husband had asked for sex "in a way I don't think a white man and woman should, or any body else," that "he was in Germany and France during the war and he said that was the way they used to do over there."[30] She reportedly carried a small gun on her person to keep her estranged husband from forcing himself on her. A Willamette Valley woman's complaint noted that her husband had insisted on viewing her while she bathed, even to the point of standing on a ladder outside their bathroom window. Historian Ellen Trimberger has shown how the emphasis on mutual sexual satisfaction and psychological intimacy in New York City's Greenwich Village served in practice to serve only men's needs; and she and Alice Echols point out that closer relationships between the sexes eroded the rich and nurturing all-female networks that women had constructed during the nineteenth century. Hence a woman recalled that when she told her husband, "I would like to go home and visit my mother," whom she had not seen for two years, he replied, "You are supposed to give up your mother when you get married."[31] Marital intimacy often occurred on men's terms. Marian Miller, a popular Portland advice columnist, commonly counseled patience and tact to women married to self-centered husbands. To an intelligent young woman having trouble attracting men she advised, "When you meet a man who seems desirable look at him with a baby stare and be dumb." "Bake them a good pie, make them talk about themselves and maybe they'll admire you," she continued.[32] Closer relationships between the sexes opened the door both for more reciprocity and for more oppression and isolation.

Women's work lives increasingly resembled men's, particularly in cities and during World War II. Joan Jensen has noted that rural women's household production and sale of commodities like butter declined as farms became more specialized and as farm families purchased more household goods. At the same time the proportion of Oregonians working outside the home who were women rose steadily: 11 percent in 1900, 17 percent in 1920, 20 percent in 1930, and 22 percent in 1940. The proportion of wives in the work force also rose, from 4 percent in 1900 to 14 percent in 1930. World War II brought the greatest influx of women and wives: 41 percent of a group of women shipyard workers said that they had been housewives before the war. Portland women earned wages more commonly than did their rural counterparts, even before the shipyard boom. They constituted 30 percent of Portland's employees by 1940, compared to only 10 percent of employees living on farms. Cities acted as a magnet for single and divorced women: in 1930, Oregon's urban women were more than three times as likely to be divorced than were rural farm women. Females headed 17 percent of Portland families, but only 5 percent of rural farm families. The quality of women's jobs also improved in the century's first decades. Clerical and sales work expanded dramatically. More women worked as professionals—though usually very low-paid ones—than as domestics, women's chief vocation until early in the twentieth century. World War II brought particularly dramatic improvements, at least in Portland. Women made up 27 percent of the employees at Kaiser's three huge shipyards in 1944, thus becoming an integral part of what had been an all-male preserve.[33]

These employment trends mask a great deal of continuity and stubborn inequality. Only a small fraction of wives worked outside the home, and many who did so preferred not to. African American wives, commonly among Oregon's poorest residents, were more than three times as likely to work for wages in 1920 than were their Euro-American counterparts. Some 20 percent of homemakers among families who rented in 1930 were gainfully employed compared to only 13 percent of those who owned their homes. Relatively few of these jobs paid very well. In the nation as a whole, women's access to the professions slowed or reversed itself between the two world wars, particularly during the 1930s. Working wives invited censure during the Depression, even though their numbers increased and their wages could keep a family from abject poverty. A Portland woman noted that her husband's failure to support her and their two children meant that she had to get a job, which caused her great shame among her friends. A judge told another divorce-seeking Portland wife that "she should be in the home rearing" her two children, ages fourteen and twelve, "not out working."[34] Historians emphasize that working wives tended to define and even pursue employment as a familial rather than as a personal goal, that they interpreted it as a way to enhance their family's ability to consume.[35]

But wives' work—low pay, stigma, and family orientation notwithstanding—affected the balance of power within marriage. A Portland woman in the Depression, asked by a district attorney how her husband's conduct affected her, retorted, "Well, I don't want to put up with it. I don't see why I should support he and I both."[36] In 1945 a husband accused by his wife of severely beating her blamed their problems on his wife's full-time job at Montgomery Ward's, which had emboldened her to keep her own schedule and to obtain a restraining order barring him from their home. The prospect of supporting herself freed another woman from her marriage and freed her tongue to describe in a 1928 letter to her husband the abuses she had suffered:

> I wouldnt live with you again or any other man I remember one time when we went to Salem you never gave me a cent but tagged me around every minute and if I bought anything you had to pay for it. I was so mad I said to myself d——m a man I am to independent to live with a man no more for me. When we sell the farm I will get in to something that I can make a living at with out much work.

The woman expected this work to be less onerous than her labors as a wife. "I used to spend about half my time running from the kitchen to the wood shed for wood," she recalled. "Im off that stuff for life."[37] Even low-paying jobs could offer an attractive alternative to keeping house for a cruel husband.

Oregon's wives experienced a strong, often contradictory set of changes between the two world wars. To be sure, much remained unchanged. Only a small proportion of wives worked outside the home, aside from a couple of years during World War II, and the great majority of wives continued to define themselves as homemakers. Remarked one woman who had been deserted by her husband: "I always tried to keep the home together. I think a woman's [sic] feels a home is something sort of sacred."[38] But the nature of that home changed, even for the great majority of wives who did not work outside it. Greater emphasis on the affectionate and romantic aspects of marriage made for increased emotional intensity between spouses, a trend facilitated by smaller and more socially isolated families. Wives spent more time with their husbands, less with women relatives and neighbors. Both husbands and wives expected more care and love from each other than before, expectations that fueled a rising divorce rate. A growing, if still small, proportion of wives obtained an independent livelihood by working outside the home, albeit largely for the family's benefit. Hence both marital intimacy and wives' autonomy rose. Dorothy Cobble points out that this paradox existed outside of marriage as well, among growing numbers of waitresses who maintained close, even companionate relations with their male customers and created a highly pragmatic and independent feminine subculture cynical towards marriage and men. Growing numbers of women gained the ability to live autonomously, even as the emotional distance between women and men narrowed.[39]

Men's response to women's growing independence was not of one piece. Some saw it as an opportunity to drop the burdens of bread-winning and responsibility that the nineteenth century had so rigidly imposed. But others manifested a more complex and troubled reaction to modern sex roles.

One husband, conspicuously basking in the greater freedom of the 1920s, enclosed in a letter to his a wife a photograph of a "little jane" who "wants me to take her away with me . . . stayed all night with her, three nights, Free of charge, love at first sight."[40] Some Portland women indicated that their spouses expected them to earn wages during the Depression. One recalled her husband's remarks that "if he knew enough to work he wouldn't get married." "When the money run out and I wasn't able to work he deserted me," she continued.[41] Some husbands saw the blending of women's and men's spheres as an opportunity to do less work.

But men more often expressed anxiety over the shrinking gap between women's world and their own. Oregon literature from the 1920s, 1930s, and early 1940s strongly indicates that its men missed the nineteenth century. H. L. Davis and James Stevens ridiculed the Pacific Northwest's longstanding tradition of sentimental fiction and emerged as its leading novelists between the wars, both emphasizing a stark realism. Yet Stevens, in particular, clearly preferred the past to the present. In a draft of a 1923 letter to H. L. Mencken, who published much of his work, Stevens described himself as "a lusty young barbarian" when he was a boy in the West and recalled the "gaiety of labor, honest fatigue, stories and songs about the life, gory battles and the tribal enmity with the law, the railroads and the scissorbill." It was, he fondly recalled, "a hard violent life." But the Pacific Northwest of the 1920s was different: "Now we are regimented. Newspapers penetrate. Movies in the logging camps. We are part of the Organization. Slaves, serfs, unworried, full-bellied, chewing fudge at the movies . . ."[42] In the half-autobiography, half-fantasy *Brawny-Man*, Stevens breathed life into this portrait, describing the plight of ruggedly independent working men in the early twentieth century.

Asked one of another: "The West is won. Where'll we find our god of adventure, you great dark devil, you? Where'll we go?"[43] Paddy the Devil, the book's hero, is shot in the back, and Gager, the romantic adventurer who posed the above question, leaves to fight in France. Jim, the book's young protagonist, disappoints Gager by settling down to a mill job. The West was indeed won—or lost.

For Stevens, this loss had a feminine face. Jim's betrayal of Gager and his acceptance of a mill job is quickly followed by *Brawny-Man*'s final scene: Jim sitting with a pretty young Italian woman for whom he has bought a ring. Indeed, much of Stevens's fiction is marked by cynicism toward women, particularly pious ones who attempt to domesticate young men. In *Brawny-Man*, for example, a winsome churchgoer named Isis convinces Jim to settle down at a respectable job milking cows in order to be worthy of her love and then flees town after having been intimate with a boy who shared her devout moralism.[44]

Ernest Haycox, an Oregon novelist less distinguished than Davis and Stevens, emphasized the inherently masculine nature of the West in his very popular formula westerns. Nine pages into his first novel, published in 1928, the protagonist's father informs him, "The East is settled, it is orderly, it is governed by women's ideas. This is still a man's country. Make no mistake about that." Later, dying from a wound, the father tells his son that "some girl [in the East] took the sap out of your heart." As Jane Tompkins persuasively argues, the twentieth-century western represents not simply a reaction to modern society, but an attempt by men to reclaim their manhood from Christian womanhood, which had dominated nineteenth-century culture. The western is a protracted lampooning of domesticity as manifested in being pious, turning the other cheek, even expressing emotions. The protagonist in *Free Grass*, in a rare moment of verbosity, counsels a friend "No matter how you are hurt, never reveal it to a living creature," for "once a fellow started crying about his hurts he would never quit. This is a rough country. Nobody wants to hear about your feelings."[45]

Yet Haycox's stories, with all their stoicism, their instinctive distrust of domesticity and feminization, are love stories as well as adventure stories. His uncommunicative, fiercely independent heroes always get their woman shortly after the last villain falls. Indeed, protagonist and lady commonly find each other through this bloody act, this violence inflicted upon a bad man by a good man. It is as if these autonomous men somehow require a woman's admiration to validate their solitary and harrowing attaintment of masculinity. In most of Davis's novels, too, the reader is treated to a romantic ending once the male protagonist has managed, after a fashion, to achieve his manhood. By way of contrast, in Anne Shannon Monroe's *Happy Valley*, published in 1916 and based on her experience as an eastern Oregon homesteader, the central male character wins his love only after conquering an inner foe, alcoholism, and learning to cooperate with other homesteaders.[46] In the work of Haycox the fit between main plot and romantic ending is less harmonious, suggesting a strong tension between independence and distrust on the one hand and a yearning for closeness on the other in writer and reader alike.[47]

Edison Marshall and Charles Alexander, a pair of Oregon adventure writers from the 1920s, also depicted this paradoxical relationship between masculine independence and romantic attachment. In *The Isle of Retribution*, Marshall has Ned, a well-to-do and soft young man, shipwrecked along with Bess, a good-hearted young working woman, on an isolated North Pacific island dominated by a ruthless and gigantic Russian trapper. In the wilderness Ned becomes a man. The hardening of his body is accompanied by a hardening of his speech: "He no longer gabbled lightly like a girl, his speech full of quirks and affectations: he spoke in blunt, short sentences, with blunt, short words, and his meaning was immediately plain." Bess is swept up by this transformation, and finds Ned irresistible once nature has reworked his flaccid, urban character. "Bess was a woman," Marshall explains, "and that meant that man that is born of woman was her work and her being. She turned her eyes from God to behold this man."[48] Alexander offers a similar plot in *The Splendid Summits*. Esper and Ella, an archetypal admiring woman, are a pair of well-to-do Portlanders who experience a dramatic wilderness adventure in Oregon's Cascade Mountains. For Esper, facing down the brute, animal-like Jeopard is from the beginning a way to win the beautiful Ella, who is first captivated by the will and magnetism of Jasper, Esper's noble, but emasculating, older brother. With Jasper killed by Jeopard, Esper's path to masculinity is clear; by an act of sheer, improbable will he overcomes several severe beatings, lack of food, an attack by wolves, and a long trek through the frozen wilderness to subdue the well-rested and well-armed Jeopard with his own two hands, felling him with a blow on the point of his massive jaw. Ella, in whom "rich new depths" had been plumbed by the "very big, very male" Jasper, finds Esper "overwhelming."[49]

These stories, written by Oregon men of differing literary skills and popularity, share several themes. Unlike the disciplined Cecil in *The Bridge of the Gods*, Oregon's quintessential novel of the late nineteenth century, the modern protagonist embraces violence. Beating or killing a villain is an essential part of becoming a man and of winning a woman. Here, then, is what Gail Bederman has described as a movement from a Victorian emphasis on "manhood" as "self-mastery" to a modern embrace of "masculinity," a celebration of the more natural and violent male.[50] The wilderness is the place where masculinity is attained. It is the converse to the feminized city or the East. Yet only James Stevens is overtly hostile toward women. The other writers, even the self-consciously nonsentimental Davis, conflate the attainment of masculine independence with the attainment of romantic entanglement. This is not necessarily a contradiction. Maturity, including the ability to share life with another, requires at least a modicum of independence and self-reliance. But the fierceness and solitude with which these authors' protagonists pursue and attain masculinity seems at odds with their inevitable couplings at story's close. Furthermore, the adoring women in *The Isle of Retribution* and *The Splendid Summits* are allowed no freedom of action. Their inexorable role, their purpose, is to give themselves reverently to the man whose coming of age overwhelms them. These Oregon writers, expressing feelings present but often obscured in less articulate men, depicted a divided masculine self. The central message of Haycox, Marshall, Alexander, and even at times Davis was that man needed nothing so much as the blank slate of the wilderness, untouched by feminine civilization, on which to prove himself. But that message was undercut, even negated, by the implicit theme of reliance on woman's companionship and, in Marshall and Alexander, on woman's unreserved devotion. These writers circled through the West's stark isolation, back to the arms of she whom they had fled.

The sermons of Oregon's ministers from the 1920s and 1930s reveal an ambivalence about women that is less paradoxical and more patent. These men commonly championed and celebrated women's unique role in the family. Men were not to neglect home and marriage, to be sure. The Reverend Carrick, preaching in 1925, reminded his listeners that the Christian husband's headship of the home required him to "sacrifice himself for his wife, bear her burdens and even lay down his life for her."[51] Yet woman's very identity, unlike man's, was inseparable from the home. "Man deals more with objects and things whereas woman deals more with persons," Carrick explained. "Mothering is the chief business of woman."[52]

The ministers repeatedly identified selflessness as a mother's chief character trait. "When mother is gone," remarked another preacher, "it is a common thing for those who are left to come to the minister and say, 'Tell them that she never thought of herself.'" "That," he concluded, "is the genius of motherhood."[53] Likewise, Carrick identified "self negation" as the "most impressive exhibit in a true mother's life."[54] The ministers delighted in recounting maternal acts of self-abnegation. Remarked Goodsell: "If any body missed out on the cake it, [sic] was mother, and if anybody had to go without new clothes, it was mother, & if anybody had to stay home from the entertainment it was mother."[55] Near the Depression's close Victor Phillips, a Methodist pastor in Portland, recounted a story in which a rural schoolteacher asked a young boy named Jimmy how his seven-member family would divide a pie. Jimmy insisted, in the face of his teacher's objections, that he would get one-sixth rather than one-seventh of the treat: "I know fractions, some. And I know mother. She'd say she did'nt want any."[56] Mothers' greatest pleasure came in seeing others satisfied and happy. John Dale McCormick, a Methodist minister, defined mother as "She who suffers long and is kind."[57]

Mothers' great capacity for suffering and sacrifice located them next to God. "No one comes closer to God than a mother," observed Carrick. "Her life, primarily like the Christ's, is not to be ministered unto but to minister."[58] Pastor Phillips quoted a poem that was a staple of Mother's Day sermons:

> If I were hanged on the highest hill,
> I know whose prayers would follow me still;
> Mother o' mine Mother o' mine.
>
> If I were damned o' body and soul,
> I know whose love would make me whole;
> Mother o' mine. Mother o' mine.

He concluded: "A love like that is akin to the love of Christ; there is a touch of Calvary in it."[59] The mother emerges from these sermons as a sort of Christ figure, a Protestant Virgin Mary whose earthly love is tinctured by divine and perfect love and who leads boy and man to God.

These ministers, all well-educated and of mainstream Protestant denominations, struggled over what to make of the new twentieth-century woman. Goodsell identified Jesus as the man "who has knocked the shackles off the arms of womanhood," that "this larger freedom that women now enjoy has come through principles set going by him." But he cautioned women against "pushing her freedom too far," against casting aside the ideal of being a wife and mother for the ideal of equality in employment and education. "Our sex likes to feel its superiority," he warned, "and if a woman makes a man feel uncomfortable, take it from me, she will never get him." Goodsell hopefully predicted that once "this modern woman has tested her powers . . . she will turn with new zest to that highest of all vocations which is exclusively hers—that of mothering the race."[60] Other ministers rued the most visible signs of modern womanhood: "rouged lips and short skirts"; "cigarettes, drinking parties and divorce courts."[61] "Mother's Day has no tribute for the selfish cigarette-smoking, booze-drinking, . . . pleasure-hunting, child-neglecting, home-destroying mother," asserted Goodsell in the 1930s, "but rather for the old-fashioned mother—or the God-fashioned mother—whose worth is measured in unselfish deeds, noble character and Christ-like personality."[62] Christian and western civilization hung in the balance. Carrick warned in 1921: "let the women in our homes become corrupting Delilahs and a mightier power than Samson's will shake the pillars of state."[63]

These men clearly expected women to be touchstones of virtue and continuity in a time of great stress and change, to counterbalance modern developments rather than to lead them. "*Mothers can save the soul of the nation* by the exercise of *faith* and prayer," asserted Carrick in the midst of the Depression. "She can *infuse honesty* and *human tenderness* into the currents of business and social life. She can *change* the *jungles* of our nation into sympathetic brotherhood and fellowship."[64] "Christian mothers are the hope of the world," proclaimed McCormick in 1940, as that world slipped further into another horrible war.[65]

Mothers' salvific roles operated in an intensely personal way in men's lives, not simply for the good of larger society. As McCormick put it in 1928: "Mother holds the key to Christian manhood."[66] These ministers posited an extremely close relationship between son and mother defined by her solicitude to him. "You cannot think of your mother without thinking of her sweet and beautiful service, her tireless devotion," stated Goodsell. "There was nobody's touch as soothing and there was nobody's presence as sweet as that of your mother," he continued.[67] "I have seen a mother wait, oh so long for the lad's return home—where is he? Is he safe?" remembered Lee in a 1927 sermon delivered in eastern Oregon. "When every one else ceased to think or care—mother had ceased to think of all but he."[68] This image offered to men fulfillment of the infant-like wish of complete nurture. Goodsell, in a Depression sermon aptly entitled "Dreams That Come True," recounted a story of how a civic leader at the height of his powers returned home to "his saintly mother" and told her of his wish "to be your little boy again," to be cared for "just as you did then." This regression to childhood ostensibly restored the man's moral powers, but one also suspects that the return home represented a protest of sorts against adulthood. "God says if you want absolute perfection in comfort and assurance you can find it in your mother," he concluded.[69] Mothers, then, operated not simply as repositories of virtue in tumultuous times, but as fountains of limitless comfort in the arid world of manhood.

Oregon's ministers and writers of the first half of the twentieth century thus shared a certain view of women. Both asserted that woman's essential role and nature was to serve man: as adoring sidekick or as selfless nurturer. Both found in womanhood an antidote to the pains of isolated manhood. Among the writers this attachment was at odds with their central themes of masculine independence and adventure. The ministers' yearnings for dependence and nurture were much more explicit and included images of all-understanding mothers whose capacity for sacrifice approached Christ's. Both also found in women a threat: the prospect of smothering, civilized womanhood on the part of the writers and the prospect of independent, self-oriented womanhood on the part of the ministers. In either instance, unwelcome progress wore a woman's face.

As we have seen, ambivalence toward women was not new to Oregon or to the United States at large by the 1920s. But it had become less veiled than before. Balch's *Bridge of the Gods*, the highly popular Oregon novel from the 1890s, had portrayed women as the innocent victims of males' inability to control their brutal instincts. Fiction from the 1920s and 1930s was more apt to be concerned about women's interference with men's exploration of their natural instincts, which were now redefined as good. This increased ambivalence toward women and decreased suspicion of masculine impulses had ominous consequences for violence against wives.

Yet, in theory, good men used violence judiciously and only against other males. In Marshall's *The Isle of Retribution*, Ned automatically defends his sweetheart from the pitiless Russian trapper's insinuation of a sexual advance, "obeying a racial instinct that goes back to the roots of time."[70] In another Marshall novel, *The Strength of the Pines*, the villain becomes angry with a woman who spurned his love: "He struck her breast. The brutality of the man stood forth at last. No picture that all the dreadful dramas of the wild could portray was more terrible than this."[71] In Haycox's *Free Grass*, only Lispenard, the most despicable of the novel's low characters, strikes a woman. A more honorable villain refers to Lispenard as "trash," asserting, "I don't traffic with women, and I got no use fo' a man as does . . . I'm a dam' rascal . . . But I don' sleep with snakes."[72] Remarks one of the women in Monroe's *Happy Valley*: "no man that is a man can fight back at a woman."[73]

Nonfictional people also asserted that true men would not strike a woman. A witness in a 1924 case said as much when he found his mother being manhandled and threatened by his stepfather: "I grabbed him and told him no gentleman would ever treat a woman that way."[74] Another eastern Oregon woman recalled her husband telling her that "if she were a man he would knock hell out of her" as he shook his fist under her nose.[75] Likewise, a Portland attorney wrote his estranged and combative wife that "if you were a man—you would be merely pulp after several words," but "because you are a woman and my wife—there is nothing I can do." "It makes me want to kill or maim when those things are said to me," he continued, "and the fact that you are a woman holds me back."[76] A wife whose husband did hit her recalled that the blow "was the only thing he ever said he was sorry for."[77] At least a considerable number of men continued to view violence toward wives as unmanly and wrong.

Yet the paternalistic restriction against hitting women was not as strong in the 1920s and 1930s as it had been in the 1890s. One man allegedly told a friend or neighbor "that he had only hit or beat" his wife "about four or five times in their married life and he couldn't see why she should be so afraid of him."[78] The complaint of another eastern Oregon man admitted that "the plaintiff slapped the defendant" when she cursed him.[79] Some wives said that their husbands had spanked them, a form of violence seldom mentioned around the turn of the century. One recalled that her husband had put her over his knees to administer the blows, saying "she was but a child, and should be treated as a child."[80] Another eastern Oregon woman's attorney recalled that her husband had told him that his wife had "went into a tantrum" when he slapped her and ordered her out of his store, "so he laid her across his knee and spanked her."[81] In a time of increased familiarity between the sexes, this sort of intimate, vaguely sexualized violence seemed less objectionable than it had before. Stevens, the novelist, has Jim of *Brawny-Man* asserting that his sweetheart liked "that I was burly and rough, and would use my muscle to make her sit on my lap, and would pick her up in my arms and swing her around, head down, while she clawed and wiggled and had as much fun out of the rough-house as I did." "Any real girl likes for her man to use his muscle on her," he explained.[82] The boyish flapper seemed a more appropriate target for violence, playful or otherwise, than had the physically and emotionally more removed lady of the late nineteenth century.

Historians have outlined a complex mix of cultural and social developments that speak to this increased acceptance of violence toward wives. Carol and Peter Stearns note this era's recognition of the positive aspects of anger, and how this modified the Victorians' general condemnation of the emotion. Kevin White argues that the powerful youth culture of the 1910s and 1920s celebrated pleasure seeking, male sexual prowess, muscular primitivism, and even irresponsibility, which led to an easy acceptance of violence toward women both in popular literature and in fact. Elizabeth Pleck identifies the 1920s and particularly the 1930s as a time when Freudian ideas undermined Victorian assumptions of women's purity, that therapists interpreted wife beating as a manifestation of women's unconscious desire to be dominated and hurt. Linda Gordon asserts that Boston social workers more commonly blamed wives for husbands' violence after the 1930s than they

had before, a development she relates to the waning of a general moralistic outlook, the decline of feminism, and the fact that women no
longer seemed as helpless.[83]

Indeed, Goodsell warned that "if woman is the equal of man, . . .
she must . . . not expect favors and considerations because of her sex."
"If woman is going to regard herself as man's equal," the minister continued, "she must recognize the fact that in order to succeed she must
depend upon her efficiency and upon that alone."[84] Yet most wives,
political and economic advances notwithstanding, still relied on a husband's economic support, this at a time when the erosion of women's
separate sphere and of masculine self-control put wives at greater risk
of violence from their husbands.

Nard Jones's *Oregon Detour*, reminiscent of Sinclair Lewis's *Main
Street*, plumbs more subtle attitudes toward women and wife beating.
The story revolves around two young couples: Etta, the narrator, and
her husband, Charlie; and Peg and Swede Mongsen. Peg's easy ways
with men and liquor invite censure from the community's more cau-
tious residents. Charlie remarks that if Peg were his wife, "I'd knock
the hell out of her once or twice and then she'd come to time." "It
wouldn't do her any harm," agrees Etta, a close friend of Peg's. Yet
when Swede hits Peg in front of Charlie and Etta for cheating on him,
Charlie says, "Mongsen, you can't do that in my house." Still, as the
Mongsens drive away Etta realizes that "Charlie obtained from" Peg's
beating "a malicious satisfaction. It seemed almost to strike him as
humorous, and she could clearly see his hate for Peg and what she had
done." Charlie comes to realize "that all his hate for Peg had been a
cruelly distorted desire, a masochistic passion to beat her into an idol
of his own," for the sexy Peg "was . . . so different from Etta." Indeed,
Peg eventually dies when she accidentally falls out of Charlie's automobile during a clandestine, illicit meeting. Charlie is too afraid to
stop the car and try to help her, so only Etta learns of the affair.
Charlie is at once disgusted by and drawn to Peg's sexuality, and his
satisfaction in the violence she suffers is related to his desire for her.
Etta concludes that she had seen Peg's death coming, for "it did seem
like God had got tired of watching Peg forever breaking His com-
mandments."[85] Jones clearly intends this remark to be ironic, given the
complicity of Charlie and the rest of the community in Peg's sinning,
not to mention her death. Peg, then, is the community scapegoat, is

Charlie's scapegoat, and she suffers the consequences of his illicit lust. *Oregon Detour* is a suggestive rendering of a small community poised uneasily on the edge of modernity, and of how women, no longer protected by a separate social sphere, bore the brunt of that uneasiness.

Violence did become more common during the 1920s and 1930s than it had been in rural Oregon during the 1890s. Few wives, husbands, or witnesses indicated the sort of masculine restraint so common a few decades before. On the contrary, wives were more apt to describe frequent acts of violence. A Portland woman remarked in 1936 that her husband "strikes me at least three or four times a month and curses me all the time."[86] Another recalled that for four years her spouse had "cursed me and beat me an average of two or three times a week."[87] A third Portland woman, this one testifying during World War II, said that her husband of four months hit her "all the time. There doesn't a week go by but what he is drunk and comes home and chokes me."[88] Wives in other parts of Oregon echoed their urban counterparts. One from Coos County indicated that her husband had repeatedly struck her with his fist, frequently threatened to kill her, tried to gouge out her eyes, and often told her that he "intended to keep her as his wife merely to torture her."[89] An eastern Oregon woman's complaint noted that her husband often beat her "to point of unconsciousness," and another remarked that her husband would "shoot around over my head, he would throw knives at me . . . every Saturday night when he came home."[90]

Other wives from the Depression and World War II years described extreme forms of physical abuse encountered rarely in complaints or testimony from the late nineteenth century. A Portland woman in 1934 recalled that "I was covered with bruises from head to foot most of the time" from her husband of sixteen years.[91] Several Portland women indicated extensive abuse during World War II. One said that her husband "broke my eardrum and my finger and knocked my teeth out and caused tumors of the breast when he bruised me there."[92] Another said that her spouse, a broker before the war and a shipyard worker during it, "struck me on several occasions and broke my ribs and blackened both eyes. My nose was broken."[93] An aviator's wife said that he had frequently beat her, knocked out her front teeth, and once walked on her back with golf shoes. Yet another Portland woman recounted that her husband beat her about twice a week, and would often "take his hand and slap me back and forth . . . as hard as he could."[94] He also tried to burn out her eyes with a lit cigarette.

As discussed in Chapter 2, male violence had become more affective and less strictly instrumental by the 1890s. That is, husbands increasingly employed it not simply as a tool to coerce obedience, but also as an expression of general ambivalence toward women and marriage, an expression that occurred independently of a particular wife's actions. By the interwar period, a host of developments had fueled that ambivalence. Men found in the movement of women toward political, economic, and social equality and in their own contradictory reactions to modernity fuel for both instrumental and affective violence.

Much of husbands' violence simply served to help them get what they wanted. "If he told me to do something and I didn't think it was proper, I wouldn't pay any attention to him and he just continued slapping me that way until I did do it," recalled one woman.[95] "He feels that he can slap my face any time I do anything that does not suit him," testified a Portland resident during World War II.[96] A Coos County man reportedly told his wife in 1924 that he would "break her will or break her back" when he struck her several blows.[97] Instrumental violence often centered around men trying to get their wives' money. One man reportedly twisted his wife's hands in the early 1920s "because she wanted to save a dollar, [and] he wanted to go to the ball game" in Portland.[98]

Husbands were particularly prone to become violent over money during the Depression. An eastern Oregon woman described one such dispute: "I said 'Absolutely there must be some supplies brought in today,' and he said he didn't know how he was going to get them, and he struck me and it really hurt."[99] Another wife recalled that her husband "would come home from the pool hall at night drunk and if I told him he had to go to work he would double up his fist and swear at me and everything else."[100] Other quarrels centered around wives' employment. A woman who owned some cabins, a campground, and a service station in eastern Oregon let the man she had recently married work there because he had just lost his job. "One day he came in," she recalled, "and said 'I'll tell you right now I am going to run this with an iron hand. I am going to make some moves.'"[101] A wife who secured a job cooking for harvest hands when her husband could not support her suffered a bruised face when he accused her of intimacies with these men. Other women who worked during the Depression complained of unemployed, violent husbands who drank to excess, stayed out late, or interfered with their work.[102] Yet the Depression years apparently did not bring a marked increase in violence toward wives. The increase was instead gradual and sustained, fueled more by long-term cultural trends than by short-term economic crises.[103]

Much of the husbands' violence seemed calculated to establish their dominance at a time when many wives desired more satisfying and equal relationships. A man described by his wife as "just a ball player and a gambler and a hobo, and not good at anything" reportedly told one of their friends that the wife "came back from school with airy ways" and that he had therefore thrown "water in her face." By this act, the husband asserted, "I just took her down."[104] Several men reacted with violence when wives objected to double standards in staying out late or pursuing extramarital affairs. An eastern Oregon woman recalled that she asked to go with her husband to a party that he was taking another woman to. When she persisted "he kicked me and beat me and struck me in the mouth and the blood flew all over the bed." "She always wanted to go with him," recalled her sister. "She wanted him to take her to the show or some place, and he would just fly into a rage."[105] Some wives objected to infidelity more directly. A Portland woman said that when "I asked one of his girls to leave his car, or our car, . . . he beat up on me, he knocked me down and he kicked me."[106] Wives, influenced by rising expectations for affection and mutuality in marriage, apparently objected to adultery and other improprieties more overtly than their grandmothers had, and their husbands often punished them for it.

Such conflicts illustrate Linda Gordon's assertion that violence against wives arises not simply out of male dominance but often out of women's struggle against that dominance. A Coos County woman recounted two particularly explicit instances of this. In one case she and her husband were driving home and he became so quarrelsome that she wanted to get out of the car. When he refused, she turned off the automobile's ignition and tried to leave, and he abused her physically. Three years later, in 1931, officers raided their home and arrested him for possessing beer. His return home the next morning with a jug of whiskey "so provoked plaintiff that she broke the jug," as her complaint explained.[107] He then struck her many times and jumped up and down on her. A Bend area wife likewise recalled asking her husband if she could drive the automobile to downtown Bend. He removed its distributor head and said, "Now drive it." "It made me so peeved," she continued, "and I tried to take the thing away from him and he struck me and kicked me."[108] Another eastern Oregon woman recalled an evening in which she felt ill after supper and lay down. Her angry husband told her to get up and wash the dishes, and when she refused he threw her off the davenport. When she quickly returned to her resting place he slapped her. When she fought back he hit her with his fist, blackening her eye. This husband's violence escalated in concert with his wife's resolve to exercise some control over her life. Another wife said that her violent husband told her to mind him, "that if I would mind him we would get along better."[109]

But other women complained of violence that seemed completely unrelated to their actions. One said that her husband threw water in her face apparently because "he had to start haying. Every time haying came on he got angry and peevish."[110] The mother of a Bend area wife said that her son-in-law "would come home from the mill cross and cranky, and throw things around, and if she would try to talk to him he would slap her."[111] "He was always getting mad when things did not go his own way," concluded a third eastern Oregon woman, "and usually took it out on me."[112]

As in the 1890s, wives commonly cited their husbands' jealousy as a factor in their violence. Some husbands, sensitive to the era's preoccupation with physical appearance, threatened to disfigure their wives. One woman recalled her spouse grabbing her by the hair and saying "he would mar me up until nobody would look at me."[113] A witness in another eastern Oregon case said that the defendant "didn't want her to comb her hair or any thing like that, he was afraid someone else would look at her."[114] "Just jealously insane," remarked another wife when asked to explain the cause of her violent husband's abuse, "that's the only definition I have for it."[115]

Violently jealous husbands struggled to control their wives' freedom of movement in a time of greater mobility for women. One woman recounted an evening in 1924 when her husband jerked her out of her car and kicked her. "He thought I was out riding around when I shouldn't have, I guess," she remarked.[116] Another eastern Oregon woman said that her husband struck her when she insisted on going to a lodge meeting: "He said I just wanted to run around and go out."[117] World War II presented particular difficulties to many jealous or possessive husbands. A woman married to a serviceman stationed in Washington said that he came home on New Year's Eve 1942, found that "I had girl friends there, and he objected to them," and pushed her down the stairs.[118] Another Portland wife worked directly under the supervision of a violent husband, at Willamette Iron and Steel: "He wouldn't let me talk to anybody; . . . not even to talk to the girls around there,—I was to keep my mouth shut and do my work. He put me over in a room by myself, and he wouldn't even allow the time-checker to come in."[119] Most husbands could of course not so closely control the actions of employed wives, though many apparently wished to.

During a time when society increasingly defined women as wives first and mothers second, many women not surprisingly complained of being hit during or just after pregnancy. A woman in an isolated part of eastern Oregon recalled that her husband frequently beat the children up and threatened to kill them and her, and that when a recently born child cried and she asked him to bring it to her he instead threw it "up in a chair" and said he wished the "little devil was dead."[120] The child did die, apparently from being thrown. A Bend area woman said that when she reached the eighth month of her pregnancy she suggested to her husband that they prepare for her confinement. He then cursed her, said the fetus was not his, and slapped her so that she fell, injuring herself so severely that the fetus died. Such descriptions appeared frequently in the cases from the 1920s through the 1940s, notwithstanding the era's generally sketchy testimony and lowered birth rates.[121]

Husbands of this time commonly attacked their wives' sexuality directly. A number of beatings occurred when women refused sexual advances. One recalled that her husband "pinched me and poked me" when she refused to let him "satisfy his desires."[122] This sort of violence was nothing new; wives from around the turn of the century had also commonly complained of it. Unlike earlier husbands, however, men of the 1920s and 1930s not uncommonly tore off wives' clothing. A Coos County woman said that her husband stripped her and then beat her with a strap. Another husband reportedly hit his wife on the head and body, pulled her dress off, then drew a knife on her. A third husband's wife indicated that he tore all her clothes off and then chased her with a pitchfork. Another recalled that her intoxicated husband "tore all my clothes off my back, everything but my shoes and stockings, and cursed and swore at me" when she "came home later than he thought I should."[123]

Stripping wives of their clothing satisfied several desires. The destruction of such personal items expressed contempt for a woman's privacy and autonomy, for her person. Hence a Portland woman recalled in 1936 that her husband "tore my clothes all off once and he would grab me by the hair and spit in my face."[124] Several wives mentioned that their husbands deliberately burned or otherwise destroyed their clothing. Igniting or rending objects that a wife wore next to her skin suggested the destruction of her self.[125]

The forcible exhibition of women's naked or near-naked bodies and the destruction of highly feminine articles of clothing such as undergarments also betrayed a strongly negative focus on their sexuality. Hence a husband in 1930 reportedly ripped most of the clothes from his wife, threatened to kill her, knocked her down, called her names, and accused her of being immoral at a Coos County auto park—all in the hearing of other people. A Coos County dairy farmer took the public abasement of his wife still further. Her legal answer to her husband's suit noted that in 1924 he accused her of infidelity with her former husband, beat her about the face, wrenched her arms, tore her clothes off, and then "dragged her, partly nude, bruised and disheveled into an adjoining room and called on two young boys, who were employed on the ranch, to come and see how to treat a dirty cow" and exposed her bruised and half-naked body to them.[126] The humiliation of this woman, the literal stripping away of her privacy and the exposure of her supposed wantonness, could hardly have been more complete.

Violent husbands' images of their wives could move quickly from debasement to idealization. A 1936 letter by a Bend man to the woman he had wed nearly nine years before in Oklahoma serves as a particularly vivid illustration. It was addressed to "Oh my poor little darlin & son":

Oh God you acted so cold last nite and wouldn't let me even talk to you. Sweetheart listen to this, Wherever you've been, what ever you've done, its my fault, an Oh god Susan dont punish me any more, you've gotten even with me I love you so. Honey we've both done a great wrong . . . little girl I don't want to live with out you . . .

Please God let me have one more chance to make my wife & son happy, Honey how could you be so mean to not let Jim come down & see me. Susan who in the world has put this into your head. Ah hell, Susan, you're doing the meanest thing in the world a woman can do.

You know I never mean those cussings. Susan I found out that we been all wrong, my way's an actions have been all hay wire.

You see honey I only wanted to make you see things my way, and God Im sorry to say I went at it all wrong . . .

I told you Id never hit you again, I wont. I ment it an you know it—that was one of my biggest mistakes, with a little encouregment, I'd be the sweetest thing in the world to you cause to me you're the most perfect, sweetest, most beautiful little thing Ive ever known.

This man's intensely self-centered spiritualization of his wife dovetailed with his consternation over being abandoned, a cluster of emotions not unlike those expressed by Oregon's ministers as they spoke about mothers. Like the sermons, this letter is suffused by a tension between the author's idealization of "the most perfect, sweetest, most beautiful little thing Ive ever known" and his half-contained rage over her "doing the meanest thing in the world a woman can do." His next letter began: "Dam your soul."[127] His wife reported that he had hit her at least once or twice a week and had told her in their son's presence that she was nothing but a streetwalker.

Violent husbands also expressed ambivalence about the home in general. The plaintiff in a 1924 divorce suit said that her spouse meanly pinched their baby, "didn't want to work, and would get peevish and break up the furniture, and swear he would get rid of us." "He told my mother it made a difference after the baby came," she continued, and "he didn't think I should get up at night" to care for the infant. She had left him, and he had tried repeatedly to get her to return. "I don't think he knows what he does want," she concluded.[128] Other violent husbands also vacillated between leaving, staying, and returning. An eastern Oregon woman said that she left her husband several times on his orders and then returned on his promises to do better. A Coos County woman said that her husband left her three times and,

although he said he would not return, two times was back for breakfast the next morning.[129]

Some husbands expressed their ambivalence over marriage by
destroying the objects that symbolized it. Several reportedly tore up
their wedding certificates. A south-coast woman said that about six
weeks after their marriage and while she was ill and bedfast her husband dragged her across the floor, tore their marriage license into
pieces, and threw them in her face. Another Coos County woman said
that her husband had purposely smashed all the dishes she had received
as a wedding present. Other wives said that their husbands had burned
up knickknacks, even recipe cards. An eastern Oregon woman's complaint described a particularly vivid and symbolic destruction of such
objects in northern California during the early 1920s. The impoverished wife "had gotten a few things together" on Christmas Eve for
the children, including some gifts and a tree. The husband arrived
home late, "drunk and angry," and "upon entering the house and seeing the little tree, all fixed up, he became so angry that he took the
tree and tore it to pieces, took all the little gifts and presents off of the
tree and mutilated and destroyed them." "Not being satisfied with this,"
the complaint continued, "and while cursing and defaming the plaintiff, he took all the table linen and mattress and sheets and quilts off
the bed, took them to the kitchen and dumped them on the floor, gath-
ered up all the food there was in the house and spilled these on the
floor, put the cooking utensils on the floor and then took the stove
pipe and dumped soot over the bed linen and food and everything he
had put on the floor and then turned water all over this mess, then
broke and tore up all the furniture."[130] A month before he had sprin-
kled wine over various objects in the house, broke their bed to pieces,
and held the emptied bottle over his wife's head and threatened to kill
her. This physically abusive husband employed wine—certainly a
potent antidomestic symbol—and soot to desecrate ritualistically the
home, to violate literally its most sacred objects.

It is suggestive that this desecration occurred while he was under
the influence of liquor. As in earlier times, people often associated wife
beating with alcohol. Earl Moore, an eastern Oregon attorney, asserted
in a 1930s legal brief that "it is a known fact that drunkenness is often-
times the hand-maid of cruelty."[131] Frequent drinking "was nearly the
whole trouble" with her violent husband, asserted a Portland wife in

1937.[132] Another Portland wife, citing an instance in which her husband tore her clothes off, remarked that "he was intoxicated and I know he wasn't responsible."[133]

There was some truth in these people's assertions. Alcohol acts as a disinhibitor, and people do things when they are intoxicated that they do not otherwise do. But, as Linda Gordon points out, drunken behavior appears to be learned behavior, not simply a physiological response. Indeed, Craig MacAndrew and Robert Edgerton have argued that cultural norms are not universally suspended when people become intoxicated, that true taboos remain taboo under all conditions, while lesser restrictions are violated. Drunken people in some sense use their inebriation to overstep boundaries selectively. These violated boundaries are not regarded by society as absolute, especially if the offender is not perceived as being in his or her right mind. The decision to drink, then, can be understood as a decision to participate in a ritual in which the inebriate and the community conspire to sanction acts that are ostensibly but not truly unacceptable. Drinking becomes a way both to express submerged emotions and, as David Riches puts it, to "disclaim responsibility for what the ritual has said."[134]

A man's repugnance towards marriage and home, largely obscured when sober, could become remarkably stark when intoxicated. The man who came home drunk and tore apart his family's Christmas tree and desecrated his home's sacred objects offered a particularly patent but by no means singular example of how this process worked. Account after account, from this era as well as earlier ones, described the nocturnal arrival of a surly and intoxicated husband who tore the house apart or beat his wife. Alcohol was the symbolic converse of domesticity. Hence a Portland wife reported in 1935 that her husband "said he preferred his bottle to home life and he left on March 15 and I haven't seen him since."[135] Alcohol stripped away the norms of self-control that so commonly papered over men's widespread doubts about marriage and domesticity, revealing violent, deeply felt emotions that could rip a home apart, literally and figuratively.

Of course not every husband who drank to intoxication or who enjoyed an Ernest Haycox novel was bent on acting out submerged resentments toward marriage. But husbands who did get drunk and abuse their wives were nurtured in their violence by a masculine culture that expressed considerable ambivalence over women in general and marriage in particular. This ambivalence connected violent husbands with their nonviolent counterparts, linked repugnant acts with mainstream views preached from the pulpit and penned by respected authors. This ambivalence, closely related to misogyny, had also been present in late-nineteenth-century Oregon. But that earlier time had also emphasized self-control, a concept that had begun to unravel by the 1920s.

Sociocultural developments also affected how wives responded to and resisted their violent husbands. Informal community assistance dwindled as help from police officers grew in the 1920s, 1930s, and early 1940s, particularly in Portland. The law constituted 51 percent of the interventions described in the divorce suits, up substantially from 30 percent around the turn of the century.[136]

Police officers offered a variety of services to wives of violent husbands. A woman who ran a boarding house in the Bend area said that she called the police when her husband spent a day "raising cain and cussing and swearing through the house, and swearing it was going to be Judgment day." Ethel Johnson of Bend's Women's Protective Division came out to the home to keep him from interfering with the plaintiff's work. Johnson then called the chief of police and told him "I was afraid to leave her alone there and I couldn't stay there all night," so the chief arrived and arrested the husband for disorderly conduct.[137] Another woman who called the Bend police simply asked the chief "to help me get my trunk out of the house before he [her husband] beat me up some more. The chief stayed there until I packed up and then I left with him in the car," she continued.[138] Another Bend police officer, called to the scene of a violent quarrel, testified that he had "asked her [the wife] what she wanted me to do with him and she said 'Put him in jail,' and I did."[139] Wives had husbands arrested for assault and battery, disturbing the peace, drunkenness, and nonsupport. The prospect of such actions could deter violence. An eastern Oregon woman said that when her husband threatened to kill her, "I said, 'George, I will have you put under peace bonds or have you put in jail.'" She added, "He never made that statement again."[140]

Not all police officers were so helpful or empathetic. A woman in a 1924 case testified that her husband had been out to her ranch and threatened her life since she had filed for a divorce. "I . . . tried to get the officers to arrest him," she remarked, "but they wouldn't go without a warrant."[141] A witness in another case recalled that a sheriff had talked a wife "into going back and trying it again" after the wife had fled a husband's violence.[142] Wives of such husbands often depended on Oregon's law-enforcement officials more fully than they had before, but those officials did not always respond as the wives wished them to.

Women often had to rely on the uncertain protection of police because of their growing isolation from neighbors and kin. Indeed, third parties most commonly intervened where marital privacy remained hard to come by. An eastern Oregon woman recalled that when her husband threw her into a corner and slapped her at his lumber camp "the two boys that were there that were falling timber with him, one of them took hold of his collar."[143] A Bend woman who was "in and out" of her neighbors' home "every few minutes" recalled how that easy familiarity had deterred the husband's violence: "I came in the front door and he had her by the neck up against the kitchen door, and he said, 'You'll sleep with me tonight, you son-of-a-bitch,' and he slapped her and I said, 'What's the big idea, Curt' and he went out the door."[144] As during earlier times, co-residence could be a particularly strong safeguard against violence. A man who employed a couple recalled that "I had to call him down a time or two for cursing her."[145]

But the easy familiarity between landlords and tenants, neighbors and friends that typically worked to abused women's advantage had begun to wane by the 1920s and 1930s. This was partly a matter of household demography. As noted earlier, the average population per Oregon dwelling dropped from 5.07 in 1890 to 3.85 in 1930. Less than one Oregon family in ten included a lodger in 1930. Outsiders became more respectful of marital privacy as households shrank. A Bend man who had boarded with a couple recalled, "I was in the bedroom and I heard him say 'I'll kill you,' and I took my hat and walked up town."[146] A witness from an eastern Oregon community testified that a neighbor told her of how a husband "one night" knocked his wife "down and around the rooms, and they couldn't sleep for the noise" without indicating that the neighbor had done anything to help the woman.[147] The mother of another eastern Oregon wife spelled out her reasons for not taking any measures against her violent son-in-law: "I knew that she was very unhappy, though she did not say anything, just from little things that occurred and while I never saw him mistreat her or hit her, I knew a lot of what was going on and I realized the situation all the time but I kept out of it as it was something for her to settle."[148] Some battered wives concurred. "I always tried to shield him with my folks," remarked one. "I did Not want them to know."[149] Oregon's Ku Klux Klan, one of the most vigorous in the United States during the 1920s, attempted to stem the tide of privatized morals. A southern Oregon chapter persecuted a Spanish-Indian resident for allegedly embarrassing young women with whistles and sexual comments. Yet these racially selective efforts were but straws in the wind of a much more pervasive shift in attitudes.[150]

But if third parties were less interested in assisting abused wives, they were also less concerned with keeping marriages together at all costs. This is not to say that divorce became innocuous. A woman in 1926 explained why she had not sought a divorce in her home community: "for the one reason, we both lived there and we were both acquainted there, and it was just the scandal of having the divorce where we were both so well known."[151] The Reverend Goodsell asserted in 1937 that "the teaching of Jesus upon the permanence of the marriage relation is absolutely clear," a declaration that other clerics echoed.[152] But the ministers were swimming against the tide. A Multnomah County judge complained during World War II that "just being late to dinner" was not grounds for divorce.[153] But by then plaintiffs did not have to prove much more than that. In an era that increasingly emphasized individual self-fulfillment, a wretched lifetime of fidelity to a cruel husband struck many as pointless, not noble.

Child support and alimony more commonly accompanied divorce than in the past. In 1944 Multnomah County's Judge Crawford asserted, "Probably in the last ten days there have been ten or a dozen cases where I felt that the man should pay something for his wife's support, even when there is an understanding between the two of them to the contrary, because I feel that frequently those understandings are rather coerced than voluntary."[154] Husbands commonly evaded such payments. An eastern Oregon husband reportedly threatened to "go on the tramp" in 1935 if he had to pay more than $30.00 per month to his divorce-seeking wife.[155] Oregon's legal system did not make the collection of such debts a high priority. Yet judges' assumption that ex-husbands owed their children and sometimes their former wives at least a modicum of financial support represented a marked historical shift.

The surprising number of wives who expressed indifference or even hostility to receiving support from their ex-husbands underscored their growing independence. "I would sooner not have any thing," remarked an eastern Oregon wage earner in 1924, "because if I didn't ask for support for the baby he wouldn't have any right to come where he [the baby] was at."[156] Such assertions peaked during World War II, when shipyard and other war-related work gave many women their first true economic autonomy: "I just want to be free of him, and independent"; "I would rather be on my own . . . I would rather be independent"; "I work, and I feel capable of making my own living"; "I am working, and I figure that I am entitled to just half of what is in the bank. That is all I want . . . I have always supported myself"; "I want to be free. I don't want any reason for our having anything to do with each other."[157] The *Oregonian* remarked on this trend in 1945, noting that "the courts have had difficulty" persuading wives who had their own income for the first time to accept money from their former spouses: "The attitude of many has been that they want only to be completely free from their husbands."[158] The unprecedented employment opportunities of World War II made that sort of independence much more widely available than ever before.

For many wives, however, staying with a violent husband seemed preferable to leaving him. Fear of becoming a single mother continued to deter some. One remarked that she returned to her highly violent spouse because "I thought it would be better for the boy to be with his father and mother both."[159] An eastern Oregon woman with eleven living children who had married in 1908 remarked in 1935 that she had lived a life "of poverty and hardship and misery." "I had children and couldn't get out of it," she explained.[160] Small children in particular made it difficult to leave one's husband. "I haven't wanted to live with him for a long time under existing conditions," remarked an eastern Oregon woman in 1924, "but I had the baby and couldn't do any thing."[161] A Willamette Valley woman quoted her violent husband as telling her that "as long as he could keep her pregnant she could not leave him."[162] Children, especially infants, compounded a divorced woman's economic difficulties.

Even World War II, unique in that the federal government encouraged mothers to work, did not solve their child care dilemma. One testified that she had resigned her job of twenty-three years with the telephone company because "I couldn't get anyone to take care of the children."[163] Another boarded her children, ages six and four, in a home. A third mother shared child care with a housemate: "This other lady works day shift and I work swing shift . . . and so we take care of our children that way."[164] Another working woman, asked what provision she had made for her children, ages thirteen and eleven, while in court replied, "Well, they were in bed when I came down here this morning and I told them to stay there until I got back."[165]

Social service agencies offered more assistance and fewer threats to such mothers than they had around the turn of the century. Portland institutions such as the Jewish Shelter Home, the Waverly Baby Home, and the Albertina Kerr Nursery Home cared for children whose parents could not do so. The latter organization described the plight of a mother with a five-month-old infant whose spouse's violent quarreling caused her to decide "to take the baby and leave her husband." "She had no place to turn, no one to go to," the account continued, and "she had to have work. She knew of the Albertina Kerr Nursery Home and brought her baby there to be cared for until she could make an adjustment."[166] Some divorcing-seeking wives held out no hope of recovering their children. A Portland woman in 1935 who had left her intemperate husband said that she would have to give her infant son up for adoption: "I will have to let him go. I did want awful bad to keep him but I couldn't."[167] Another divorce-seeking wife of the Depression, asked why she did not seek custody of her six-year-old daughter, replied, "Because I cannot take care of her. I can't support her."[168] Yet several Portland institutions offered a temporary home to such women's children and were apparently less apt to refuse to return them than before.

Vengeful husbands or ex-husbands were an especially powerful deterrent to divorce. A Willamette Valley wife indicated that her spouse had said he would kidnap their one-year-old boy if she took the child with her. A wife seeking a divorce from a violent husband in the 1920s recalled that she had dropped her suit and returned to him when he took her infant and "said I couldn't have the baby unless I would go back to him."[169] Violent husbands commonly threatened to tarnish the name of wives who tried to leave them. A Portland husband typed a letter that hinted of such threats the morning after he received notice that his wife in eastern Oregon had filed for a divorce:

"I can disgrace you In that town so bad that you will have to get out if i come up there with this lawer, things that you done before and after we were married, just think hard and you will fnow [sic] what I mean." But he added, "I never in this world could get you back if I done that. And dear I love you to much [to] do it I guess, I just went up to see the lawer to satisfy my curiosity."[170] Likewise, a Portland woman asserted in 1934 that her husband "said if I sued him for divorce he would just put me right out in the street . . . and he would prove I was a prostitute."[171]

Husbands not uncommonly threatened to kill or otherwise harm wives who left them. An eastern Oregon woman recalled telling her husband "a number of times that if he didn't behave himself and treat me right I would file for divorce, and he said if I ever filed for divorce he would kill us all."[172] Violent threats and acts often escalated once wives left. A south-coast woman indicated in 1924 that her spouse, whom she had left about seven months before, had recently come into her home late at night, tried to force her to have sex, and, when she refused, bruised and wrenched her limbs. An eastern Oregon woman testified that two months after she had left her husband he "put up his usual line that he wanted to make up again." When "I told him no, that there was absolutely no use, . . . he got a pistol that was there . . . and threatened me with it, and nearly scared me to death and Annie, my child, and then he cocked it and held it at his own head."[173] A woman who had lived on a ranch near Prineville in the early 1940s recounted a particularly harrowing history of what happened when she left her violent husband. He drove to their ranch drunk; shot two pigs, nineteen chickens, and the family dog; and then returned to Prineville, where he held a knife on her to force her back to the ranch, all the while threatening to kill her and their children. Not until over two months later was she able to hide enough money to flee to her sister's home in Portland with her two young boys. But her husband then went to Portland and threatened to kidnap the children and to kill her if she did not return. His persistent intimidation apparently worked. Nearly three years later, in 1947, the court dismissed the suit for want of prosecution.[174]

This incident illustrates the extreme risk that wives of violent husbands faced when they elected to resist that abuse. Yet these risks did not deter such wives from fighting back. Linda Gordon identifies the

1930s as a crucial decade in struggling Boston wives' invention of the right not to be beaten, an invention made possible by expanded opportunities as wage earners and the increased availability of divorce.[175]

Several sorts of evidence suggest that the years between the two world wars were also a dividing line for how Oregon women reacted to their husbands' violence. We have already seen how the rate of divorce climbed as women's employment opportunities vis-à-vis men's improved. Wives also tended to resist violence more directly than they had in the late nineteenth century. In 1936, for example, a rancher said that his wife had struck him on several occasions before leaving him. His large wife did not deny using violence on her husband:

> We got into a dispute as to something concerning the work on the ranch at that time, and Kurt called my dad a name, and I said, "Well, my dad is no worse than your dad," and he called him a Missouri son-of-a-bitch, and I picked up an empty coffee can and threw it at him, and I finally went around between the bed and the stove and stood with my back like this, with my back to the bed, and he shoved me over on the bed and then jumped onto me and hit me and I finally managed to get away from him and then he ran.[176]

Other wives also admitted to using violence. A woman from eastern Oregon recalled a day in 1933 when she repeatedly told her husband to get up and eat breakfast so she could get their son to school on time: "He cussed me and he called me all kinds of names and he said that he would get up whenever he pleased. And that aggravated me, and he reared up in bed and he says 'I don't have to listen to you and I am not going to any more.' I threw an egg at him, he jumped up out of bed then and shook me by the shoulders, and I struck at him and I hit him and he hit me and left marks on my arm."[177] Likewise, a Portland woman's complaint noted that her husband on one occasion "so conducted himself with another woman that this plaintiff did slap him and take him home," but later that night, "and while plaintiff was nursing her baby, the defendant did strike this plaintiff and black her eye," one of many times he had hit or otherwise abused her.[178] Husbands could usually trump a wife's blow with a greater one of their own. Yet women's choice of violence as a way of resisting male violence or male dominance expanded the problematic options available to them.

The shrinking gap between the genders' spheres and the rise of a culture based on self-expression and freedom rather than self-restraint and responsibility opened up more possibilities for the wives of violent husbands. It made women's use of force less repugnant and allowed wives to leave violent husbands more frequently and more promptly than they had a few decades before. But wives found themselves increasingly reliant for protection not on an intimate web of neighbors and family, but on police officers, men who were often disinterested strangers. The twentieth century brought increased permission for abused wives to act on their own behalf, but a decreased likelihood that anyone else would.

The nature of violence against wives and the ways in which wives resisted that violence shifted as Oregon entered the modern age. In the first decades of the twentieth century, Oregon, like the rest of the nation, moved decidedly from a culture based on production to one based on consumption. The widespread distribution of automobiles and other consumer goods and the proliferation of movie theaters and radios, tireless messengers of the good life of leisure and enjoyment, facilitated this shift to self-gratification. Not surprisingly, then, abusive husbands of the 1920s, 1930s, and early 1940s less often practiced the sort of restraint that their counterparts of the 1890s had commonly done. Violence increased as self-restraint decreased.

This increased violence had both affective and instrumental causes. Husbands frequently beat their wives over baseless sexual jealousy and around the times that wives gave birth. Some shifted quickly between idealizing and debasing their wives, vacillations similar to those expressed by Oregon's novelists and ministers. Yet much of husbands' violence was also a response to more concrete developments, often to a wife's attempts to establish control over her life, to assert her identity as a person in her own right. The waning of self-restraint and the blurring of the line that had distinguished the genders' spheres made hitting one's wife a more acceptable option to husbands, regardless of whether that blow arose from general resentments and anxieties or from a desire to control wives participating in the broad social movement toward sexual equality.

Women's growing sense of individuality and equality often emboldened them to resist or escape abusive marriages more directly than their counterparts from the late nineteenth century had. They seemed less hesitant to use physical force, and they left husbands more promptly and more commonly. The same cultural and social developments that had begun to put wives at greater risk of being hit by violent husbands also helped them to respond more strongly and effectively to that violence.

This ironic relationship between wives' vulnerability to violence and their ability to resist it was not new in Oregon's history. The nineteenth century had featured a similar tension until the ascendance of self-restraint had reversed it, leaving wives both safer from husbands' violence and less able to resist it. This latest paradigm, recognizable in Portland early in the twentieth century and well established elsewhere by the 1920s, would prove to be much more durable. The post–World War II era would bring not a moderation of forces unleashed in the quarter-century before it, but their florescence.

5

"We Found That We
Were Not Alone":
The Years after World War II

The decades since World War II constituted a coherent era in U.S. history. Sustained prosperity in the postwar period created an environment in which the consumption-oriented culture forged earlier in the century could mature, unimpeded by the frictions of a major depression or a world war and abetted by the miracle of television.

This accelerated emphasis on pleasure and self-fulfillment accentuated early-twentieth-century trends in the history of violence against wives. The years after World War II and especially after the mid-1960s saw a further rise both in that violence and in wives' capacity to escape or resist it. These decades also ushered in an unprecedented development: a powerful grass-roots movement against wife beating. The last half of the twentieth century has been a time of extremes and paradoxes, of ironies and contradictions inherent to a culture based on self-realization.

The late 1960s and early 1970s marked a watershed in U.S. history. James Lincoln Collier, in *The Rise of Selfishness in America*, argues that the twentieth century's trend toward self-indulgence quickened in the early 1970s due to several developments: the coming of age of vast numbers of children born into prosperity, the pervasiveness of television and advertising, the counterculture's hedonistic strain, the human potential movement's emphasis on self-help and self-improvement, and a break in national morale precipitated by the Vietnam War and the Watergate scandal. Drug use and divorce rates rose markedly in the mid-1960s, as did sexual promiscuity. Yet these were also years of striking reform and idealism: the extension of true civil rights to African Americans; widespread concern over poverty; the end of the Vietnam War; large-scale movements for equality among people of color, women, gays and lesbians; and a pervasive sense among many young people that the course of U.S. history, of western civilization, needed to be radically altered and rendered more humane and inclusive. A commitment to self-realization survived and prospered as a common denominator that has united a diverse nation. Of the many slogans the 1960s birthed, none has proved more durable than "Do your own thing."[1]

Social critics have typically interpreted modern individualism in largely or wholly negative terms. Philip Slater, in the aptly entitled *The Pursuit of Loneliness*, asserted in the 1970s that the nation's culture effectively frustrated people's desire for community, for engagement and accountability with the social and physical environment. Christopher Lasch, as the title of his 1979 book *The Culture of Narcissism* implied, characterized modern people as anxious and self-absorbed as they restlessly pursued the consumer culture's promise of total gratification at the expense of deeper social, intellectual, or aesthetic commitments. The era's cynical self-aggrandizement is perhaps best summed up by a bumper sticker popular in the 1980s that read: "He who dies with the most toys wins."[2]

But the movement toward self-fulfillment can be interpreted positively. Daniel Yankelovich pointed out in 1981 that this ethos could be an exacting master, such as when a wife who is married to a wealthy but indifferent husband chooses the more demanding option of single motherhood. Peter Clecak in 1983 argued that the 1960s and 1970s marked a time when the quest for an "ideal self" became more intense and more broadly shared, as groups that had been on the margins of the nation's economic, legal, and political life gained the ability to develop their lives much more fully than before. This movement affected even conservative Protestants. By the 1950s evangelical leaders openly championed an end to the patriarchal family, and by the 1970s they had embraced a positive image of the self sharply at odds with their tradition. The modern credo of self-realization has proven

to be remarkably adept at transforming even its most determined critics, in part because of its inclusiveness. For Clecak, modernity had ushered in a vast expansion of possibilities, and the selfishness and anar-
chy that critics such as Lasch lamented were simply extreme and
unavoidable by-products of a larger, more salutary trend.[3]

The costs of pursuing self-fulfillment have been substantial, however. A national survey comparing attitudes from 1957 and 1976 found
that people of the latter period had a more positive view of the self but
less concern about the social aspects of their identity. The search for
individual satisfaction has been almost by definition an isolating experience, one that has often brought separation from one's community,
one's spouse, even one's children. Modern individualism, freed from
the nineteenth-century fetters of social obligation and self-restraint,
had by the 1970s created both greater opportunities for personal happiness and an impoverished community life.[4]

Oregon, though still much more staid than California, its trend-
setting neighbor to the south, marched in step to the nation's larger
trends. As with much of the West, the influx of federal dollars and
defense workers during World War II precipitated sustained growth
and urbanization. Oregon's population rose from 1,090,000 in 1940 to
1,521,000 in 1950. By 1970 it had surpassed 2 million, and in 1990
Oregon had 2.8 million people, over 70 percent of whom were urban.
Indeed, a large proportion of Oregon's growth from 1940 to 1990
occurred in its three largest cities, Portland, Eugene, and Salem, as
well as in the rapidly expanding band of suburbs around Portland. Oregon's farms declined in number, though not in acreage, and they constituted a diminished portion of the state's economy. Timber remained
an important, though mercurial, employer. Oregon's reputation as a
progressive, relatively uncrowded state with a temperate climate and
beautiful scenery drew many well-educated people as permanent residents and helped stimulate its electronic and tourist industries. By
1993, a century and a half after the first wagon train had made its way
to the Willamette Valley, Oregon had long since ceased to be a frontier in any conventional sense of the word, though it still symbolized
relative stability and moderation.[5]

Yet modern Oregon was not of one piece. African Americans and
Spanish-speaking Americans made substantial population gains in
Portland and the northern Willamette Valley, though most of the rest

of the state remained overwhelmingly white. Urbanization proceeded fitfully in eastern and coastal Oregon, as did economic development. Many of these communities depended heavily on a single industry and consequently suffered deeply when, for example, a local mill closed down. By the 1980s Oregon offered startling economic and cultural contrasts between prosperous suburban communities, such as Lake Oswego just south of Portland, and economically depressed, working-class towns, such as Coquille on the south coast. Modern Oregon was both "Nike Town," glittery showcase of Michael Jordan's athletic shoe, and glum mill towns, where unemployed loggers fumed at environmentalists and struggled to keep their homes and their hopes.[6]

In Oregon, as in the United States as a whole, residents remained united not so much in their circumstances as in their hopes. The 1980s deepened economic cleavages between metropolis and town, the well-to-do and the working class. But the twentieth century's long-term trend toward self-fulfillment enjoyed broad support from Oregonians. The florescence of a consumption-oriented ethos provided a certain coherence to post–World War II life.

The history of sex roles in the years after World War II defies pat generalizations. Romantic relationships have seemed at once more intense and more tenuous, wives more independent and more vulnerable, husbands more autonomous and more dependent.

Marriage continued to grow more insular. Elaine Tyler May, writing of the 1950s, argues that people saw the family as a place of adaptation and containment, a place where the new age's potential dangers could be moderated. Indeed, the 1950s marked the slowing of some demographic trends and the reversal of others. The birth rate rose, as did the proportion of people who married. These couples, particularly those belonging to the expanding middle class, lived more privately than they had earlier in the century. Richard Steiner, a Unitarian minister in Portland, remarked in 1961 that "the typical metropolitan family usually lives far from whatever roots its members may have once had, cut loose from the moral sanctions of a small community and beset by the temptations of . . . anonymity."[7] The 1950s' overriding emphasis on early marriage and reproduction proved to be something of an anomaly, but the family's increasing isolation was not.

Growing numbers of marriages buckled and cracked under the weight of rising expectations for self-fulfillment and intimacy. The divorce rate remained fairly stable through most of the 1950s, at a level not much above what it had been during the 1930s. But from the mid-1960s to the mid-1970s it rose dramatically. By the late 1970s there were 38 divorces for every marriage in the nation, 40 for every marriage in Oregon. As a Portland woman who divorced in 1975 put it: "Today's attitude of 'me first' is not conducive to working together as a unit."[8] To be sure, the soaring divorce rate indicated exacting standards for companionship and intimacy, not just self-preoccupation. But the search for more satisfying marital relationships could arise from a desire to exploit, not to share and reciprocate. Howard Gadlin cautioned in his 1976 historical overview of intimate relationships that "we have moved toward a new form of consumerism in which the products consumed are other persons who are appreciated in terms of their ability to satisfy our fragmented needs."[9]

As before, gender played a key role in determining what spouses invested in and reaped from marriage. Judith Armatta, an attorney with Oregon's Coalition against Domestic and Sexual Violence, recalled growing up in the 1950s: "We were . . . taught to find a man, serve him and live through him. His ego needed boosting and we were encouraged to lie to do it . . . Women's primary responsibility for children included keeping them quiet and out of dad's way. Children came second to the man of the house."[10] Steven Mintz and Susan Kellogg concur, noting that although the wife of the 1950s had gained theoretical equality with her spouse, her "primary role was to serve as her husband's ego massager, sounding board—and housekeeper."[11] Women continued to devote more of themselves to their marriages than their husbands did.

The 1960s and particularly the 1970s brought unprecedented and direct challenges to men's marital domination, a challenge that many historians locate in changing patterns of women's employment. In 1960, most U.S. households had a male breadwinner, a female housewife, and children. By the late 1980s fewer than 15 percent of the nation's households fit that description. Oregonians participated in this shift. The end of World War II brought widespread unemployment to Portland women. But Oregon women's participation in the paid work force grew steadily, albeit usually in jobs much less remunerative than shipbuilding had been. In 1950 29 percent of them were in the paid labor force, by 1980 50 percent. A large proportion of wives who worked outside the home had low-paying jobs in the service sector or the helping professions, and they typically defined their work as a service to their family. Some 57 percent of Portland wives in a 1978 study indicated that they had taken jobs to help meet living expenses, 45 percent to provide money for extra family expenses. Only 27 percent said that they had sought work to follow their own professional career, barely more than the 26 percent who had gone to work to support their husband's education. But these responses should not detract from the revolutionary development that had been slowly growing since early in the century and that had blossomed during its second half. The rapid growth in women's paid labor, particularly by wives, had greatly loosened the bonds of economic dependency that had provided much of women's incentive to marry and to stay married. Women's expanded employment—lack of child care and pay equity notwithstanding—opened up a new universe of possibilities for independence and achievement hardly imaginable a century before.[12]

Women's rapidly increasing employment mixed with rising expectations for self-fulfillment to fuel a feminist revolution inside and outside the home. May detected discontent even among wives of the 1950s, citing a survey in which women respondents often expressed ambivalence over marriage in general and their husbands in particular. That discontent had become patent by the 1970s. Morris Tiktin, an Oregon psychologist, spoke in 1978 of "a redistribution of power in relationships, away from the husband-dominated family." "There is an awareness by the woman that she wants a 'piece of the action,'" he continued. "She would like to be a person. The emergence of women and their self-actualization is another way of stating it."[13] Simply put, wives expected more consideration and reciprocation from their husbands than they had in earlier decades.

Not all wives welcomed the movement toward equality, however. Most women agreed that they faced special barriers. In 1974 two-thirds of women surveyed said that they were victims of discrimination, a reversal of the results found only twelve years before. But these women did not necessarily identify themselves as feminists or embrace an agenda of across-the-board equality. As Barbara Ehrenreich has persuasively argued, conservative women often had a more negative view of men than did their radical or liberal counterparts. They argued that such developments as employment for women, birth control, and no-fault divorce simply encouraged male irresponsibility without taking into account women's vulnerabilities. "From the vantage point of the antifeminists," remarks Ehrenreich, "the crime of feminism lay not in hating men, but in trusting them too well."[14] Freed from the restraints of paternalism, men would simply exploit women more fully than they had before. Vivian Estellachild, writing of hippie communes, put it more bluntly in 1970: "The idea of sexual liberation for the woman means she is not so much free to fuck as to get fucked over . . . Our mothers could get a home and security, a prostitute—money, but a hippie woman is bereft of all that."[15] Modern man tended to perceive equality between the sexes not as a condition to strive for, but as an accomplished fact. Hence they could both enjoy traditional prerogatives, even while lamenting their passage, and jettison traditional responsibilities. This development has alarmed many conservative women, in particular. Judith Stacey argues that many fundamentalist wives embrace a religion that requires them to defer at least outwardly to their husband's authority because that same religion requires husbands to be responsible family men.[16] Many other women have steered something of a middle course, at once desirous of economic and social parity yet fearful of undermining the increasingly flimsy structures that encourage men to be considerate husbands and fathers. One of the many ironies of individualism is that it offered women the prospect but not the fact of gender equality while eroding many of the ways that women had survived and moderated that inequality.

Men responded in a variety of ways to the new possibilities and standards that modernity confronted them with. Some, at least beginning in the 1970s, took women's demands for reciprocity seriously and worked hard to create marriages in which all tasks, from child nurture to home repair, ceased to be gender specific. Yet most seemed more influenced by individualism than egalitarianism. Peter Stearns notes that the emphasis on truly companionate and mutual marriages was undercut by men's tendency to see the family as a place to have fun, while women typically viewed it as a place for intimacy and commitment. Indeed, Ehrenreich argues persuasively that men's "flight from commitment" began in the 1950s, well before feminism's frontal assault on male privilege. Many men used the growing emphasis on self-fulfillment to escape familial responsibilities both before and after large numbers of women openly questioned sexual inequality.[17]

Yet post-World War II society brought men new difficulties as well as new possibilities. The long-term economic boom that followed the war quickened the nation's movement toward an automated and service-oriented economy. By 1956 white-collar workers outnumbered blue-collar ones. Working-class occupations shrank dramatically in places like Coos Bay, Oregon, where young men could no longer count on making a good living in the woods or in the mills. Managerial jobs offered a much better financial return, but not the occupational autonomy that men had traditionally craved. At home, men found themselves frustrated by new familial standards that stressed reciprocity and undermined traditional paternal authority. Postwar popular culture swarmed with beleaguered husbands at the mercy of these forces: Dagwood Bumstead, the napping businessman perpetually bemused at work and home; Ralph Kramden, the poorly paid bus driver incessantly bested by life in general and Alice, his quick-witted wife, in particular; and, more recently, Homer Simpson, the snacking nuclear power plant worker who has set a new, pitiable standard as an employee, husband, and father. This sort of exaggerated incompetence indicated men's fear that modern life had become too much for them, that they had lost their mastery.[18]

As during the first half of the twentieth century, men often associated the negative aspects of modernity with women. Rupert Wilkinson has pointed out the irony in this association: men's success in business facilitated the very material softness they feared—and attributed to feminization. Ehrenreich remarks that male culture's "common drift, from *Playboy* through the counterculture of the sixties and the psychological reevaluation of masculinity in the seventies, has been to legitimate a consumerist personality *for men*," although "if this movement has had a sustaining sense of indignation, it has more often been directed against women rather than against the corporate manipulators of tastes and dictators of the work routine."[19] Men were ambivalent over the society of ease they had helped to create, and they tended to feminize the parts of it they liked least.

Ken Kesey, arguably the most prominent author in Oregon history, certainly conflated progress with femininity. *One Flew Over the Cuckoo's Nest*, published in 1962, is set in a mental hospital presided over by Miss Ratchet, the emasculating, buxom "Big Nurse." Ratchet's joyless, well-regulated institution is a metaphor for the larger society:

The ward is a factory for the Combine. It's for fixing up mistakes made in the neighborhoods and in the schools and in the churches, the hospital is. When a completed product goes back out into society, all fixed up good as new, *better* than new sometimes, it brings joy to the Big Nurse's heart; something that came in all twisted different is now a functioning, adjusted component, a credit to the whole outfit and a marvel to behold. Watch him sliding across the land with a welded grin, fitting into some nice little neighborhood where they're just now digging trenches along the street to lay pipes for city water. He's happy with it. He's adjusted to surroundings finally.[20]

The nurse's routine is disrupted when McMurphy, the consummate male individualist, arrives. McMurphy eventually succeeds in breaking the nurse's power over the ward's men when he physically assaults her, not coincidentally exposing her large breasts. Kesey's next novel, *Sometimes a Great Notion*, treats women much more sympathetically than *Cuckoo's Nest* had, but here, too, the story is suffused by the theme that modern man's individuality is at risk, that progress—here represented by a bureaucratic labor organizer—is bleeding man white. The West remains man's last best hope, for at book's close the effeminate Leland chooses to stay on the Oregon coast to pursue manhood while Vivian, the book's central woman character, takes Leland's bus ticket to New York in search of a life of her own.[21] In Kesey's post–World War II West, woman was out of place at best and responsible for man's dilemma at worst.

Comic strips, too, revealed modern man's growing fears over modern woman. Ones from 1950 showed marriage robbing men of their strength and interfering with their true vocation, namely the pursuit of excitement. Only 31 percent of domestic strips depicted men as more intelligent than women compared to 80 percent among the adventure strips. The comics saved their strongest caricatures for husbands, who tended to become fat and bald once they were married.[22]

The rapid growth of pornography expressed men's anxiety over modern women even more directly. May has examined men's fear of women's sexuality in the 1940s and 1950s and how its associations with the destructiveness of atomic energy led to such terms as "bombshell" and "bikini."[23] Pornographic images, defined as the persistent sexualization and debasement of women, became much more common in the late 1960s and the 1970s, just as women became more assertive. As

Susan Griffin persuasively argues, such images have offered men a means to possess, control, and punish women. Hence pornography has commonly featured not only the domination of women, but the gagging of their mouths and the mutilation of their bodies. Violent pornography has not been limited to hard-core magazines or films. One set of researchers found sexual violence in about 10 percent of the cartoons and nearly 5 percent of the pictures in *Playboy* and *Penthouse* magazines in the mid-1970s. Joyce Hammond's analysis of *Playboy* cartoons from the 1970s suggests pornography's broader context. She finds that the images emphasized the opposite nature of masculinity and femininity and that men would inevitably lose ground if women gained it. At a time when women were indeed gaining ground, though less rapidly than men tended to believe, pornographic magazines expressed both men's general antipathy toward women and their fears over the possibility of sexual equality.[24]

Paternalism lost much of its potency after the mid-1960s. This erosion was well under way by the 1950s. Indeed, cartoons from the start of that decade commonly featured wives who exceeded their husbands in size, and the images depicted women as being more aggressive than men nearly three-quarters of the time. Domestic violence had become not an example of male depravity, but a sort of roughhousing in which husbands like Jiggs or Andy Capp were lucky to hold their own. Judith Armatta recalled in 1989 a childhood of "eroticized male dominance and female submission. John Wayne spanking Maureen O'Hara; Rhett carrying Scarlett off to bed against her will . . ."[25] The cultural watershed of the late 1960s and early 1970s accelerated the decline of paternalism. Self-restraint had become passé, and all types of violent crime increased dramatically. Furthermore, many men saw little need to defend a gender that appeared to be gaining equality. "As male supremacy becomes ideologically untenable, incapable of justifying itself as protection," remarks Lasch, "men assert their domination more directly, in fantasies and occasionally in acts of raw violence."[26]

Even by the 1950s, husbands who appeared in Oregon divorce cases admitted to using violence against their wives more readily than they had during any era since the settlement period. One man's affidavit conceded that he "hit and pushed at" his wife "to get her away from me."[27] Another eastern Oregon husband, who complained of his wife's going out with other men, asserted in his affidavit that he had "always slapped her back in self defense" when she had slapped him and had also hit her "to protect my pride because of the way she mistreated me."[28] A third husband's affidavit went further in asserting a right to use violence: "She had come home so drunk that she didn't know what she was doing . . . If ever a woman needed a good beating the defendant needed it at that time and my possible error was that I did not do a better job of it: That may have straightened her out and made her come to her senses a little bit."[29] Husbands in earlier decades had commonly hesitated before taking such measures, certainly before admitting to it in court.

The testimony of wives in the 1950s indicated an actual rise in husbands' violence. To be sure, some described abusive husbands who seemingly hit with reluctance, if at all. But more depicted highly violent men who broke their wives' bones or beat them so frequently that they were bruised for weeks or months at a time. One woman's legal answer to her husband's divorce petition described a beating and kicking that hospitalized her for three days. Another eastern Oregon wife recalled that her husband had "hit me so hard he broke his hand," that he had beat her one to two times a month, and that he had cracked her nose and broken her ribs.[30]

Descriptions of extreme violence were commonplace by the 1980s and 1990s. A wife filing for a restraining order against her ex-husband cited "broken arms legs etc."[31] Another recalled her husband "beating me slapping me around kicking me . . . almost every day" for three weeks.[32] A third described a day when her husband "severely & repeatedly beat me about the face & head threw me about drug me by the hair & 'head butted' my nose causeing my nose to be fractured & threatend my life—even to the extent of fireing my 22 rifle to emphasis the point."[33] Other husbands went to even greater lengths to terrorize their wives. One woman offered a particularly harrowing account of abuse: "He burned me with a lit cigerette on the shoulders & legs. he killed my two puppy by chocking & squeesing there guts out. he tried to chock me and smother Virginia [her daughter] . . . he has tried to make me miscarrge by sticking things in me while p.g. [pregnant]."[34] Mary McGuire, convicted in 1977 of hiring men to kill her husband, described a similar life of terror, including broken ribs and pelvic bones, cigarette burns, and the decapitation of her horse. Another wife, also in the late 1970s, recalled a particularly brutal beating: "he beat and he beat and he beat. He picked up a television set and hit me with it. I had on a white dress and he kept beating and the dress was soaked with blood all over. I asked him for a wash cloth for my eye because it was beat so badly I couldn't see, and he said 'Don't worry about it. You're going to be dead one way or another.' "[35] This assault lasted three and one half hours.

Quantitative evidence also indicates that violence against wives rose late in the twentieth century. Studies from across the United States showed that violent husbands used physical force frequently by the 1970s, with most such husbands hitting their wives at least once every few months or weeks. A late 1970s sample of 96 Oregon women who had been hit by their partners identified 6.2 percent as suffering continual violence and 50.5 percent several acts per month. Oregon's homicide rates for wives also rose over the course of the twentieth century.[36]

Oregon women responded in an unprecedented way to this escalation of violence. A grass-roots collection of women's shelters and crisis lines began forming in the 1970s. These feminists related male violence to broader gender patterns. In 1981 one remarked that such abuse "is part of a larger system of violence outside the home, including rape and sexual harassment at work, that functions to control and limit women's public and private activities."[37] Likewise, Multnomah County's Family Violence Intervention Steering Committee asserted in 1991 that "domestic violence is an expression of the unequal power that exists in relationships between men and women," an "inequality . . . supported historically by the social norms, roles, and institutions of this culture."[38] By the 1980s this sort of radical critique of wife beating and male dominance was widely articulated in the state's small-town and urban shelters alike.

This is not to say that the feminist battered-women's movement did not meet considerable resistance. Mary Henderson, the first director of a shelter in the northern Willamette Valley, recalled speaking to various service clubs, churches, businesses, and agencies in McMinnville: "People still had a hard time believing that domestic violence happened in their quiet community, after all they had never heard about it before. Some of the attitudes I confronted were: If women would keep their mouths shut, they would not get hit; I'm sure they deserved it; So, she made her bed, let her lie in it; No worse for her than for us."[39] Nor did those working to end violence against women necessarily agree on methods or even goals. Tensions were particularly salient around 1980 between the short-lived Family Violence Program, overseen by powerful government administrators in the Portland area, and grass-roots feminist organizations. Leaders of the latter groups criticized the federally funded program for, among other things, not assigning a "higher priority to meeting the needs of victims than to meeting the needs of batterers," a criticism that a member of the program met by asserting: "families are our concern."[40]

Yet the existence of a well-funded program designed in large part to end violence against wives constituted a major historical departure. Commissioner Charles Jordan of Portland's Office of Public Safety, an instrumental player in establishing the eighteen-month program, asserted in 1979 that the "community needs to become aware of the extent of violence in its home and it needs to become intolerant of that violence."[41] In 1983 Republican Governor Victor Atiyeh proclaimed a Domestic and Sexual Violence Awareness Week and a Unity for Battered Women and Victims of Sexual Assault Day. Such pronouncements indicated growing public concern over violence toward wives.[42]

The battered-women's movement has had a profound and tangible impact on violence against wives in Oregon. Its most visible contribution has been a network of shelters, safe homes, and crisis lines (discussed later in this chapter). The movement's sustained advocacy, carried out both at the local level and at the state legislature, has also changed the face of public attitudes and policy. Relatively sensitive treatments of wife beating began appearing in Oregon newspapers in the 1970s. This is not to say that public views have changed completely. A 1955 article in a Portland newspaper listed selfishness, money problems, sex relations, conflicts with in-laws, children, unfaithfulness, lack of mutual interests, distrust, nagging, drinking, and varied family backgrounds as "the main reasons marriages fail."[43] The conspiracy of silence about male violence persisted into the 1980s in many places. An Astoria woman described how "traditional sources" responded to her plea for help from her violent husband: "My minister told me to pray and be more supportive of my husband; my doctor took X-rays of my injuries, prescribed tranquilizers and sent me to a mental health clinic. The therapist suggested that I was harboring feelings of inferiority and suggested more tranquilizers."[44] Due in large part to the dedication and skill of Oregon's battered-women's movement, reactions such as this are becoming more rare. Increasing numbers of people are aware of domestic violence as a serious social problem.

Violent husbands, furthermore, are now much more likely to face legal consequences than at any other time in Oregon's history. Domestic violence legislation passed in the late 1970s required police officers responding to a family fight to arrest a man if he had assaulted his wife, even if the wife did not then say that she would prosecute, and to arrest when they had probable cause to believe that an assault had occurred, unless the victim objected. By the late 1970s thousands of Oregon wives annually won restraining orders that barred their husbands or ex-husbands from interfering with them for twelve months. Violators could be jailed. Such orders have been no guarantee of safety from a violent husband or ex-husband. Yet it seems highly likely that these orders commonly deter violent men. Vietta Helmle, executive director of a women's crisis service in Salem, remarked in 1992 that restraining orders often worked "because most people really, really don't want to talk to police officers, they don't want to go to court, they don't want to go to jail."[45] The court-mandated men that I have counseled at Portland's ASAP Treatment Services seldom exhibit much empathy for their abused wives or partners, but they are almost unanimous in adamantly asserting that they will give up hitting these women to avoid going to jail. In 1993 Portland police arrested about one hundred men monthly for hitting their partners. Early in the century they arrested an average of just over two husbands a month.[46]

Treatment for violent men is another component of the modern movement to end violence against wives. Group counseling became common in Oregon during the 1980s, and by the early 1990s individual or group therapy was available across most of the state. Such programs reached only a small proportion of violent men, and their success has been difficult to measure. A wife beater who went through such counseling asserts that at least two years of it is required. The majority of men in such programs are court-referred; they choose counseling as an alternative to a felony conviction with possible jail time. The programs typically last only six months and emphasize group rather than individual work. A survey from the late 1970s showed that only 9 percent of battered Oregon women reported their battering partner to be in counseling. Portland's Men's Resource Center, apparently the state's largest such service, treated 496 male batterers from July 1990 to July 1991. Only a small fraction of Oregon's violent husbands receive treatment and, as one recovering abuser points out, participation is no guarantee of actually changing one's behavior. Yet the presence of such programs, many of them court mandated, represents a growing, if still modest, public commitment to ending violence against wives. Some Oregon men have begun the hard work of confronting deeply ingrained patterns of abuse and violence.[47]

Robert Robertson asserted in 1992 that "all of the men I know who are abusive are deeply ashamed of their behavior."[48] My experience as a group counselor largely supports his generalization. The men not uncommonly remarked of their violence that "I never thought I would sink to that level" or "it makes me feel like an animal." Men who hit their partners, then, seem to regret their actions, even to view it as unmanly and unacceptable. Yet violence against wives has increased during the twentieth century, particularly in the past few decades.

If even violent husbands condemn their violence, why does it continue to flourish? In the first place, violent husbands are skilled at finding loopholes to any no-hitting rules. Men in my groups commonly asserted that they would hit a woman who hit them first, or that it was their right to punish physically a partner who had sex with another man. Violent husbands are also adept at denying that violence, both to others and to themselves. One group member sat through several months of group counseling without being able to cite a single instance of abuse before acknowledging that he had used violence extensively against two former partners. But another key to the paradox of men's violence and their shame over it lies in the tension between two broadly influential and contradictory values: self-indulgent individualism on the one hand and idealistic consideration on the other. Modern husbands live in a society that in many ways proscribes violence against wives, a society in which wife beating is regularly condemned on the Oprah Winfrey show and in popular movies. But these husbands also live in a society that has removed much of the cultural wherewithal for curbing violent impulses. The twentieth century, especially the late twentieth century, has eroded people's capacity for self-discipline. Nor is U.S. society of one piece in decrying violence toward wives, even in the abstract. The contemporary era is a time in which violence against wives has become both a staple of the male-entertainment industry and grounds for court-mandated counseling, a common source of humor and the subject of a public-service announcement televised during the 1993 Super Bowl.[49]

The immediate causes of violence against wives since World War II have remained complex. Previous chapters have traced the rise of affective violence beginning late in the nineteenth century, of violence prompted by anxieties related more to women in general than to the particular actions of a particular wife. Affective violence has continued to be salient since the war, though it has by no means supplanted instrumental violence.

Wives from both the 1950s and the 1980s reported husbands using violence as an instrument of control. An eastern Oregon woman recalled that in 1954 her husband suddenly "kicked me very hard in the back" when "I asked . . . for some money to buy the children some shoes."[50] The complaint of a Multnomah County wife of the same period recalled an instance in which her spouse used angry, "very indecent language" toward her because she had been instructing her son in the Seventh Day Adventist faith. When she "gently patted defendant's lips and said, 'Please don't say those terrible things,' " he "doubled up his fist and struck the plaintiff in the mouth and stated that the plaintiff was no wife of his and that she could move out and take her kid with her."[51] A woman who filed for a restraining order in the 1980s quoted her husband as telling her, "What does it take to get you to shout [shut] up or leave. You want me to slap the crap out of you."[52] Another noted that her husband told her that "if you don't quit antigonizing me I'm going to hit you." "If I don't agree with his terms on things," she explained, "I'm antigonizing him."[53]

As during the settlement era, contemporary violence against wives has commonly served to compel wives' obedience. A couple interviewed in 1977 described how wife beating occurred as part of a larger struggle for control. The husband remarked that he used violence "to make her think the way I was thinking no matter what it took." His wife provided more details. Most of the fights occurred over money, she recalled: "He'd fly off and say, 'I'm supposed to be the man who wears the pants in this house.' And if I didn't agree with what he said, instead of sitting down and reasoning it out, he'd just get mad."[54] My counseling experience also indicates that violence toward wives often occurs as part of a broader struggle for male control. Much of these men's energy is devoted to maintaining traditional male prerogatives, to keeping their partners "three steps behind" them, as one put it. Such men expect a level of obedience that few modern wives are willing to comply with. A woman's petition for a restraining order in the 1980s described an evening when her husband told her to assist him in bathing, this while she had "the kitchen to clean up; 2 kids to get ready for bed; the house to pick up; laundry to do," and a spilled baby bottle to deal with. When she persisted in doing this work her husband hit her in the leg with the shampoo bottle, jerked her arm and kicked her, then "*ordered* me several times to get in the bathroom & help him." She retorted that "I already have 2 babies to take care of, I don't need 3," and "he finally gave up & went back to the bathroom." The next evening he told her: "If you defy me, tell me 'no' again, you'll get worse than that; you'll get what you deserve," to which she replied that she would go to an attorney "if he ever beat-manhandled me again." A few days later, when she remarked that "it wasn't easy to live with, wondering when the next time [violence] would happen," he countered that he would hit her "the next time you get out of line."[55] This man's physical abuse clearly served as an attempt to compel the obedience of a wife who rejected his claim of authority over her.

Working-class men may feel particularly threatened by women's growing autonomy. Oregon's working class, traditionally central to its economy, became increasingly marginalized after World War II. These men commonly find themselves unemployed, or, if they are employed, making less money than their white-collar wives. Several quantitative studies from across the United States indicate a positive relationship between unemployment and wife beating, as does some anecdotal evidence. A wife in one of Oregon's highly timber-dependent communities, for example, remarked in the 1980s of her husband that "I am afraid he will kill me and my children because he drink every week because he is not working."[56]

This is not to say that the state's well-to-do husbands have not been beating their wives. Robertson had a graduate degree and his own contracting business: "My life centered on my family, church, and career. I projected an image to my associates of the ideal, successful family man."[57] Divorce petitions described violent abuse from powerful professionals and business executives. In 1983 Robert Galloway, president of one of the ten largest remodeling contracting businesses in the nation, killed his wife, his four children, and himself in what was apparently the largest murder-suicide in Portland history.[58]

Violent husbands often paired strong physical and social resources with meager psychological ones. Robertson, so outwardly successful, recalled a childhood dominated by an abusive father and by the trauma of losing his mother in a car accident. Since "the fear of abandonment continued to contaminate me as an adult," he "became as dependent on my wife as I had been on my mother and was terrified of being abandoned by her." "I wanted to control her so she would never leave me," he concluded.[59] Women, too, have perceived this link between a husband's fears and his violence. One who recounted her husband's habit of "poking and hitting me rhythmically in the back" saying, "You bitch, you bitch, you bitch, you bitch," remarked that "he was just so unhappy at himself that he began beating me and he just kept beating and beating. He was beating himself."[60] "He had no love for himself, and none for anyone else," remarked a wife at the McMinnville women's shelter of her violent husband in 1982.[61]

Husbands often became violent over seemingly trivial events. A resident of Portland's Bradley Angle House, a women's shelter, described a particularly vivid example in the late 1970s:

> A couple of days before I came here—now I know this isn't gonna make any sense—he woke me up because he was hungry. So I got up and went into the kitchen and I made him a Spam sandwich. He don't like mustard usually so I put some mayonnaise on it and come back with it and sit down on the couch. He looks up. Then he threw the sandwich and says "I want mustard, I want tomatoes, I want lettuce." Now there ain't no tomatoes, there ain't no lettuce. So it's there. It's gonna happen.

What happened was that her husband hit her so hard that "my knees didn't even bend."[62] This man seemed determined to manufacture a pretext for hitting his spouse, despite her best efforts to serve him and to anticipate his wishes.

Men's violence around extreme jealousy also illustrated how abuse occurred independently of a wife's actions. "The baby got older and he was jealous of the baby," remarked a wife of her husband in the late 1970s.[63] A divorce-seeking woman in 1954 recalled being hit for taking a walk. "I can't do anything at all without his permission or being afraid that he is going to beat me," she concluded.[64] Another wife from that period said she "was allowed only one trip to the store and had to come right home," that "if I stopped to talk over the fence with the neighbor woman, he would be quite mad about it, but if I went into the house with her, he would get real mad about it." "I have even snubbed my friends in order to keep him from being jealous," she remarked.[65] A quarter-century later a group of battered women at the Bradley Angle House discussed this sort of abuse. One spoke of how her husband accused her "of having incest with my brother because we have always been close." "It got to a point," she continued, that "I felt guilty if I walked three blocks to the grocery store without telling him exactly where I was going and how long I'd be gone." "He resented you focusing energy on anything besides him," remarked a second woman. "Same thing," asserted a third. "I couldn't talk to anybody. I couldn't have no friends at all."[66] Violent husbands' jealousy often became generalized to include contact with anyone.

Jealous possessiveness often expressed itself as an attempt to control one's wife completely. "He has treated me as a piece of property, rather than as a wife," remarked the woman whose husband had allowed her only one trip to the store.[67] Another divorce-seeking wife of the 1950s said that her husband "tries to make me obey him as if I were a child" and "seems to take delight in the fact that I have to beg him to go out and in showing me that he is the boss of the family."[68] A wife in the late 1970s said that even her interest in pre-Columbian art upset her husband, that "every little thing threatens him."[69] Such husbands not infrequently told their wives that they could never escape them. A woman in the 1980s reported that her husband declared "that if he can't have me, no one else will either."[70] A woman from the 1990s noted that her husband "told me to pack my bags and leave several times—not thinking I would," and that when she did leave, "it's like—if I can't have you no one can."[71]

Some women detected in violent men's desire to control them a sort of dependency. A shelter resident in the late 1970s reflected on this: "He shut me away from society. He turned to me totally. I was his life. He tortured me with water, beat me and said things to me. In order to break me. In order to make me go crazy or die. My life was put in the closet and shut away. My life was only for his life, to stop his pain."[72] A few years later another woman recalled a violent episode that began with her husband saying "everything is hard for me, noth-ing goes right."[73] A wife who filed for a restraining order in the 1990s offered a lengthy description of a husband who mixed violent abuse with self-pity and dependency:

> Eric and I talked about the divorce. He begged me not to leave, not to divorce him without giving me a chance to see how he had changed.
> I said I was leaving him, and that was that. He says I have wife duties.
> Now he decides that I have to take the kids and leave. It's 12:30 at night, and I have no place to go. So hes going to physically make me leave. He pulls my legs off the bed and I hit the floor. I said no way, we scramble around on the floor—he started to throw my things out the window and shoved me to the ground again. I got up and he shoved me on the floor—I picked a shoe and hit him in the head— He slapped me and I fell on the bed, he was coming at me and I threw a glass at him—realization came to him and I, we were both crying and upset—he was shaking me yelling in my face I was mak-ing him do it—I married him and I had to give him a chance, and then he let me up—of course he was so sorry.

Only a few days later, apparently, a similar episode occurred:

> I went downstairs to shower—I walked out to the kitchen and got some juice. Walking back into the bathroom, Eric got in my way and gave me a shove, he told me I wasn't going anywhere but home and work—I said he was upset and looking for a fight, and I wasn't play-ing—I just wanted to get ready for work—He grabbed the juice out of my hand and dumped it on my head. I shoved past him and rinsed out my hair—we were arguing and he grabbed my hair dryer out of my hand and threw it out the window—shoved me down—my knee smashed into the dresser leg. I was just laying there on the ground crying. I was going for the phone and he ripped the phone out of the wall jack—and tried to hold me saying how sorry he was—I pushed him away and said something about him being pathetic—I landed back on the bed—his clothes were on the bed—I threw them at him as he came at me—he took his belt and hit me twice on the bottom— all I had on was my undies—leaving 2 welts and bruises. I got up went into the bathroom to get my stuff to go to work—he wasn't going to let me leave—we struggled again—he picked up a bottle of soap and threw it at me—I was not really looking at him and it hit

me on the head leaving a bloody bump—he came towards me—of course he was sorry, it was my fault he loves me so much, I told him to basically shove off he took shaving creame and sprayed in my face and hair—Now I'm screaming it was in my eyes—He put me in the shower and rinsed me off—I begged him to let me get ready for work—I got dressed and left the house, my hair wet my knee sore, my head bleeding—[74]

This man mixed bloody assaults on his wife with "pathetic" pleas for a second chance, orders to get out with frantic and violent attempts to intimidate her into staying. Robertson recalls a similar pattern of dependency on his wife, that he thought she would "love me and fix me and be my everything."[75] Abusive, emotionally repressed men "don't have relationships," he asserts, "they take hostages."[76]

This desire to control one's wife completely has led to horrible sexual assaults. Several wives, as earlier in the century, described instances in which their husbands tore their clothes from them. One woman, testifying in 1956, remarked that her husband "knocked me down and beat me, and ripped part of my clothes off, out in the middle of the road."[77] This sort of abuse had become more gruesome by the 1970s. Near the end of that decade a woman described a husband who used severe physical punishments on her when she did not find work: having sex in her anus; hitting her with a studded belt; and shoving articles into her vagina. A wife filing for a restraining order in the 1980s asserted that her spouse had shot a BB gun at her buttocks and breasts. Another described a husband who had employed sadistic sex against her for at least five years, including an instance in which he beat her with a heavy belt buckle on her pubic area until it "felt like the bones were on the surface of her skin," until "it was if the flesh on her pubic area were gone."[78]

Husbands' violence often seemed directed at their wives' femaleness. The woman whose husband had beat her pubic area bloody said that he had also slapped "her breasts around like they were something he loathed" and, while beating her, called her a "bitch," a "fucking cunt."[79] Another woman from the 1980s quoted her husband as yelling "you are a fat, lazy cunt" and "I guess I have to slap you around to get you to listen to me."[80] Another woman recalled that her partner resented her enjoyment of sex. After virtually withholding it from her for six months he came home one day and tied her up and raped her. This man "became extremely violent during pregnancy" and "had a deep resentment of femininity—he believed that women have powers much greater than men and a moral courage men may only wish for."[81] Another woman, also speaking in the late 1970s, said that her husband had "literally beat me to a pulp" and had kicked her pregnant belly when she refused to stop feeding her girls "and go to the bedroom with him." "They resent the life that's in you," she asserted. "All of them. They act like it's a threat to them."[82] A woman testifying in 1956 noted that her violent husband's abuse was worst "when I was carrying a child."[83] Many others indicated suffering physical abuse while pregnant. A survey of battered Oregon women in the late 1970s showed that 39 percent had experienced violence during pregnancy. In many instances, as the two women suggested above, this violence had to do with men's resentment of "the life that's in you," of womanhood itself.[84]

Several researchers have explored the complex relationship between men's anxiety about women and their violence toward them. Such men commonly feel both drawn to and afraid of women and fear both being engulfed and abandoned by them. This latter fear leads to intense jealousy that can focus even on the birth of a child. Violent men are often obsessed with controlling their wives, and they are apt to interpret the slightest indication of assertiveness by their spouse as a betrayal. These sorts of anxieties help to explain the prevalence of affective violence, of violence that appears to happen randomly and nonsensically, without any apparent relation to a woman's actions.[85]

Nancy Chodorow, with others, has located men's ambivalence and anxiety about women to fathers' absence from their sons' infancy. Hence young males quickly bond with their mothers, a connection they must repress to establish their identities as men, usually without the benefit of a strong father figure to take the mother's place. A boy's sex-role identification, then, is more harrowing, abstract, and antifemale than is his sister's. Yet, as Chodorow points out, women nonetheless come to represent for males a lost, golden age of security and gratification. Men therefore both dread and yearn for the emotional security that women represent. In sum, women are an extremely potent symbol of male vulnerability.[86]

Jan Horsfall, together with a few others, has linked males' early childhood experiences to wife beating. She argues that "intimacy is likely to raise anxieties about regression . . . He has a fear of intimacy as well as a need for it."[87] Marital intimacy, particularly sexual intimacy, so often triggers violence in husbands because it recalls unfinished business with their mother. In a suggestive cross-cultural analysis, Jacquelyn Campbell finds that the absence or near-absence of the father correlates positively with violence against wives.[88]

Infants' psychological development is extremely difficult to trace even in the laboratory, let alone through historical documents. Yet it is likely that men's gradual movement away from the home has increased their sons' ambivalence toward mothers and, later in life, toward wives. This is not to say that father absence or indifference is the cause of modern wife beating, or even a clearly distinguishable major cause. What does seem likely, however, is that modern men's general lack of interest in child rearing has played a major role in reproducing and exacerbating within their boys a pronounced ambivalence toward women. This ambivalence is much larger than wife beating. It strongly informs the "sexual politics," to borrow Kate Millet's term, of popular masculine culture from Norman Mailer and Ken Kesey to Larry Flynt.[89] Not all men act out that ambivalence by hitting the women they love. But this ambivalence, this misogyny, has grown so potent that it essentially puts all men at risk of using violence, particularly at a time when men's capacity to separate misogynistic thought from violent action has weakened.

It is certainly true that male violence is rooted to a large degree in male psychology. Consider, for example, this woman's description of her violent husband from the late 1970s: "My husband told me that there is inside him a door that is closed and locked. Behind that door is something that he will never look at, nobody else is ever going to make him look at, and no one else is ever going to see. It frightens him so much, that he refuses to even discuss opening it."[90] This man's deep anxieties, common enough in nonviolent as well as violent husbands, certainly had something to do with the physical abuse he inflicted on his wife.

A battered woman's observance, quoted above, that her husband viewed her life as "only for his life, to stop his pain" is an incisive and chilling insight into the affective roots of modern violence against wives. To be sure, instrumental and affective motives cannot be made discrete, cannot be wholly separated from each other. The violent husband whose wife described him as "pathetic" had a consistent goal: to control her actions, certainly to keep her from leaving him. The feminist movement, in challenging such control, no doubt impressed many violent husbands as a direct threat to their agenda. But descriptions by modern wives suggest that these men often sought a level of control that no woman could provide, regardless of how tractable she might become. Violent husbands' common fear of even the most innocuous acts by their spouses, together with their often pitiful fears of abandonment and expressions of self-loathing, do not suggest an allpowerful patriarch. Yet these stunted emotional resources are typically paired with substantial physical and economic ones. The noninstrumental and pathetic aspects of male violence have not made that violence any less dangerous or appalling.

Post–World War II women's resistance to their increasingly violent husbands has become increasingly explicit. One Portland resident used a hammer in 1964 on her spouse after he broke into her room and began throwing potted plants about. A wife in the 1980s recounted that when her husband pushed her down, "I kneed him and started to run," then grabbed a knife.[91] Another recalled that when her husband kicked her in the leg, grasped her hair, and began to hit her, "I hit him back."[92] A third, describing an instance in which her husband slapped and pushed her, remarked "naturally I fought back."[93] A booklet distributed by the south coast's Women's Crisis Service advised women that "there are varying opinions as to whether to fight back," that one should consider "your own strength and your batterer's personality" in making that decision.[94] A few women killed their attackers, intentionally or unintentionally. This act was often a woman's last resort, employed only after a broad array of other means had failed. Alta Bryan, whose ex-husband had broken into her home to beat and rape her for years after their divorce, shot and killed him a few days after he had told her that "he would come back anytime he wanted and do anything he wanted to do to me, anytime he felt like it." "There is nothing you can do about it," he concluded.[95]

Native American women have been particularly apt to use lethal force against their partners. In 1977 Janet Billey, who had grown up on the Warm Springs Reservation, stabbed and killed her husband as he came toward her. "He was going to hit me," she recalled. "I told him to stay back . . . I told him I was going to stab him."[96] From 1989 to 1993 Native Americans accounted for at least three of the twenty-four women who killed a boyfriend, husband, or ex-husband in Oregon, despite making up only about 1 percent of the state's women.[97]

Oregon's Native American women have a long legacy of autonomy and independence, one that has persisted into the twentieth century. Nora Caisse in the early 1910s charged her husband, apparently a non-Native American, with cursing her, accusing her of adultery, and trying to wrench a ring from her hand. Antoine contested her suit and wrote to her that "I have the whip hand right now. The matter of divorce is entirely at my pleasure—and you will never get it—and you cannot come back." Antoine explained that he did not "need a divorce, as my plans are to get a housekeeper, . . . a paper doll, so to speak." Two months later he asked Nora to return: "I cannot believe you hold your marriage vows so lightly." Nora's letters revealed a contrasting resoluteness that she apparently sustained throughout the case: "I will never in my life time go back to you. I hate you. I despise you. Even if I lose I shall never, never, go back to you."[98] Nora won her divorce.

Native American women married to Native American men exhibited a similar resolve and independence. Several early-twentieth-century divorce suits from the Warm Springs Reservation in eastern Oregon described wives who ordered their husbands to leave. The complaint of one husband noted that his wife "has repeatedly driven plaintiff away from their home" and would neither prepare meals for him nor let him prepare them for himself.[99]

These women drew on Native American traditions in asserting themselves against their spouses. A husband who recalled that his wife had "run me out of camp," saying that she "thought of me as [a] pile of manure," asserted that she particularly opposed his interest in Euro-American ways: "From childhood, I was raised in a pretty good home, always heard good talks, and then also . . . I am fond of reading and studied, then also I believe in the Supreme Being, and this did not agree with my wife, she did not want me to do this." At one time he had even hoped to prepare for the ministry, but her objections held him back. She also refused to be available for her husband's seeding and harvest work, choosing instead to go out and pick huckleberries "whether he wanted her to go or not."[100] This woman's opposition to Euro-American religion and agriculture and her resistance to her husband's authority seemed to be of one piece.

Nineteenth-century Native American women had often used divorce and separation to escape violent husbands. Those options became widely available for post–World War II Oregon women of all races. In the early 1970s a Multnomah County judge recalled that the grounds of cruel and inhuman treatment once "meant exactly what it said, hitting someone over the head when they didn't do what you wanted," but that it later "was diluted to mean something as simple, perhaps, as saying you didn't love the other person."[101] In 1971 Oregon made marital dissolutions still easier by instituting no-fault divorce, in which the plaintiff could simply cite irreconcilable differences. "The adoption of the 'no fault' concept of divorce is indicative of the state's policy, as exhibited by legislation, that marriage between spouses who 'can't get along' is not worth preserving," remarked the Oregon Supreme Court in 1973.[102] By the 1960s, assistance from legal aid or fee waivers for low-income plaintiffs made the financial cost of divorce much more affordable, as well.

The same forces of marital privatization that made divorce available for the asking also made family members and especially neighbors more reluctant to intervene in violent marriages. Women's ties with their families of origin tended to become more attenuated after World War II, as upwardly mobile couples moved away from their childhood homes. Younger and working-class women, however, often remained close to parents and siblings who might assist them against violent husbands. An eastern Oregon wife wed less than four years recalled such assistance when her husband returned home from the armed services in the 1950s and immediately began to threaten and roughly handle her. The woman's mother quickly called several relatives, whose presence caused the violent husband to become quiet and then to leave. Wives filing for restraining orders in the 1980s and 1990s recounted similar instances. One, upon being pinned to the floor by her husband, "yelled to our [child] to run get the police—He took out of the house & called my father . . . & he came down immediately to the house to protect me."[103] The increased social fragmentation of modern life affected women and men alike, but wives' ties to kin typically remained much stronger than their husbands' did, a factor that offered abused women a continued, if diminishing, source of support. Nonrelatives were, as a rule, more reluctant to intervene. One woman recalled in the 1980s that when her partner pulled her down by the hair as they and their children walked to church, "I screamed and [a] neighbor, Florence McCarthy, opened [the] door and saw us, then shut it."[104] Another woman, speaking in the 1970s, recounted how she had fled to a neighbor's house barefooted after a beating: "I was crying and yelling and screaming. She came to the back door and I told her what was going on and she could see and I asked her if she could help me and she said 'We don't want to get involved.' "[105] Police officers in Coos County said in 1992 that neighbors of quarreling couples often called them, but generally because they found the noise a nuisance, not out of fear for the woman's safety.[106]

Police intervention appeared to dwarf other forms of third-party interventions by the late twentieth century (see table). The scale and effectiveness of this intervention has increased markedly. The 1957 affidavit of an eastern Oregon woman noted that when she complained to a policeman that her estranged husband had smashed into the back of her car, "he advised me that he was a friend of both Kent Jones [her husband] and myself, and that I must contact my attorney."[107] By the late 1970s legislation had made restraining orders relatively easy to procure. Thousands of Oregon wives annually secured court orders that barred their husbands or ex-husbands from interfering with them for twelve months. Many thousand also telephoned the police. Multnomah County law-enforcement officials reported nearly 16,000 calls on domestic violence in 1990.[108] This is not to say that police have consistently treated such calls seriously. A 1979 study by the Governor's Commission for Women asserted that "officers continue to view

Third-party interventions

Year	Family of origin	Children	Neighbors/ Friends	Police
To 1870–1875	8 (15%)	9 (17%)	25 (46%)	12 (22%)
1890–1900	13 (18%)	13 (18%)	26 (35%)	22 (30%)
1900–1911	23 (21%)	13 (12%)	40 (36%)	34 (31%)
1924–1945	10 (10%)	15 (16%)	22 (23%)	49 (51%)
1954–1956	2 (7%)	5 (18%)	4 (14%)	17 (61%)

Source: Divorce suits described in appendix.

their primary function in a domestic disturbance as involving mediation and prompting reconciliation," that they were "trained to respond to the disturbance in terms of 'crisis intervention' rather than 'crime intervention.' "[109] Ignorance of pertinent laws has also been a problem. Doreen Binder, director of the south coast's Women's Crisis Service, said that in 1990 she did a police training and found little understanding of legislation passed many years earlier.[110]

But Oregon's police force appears to be treating wife beating as a serious crime much more consistently than it ever did before. Grassroots advocacy and training by women like Binder together with determined lobbying at the state level have led to increased sanctions against violent husbands, both on paper and on the street. Oregon courts are "light years" from where they were a decade or two ago, notes Armatta.[111]

Oregon police have commonly expressed frustration over the apparent reluctance of many women to leave a violent husband. Portland Chief of Police Bruce Baker asserted in 1977 that officers' most salient question about domestic violence "is why—eliminating masochism—does a woman continue to stay in the situation?"[112]

Economic reasons go a long way toward explaining why modern wives have so often remained with violent husbands. Women have typically lost a substantial amount of financial resources from separation and divorce. Oregon courts usually awarded such support to divorcing mothers by the 1950s. Yet they also noted that they had little power to compel husbands to obey. In 1956, for example, a Multnomah County judge cautioned that "rigorous enforcement" of a judgment against a husband might "result in chasing him off so he wouldn't pay anything."[113] A 1978 survey of 499 divorced Portland women found that 91 percent of the mothers had been awarded child support, but that only 57 percent of the awardees had received it regularly. "This making the fathers pay support money is one of the biggest farces there ever was," asserted a divorced woman in 1968.[114] Even women who received payments often lived in poverty. In the 1978 survey, 71 percent of the women said that they had to lower their standard of living after divorce. Remarked one: "I no longer have a middle class lifestyle. I began a life of poverty and am still in it 8 years later."[115] Leaving an abusive husband, as earlier in Oregon's history, often meant living with very little money.

A comparison of the wages earned by divorce-seeking women and their husbands illustrates why divorce so often brought poverty. Public assistance often provided such mothers with a base income, but one much lower than even an unskilled man could earn. In the 1950s, for example, two wives with several dependent children reported monthly public assistance payments of around $185, compared to the $400 to $500 their husbands could earn as loggers. A group of Multnomah County cases from the late 1960s showed striking disparities in what wives and husbands received in the labor force: a secretary who made one-half to one-third of what her husband did as a crane operator; a secretary who netted $250 a month compared to her laboring husband's $400; a wife employed by the Department of Motor Vehicles who barely earned half of what her husband did as a journeyman baker; a waitress who earned about half of what her husband did as a construction laborer; and a bookkeeper of six years who made less than her husband did after three months as a service station attendant.[116] Divorced women so often lived in poverty because expanding employment for women did not bring wage parity.

Wives with children had particularly difficult choices to make in deciding whether to leave a violent husband or not. On the one hand, such abuse harmed children. A divorce-seeking woman in 1956 said that she left her violent husband in part for her daughter, who "was having nightmares and crying in her sleep about him."[117] Some two decades later a shelter resident who had suffered a severe beating asserted: "I am the mother of two black female children and I have to give them something . . . If I continue to allow these things to happen it is like saying to them that it's okay, if you love a man, to let him beat you."[118] Concern for such children could lead women to leave husbands with whom they might have otherwise remained.

But, as earlier in Oregon's history, women more commonly cited concern for children as a reason to stay with violent husbands. Wives throughout the post–World War II era explained, as one of them put it in the 1980s, that they "remained as long as I did for my 2 children's sake."[119] Battered wives worried about much more concrete problems than the psychological effects of children's separation from their father. Marilyn Miller, executive director of the Governor's Commission for Women, described a broad set of concerns in 1977: "So many women say, 'I couldn't leave. I had no job. I couldn't support myself. I had children. Where was I going to take my children?' "[120] A year later a clerk remarked that her divorce had put her "under the poverty level," that her three children "are doing without necessities, and eating poorly."[121] Indeed, 81 percent of the divorced mothers in the 1978 survey identified single parenthood as the greatest difficulty they faced. "I am always tired," said one, "find it virtually impossible to work, raise my child, be mother, housekeeper, teacher and hold it all together."[122] Lack of money, lack of time, and lack of reliable child care brought a great deal of stress and hardship to divorced women and their children.

Until at least very recently, divorced women also faced residual social prejudice. A woman in the 1968 survey of single mothers observed, "As modern as the world is, there is stigma on women alone with families to raise."[123] A participant in the 1978 survey of such women complained of "ferocious" discrimination in housing against single mothers.[124] Mary Henderson, the director of a women's shelter in McMinnville in the early 1980s, recalled a woman who "told me she often wanted to leave" her husband, "but her folks told her once you're married, you stay." This woman "never told anyone of the abuse she suffered," for "she was too ashamed."[125] Not even the sustained individualism of the 1980s could free women completely from the tradition of staying with one's husband, regardless of his treatment of her.

The threat of escalated physical violence has constituted perhaps the most daunting barrier to modern women leaving abusive husbands. In the 1990s a woman filing for a restraining order remarked that her husband had threatened that "if I ever left him he would kill himself, all the children and me."[126] Another said her husband had threatened "to burn house down with me & kids in it if I tried to leave him or get a restraining order."[127] Some men have followed through on such threats. An eastern Oregon woman in the late 1950s said that her estranged husband had forced her into his car, choked and beat her, and tried to rape her. A woman in the 1980s reported that her ex-husband broke into her house even after she had remarried. For four years Alta Bryan's former husband regularly forced his way into her home where he would beat and rape her. Calls to the police resulted in his inflicting more severe beatings. The abuse ended only when she shot Jerry Bryan dead in 1978. "I just couldn't stand any more hurt," she explained.[128]

The phenomenon of battered wives killing their tormenters received substantial public attention in the 1980s, but wives of violent husbands more commonly faced rather than inflicted murder. In 1982, for example, Steve Irwin of Portland shot and killed his estranged wife less than one week after he had been arrested and released for violating a restraining order barring him from contact with her. Likewise, in 1991 Joseph Jones killed his estranged wife in suburban Portland one day after being released from jail for his third violation of a restraining order. Such killings apparently peaked in 1989, when eleven Oregon women died at the hands of husbands or ex-husbands and another seven at the hands of boyfriends. This accounted for one-third of all the state's female homicide victims.[129] Leaving a violent husband offered not only the prospect of a life free from abuse, but also the possibility of more extreme forms of violence, even death.

No-fault divorce, greater interventions from police, expanded job opportunities, and, perhaps most important, a culture stressing self-fulfillment made escaping a violent husband less problematic than it had been. But strong economic and social considerations together with violent threats often made the costs of leaving very steep.

Yet not all the ties binding modern women to violent men have been structural or material. Deeply felt romantic love has constituted another, often overlooked, factor. One woman, living at the Bradley Angle House in the late 1970s, reflected on how painful the destruction of that love had been: "When I felt love the feeling was so strong. When he started tearing me down it hurt so much. All that nice feeling, all that loving that I used to have inside me, that I had saved for someone ..."[130] Leaving one's partner sundered a relationship in which one had invested years of work and perhaps a lifetime of expectation. Binder notes that battered women are often "deeply in love with their partners." Particularly for women with difficult childhoods, these men, with all their flaws, are "their family."[131] The fact that many violent husbands can be at times caring and considerate makes the decision to leave all the more difficult. "People who haven't been through it find it hard to believe that there could have been good times," remarked one woman who had left an abusive husband.[132] Such husbands typically display the most affection and remorse right after beatings, at the moment when women are most apt to leave. In 1992 a woman recalled her first meeting with the partner she had escaped:

"he met me on hands and knees, he took off his hat with one hand and handed me flowers with the other. He admitted he was a drug addict. He told me he'd been in denial."[133] This woman declined to return. But many others, socialized to seek and maintain romantic relationships with men as their first priority, have chosen to give violent husbands another chance.

Tonya Harding, Oregon's most famous resident, appears to have been such a woman. Harding separated from the violent Jeff Gillooly several times and filed at least two restraining orders against him. Yet a man she dated during one of these separations noted that although Harding often spoke disparagingly of her husband, "she couldn't stop talking to him." Michael Rosenberg, a former sports agent of Harding's, said of her relationship to Gillooly that "I think she loves him and holds on to him and she hates him and is afraid of him."[134] Her fear and her love apparently combined to keep her in the relationship.

Lenore Walker refers to women who stay with their abusers as being in a condition of "learned helplessness." She likens the repeated violence that batterers inflict on their partners to the plight of a laboratory animal subjected to random shocks. The battered woman loses her sense of agency and choice.[135] But even among the wives featured in this study, wives who typically left violent husbands, a host of factors made escape difficult and dangerous. Women who did not elect to run these risks often acted on their best judgment. Nor were they necessarily helpless. Harding, described as a "stud" by members of her fan club, apparently used a wide variety of personal and legal resources to resist Gillooly's abuse.[136] Loving and staying with a man was not tantamount to submitting to him.

Wives probably stay with and return to violent husbands whom they could safely leave not so much because the process of abuse has infantilized them as because women are so commonly encouraged to get and keep a man at any cost. Chodorow notes that "women in our society are primarily defined as wives and mothers."[137] "Maintaining herself as a separate person in the context of an intimate relationship is the dominant issue" women face, remarks Lillian Rubin.[138] The behavior of battered wives, like that of violent husbands, is conditioned by common cultural norms.

Shelters have become a crucial resource for women attempting to free themselves from violent men. Such refuges first appeared in Oregon in the late 1970s, part of a national and international effort to provide a supportive haven for abused women. By 1979 the Portland area had four such shelters, plus a transition house, which offered a home for women recently in a violent relationship but no longer in crisis. By 1993 shelters existed across Oregon, including several east of the Cascades Mountains, still the state's most thinly populated area. These shelters could serve only a fraction of the women who needed them. During 1990 those in Portland housed 746 women and turned nearly 4,000 away. Nonetheless, the statewide network of crisis shelters and safe homes have made an incalculable impact on many people's lives. One woman filing for a restraining order in the 1980s remarked that the officer who arrested her husband "telephoned the women's crisis center" which "sent a woman out to help me and she took me to the emergency hospital." The wife then "was taken to a SAFE Home where I have been ever since."[139] Another wife of the 1980s, citing numerous acts of abuse, noted: "The womens crisis center has witnessed my physical state and is backing me up."[140] This sort of grass-roots support, often rendered by women who had themselves escaped abusive men, was a radical departure from the days when wives of violent husbands depended wholly on the often untrustworthy support of law-enforcement officials, family, and friends.

For many women, these homes constituted the only safe place they had. "Believe me," remarked one, "if I had" known of the shelter "I would have been out a long time ago. There was no place I could go. He knows everyone I know."[141] Two residents of the women's Crisis Service in Coos County spoke of the healing that battered wives experienced in such sanctuaries. "Once here," they remarked, "we found that we were not alone in our fear, anger, frustration, and pain." They began to realize "that we were not to blame for these violent acts against us by others. Through the one-on-one and group counseling we found support to begin the decision-making process, to take control of our lives."[142] Mary Henderson, the early director of the McMinnville shelter, spoke of a resident who was at first so timid that she spent "all night huddled in the basement because her daughter had seen her husband driving around town."[143] Yet this woman gradually gained confidence and eventually became a volunteer at the shelter. Claire Mead, the daughter of a battered woman and formerly a battered wife herself, shared what these organizations had meant to her in an address to the 1983 annual meeting of the Oregon Coalition against Domestic and Sexual Violence. "It has taken the assistance of this grass-roots movement for me to open my prison door," she proclaimed, for "you are my reflection of who I am and who I want to become." "We are," she concluded, "like a mirror for each other in which we discover, support, share, and celebrate each other."[144] Amidst a rising tide of violence, and notwithstanding a chronic scarcity of funds, the battered women's movement offered a precious haven and vision for many Oregon women.

The post–World War II era, particularly after the great cultural divide of the 1960s, has been a time of paradoxical extremes in the history of violence against wives.

Gender roles changed markedly, following trends established earlier in the century. Marriage continued to become more private and more focused around romantic love rather than social, economic, or other more prosaic roles. Women's status within the family more closely approached men's, first as their participation in the paid labor force rose substantially in the two decades after the war, then as the most widespread women's movement in the nation's history touched every couple's life during the 1970s and beyond. Men did not, for the most part, adopt the feminist agenda of egalitarian partnership. From their perspective, modern woman at once demanded too much independence for herself and too much openness from men. The ideal woman, like the pliant image of a *Playboy* centerfold, had no boundaries of her own and presented no demands.

Increased individualism, the further erosion of general self-restraint, and men's perception that women's demands for equality rendered men's still substantial advantages void or irrelevant led to greater violence against wives. But the roots of that violence were not simply— perhaps not even primarily—located in an overt struggle between the genders for power. Wives who described the context of their husbands' violence in detail frequently depicted physical abuse of a highly affective nature. That violence suggested not just a desire to dominate, but a desire for such complete control that it bespoke a sort of abject dependence. The psychological or emotional weaknesses of such men did not render their violence innocuous. It often made for extreme and unpredictable acts of physical cruelty; violence rooted in insatiable cravings for complete control or in general anxiety operated largely independently of a wife's actions. It transformed her into a scapegoat.

Against such violence women employed a shifting set of resources. Family members, friends, and particularly acquaintances proved less useful than before, as notions of individual freedom and privacy became more entrenched. Yet the credo of self-realization and self-fulfillment also liberated many wives from the social expectation of staying with their husbands no matter what. Men seemed more likely to continue abusing wives after those wives had left or even divorced them than they had before, and police officers and tougher laws provided only a fragile barrier against that abuse. But women's growing assertiveness emboldened them to take measures of their own. As individuals they increasingly fought back, and collectively they founded and maintained a network of feminist-based safe homes and hotlines that constituted a radical and promising departure from historical precedent.

The modern cult of freedom has carried often contradictory messages regarding violence toward wives. For abusive husbands, freedom has meant escaping the strictures of self-restraint and community oversight. For their wives, freedom has meant escaping a violent husband. For growing numbers of women, the ideal of freedom has prompted a broader social vision. Members of the battered-women's movement have imagined a society in which all women will be free from the fear and the reality of male brutality, a society in which the history of violence against wives will end.

Conclusion

The nature of violence against wives in Oregon varied over time in concert with the rise and fall of a widely shared ethos of self-restraint. In the mid-nineteenth century, during the settlement era, husbands used violence largely to enforce claims to patriarchal authority. Wives commonly faced violence in part because they often contested that authority. The hard, physical nature of women's work facilitated their ability to act on their own behalf, and their isolation from kin, neighbors, or police underscored the importance of feminine self-reliance. Later in the nineteenth century, violence against wives became less common as an ethos of self-restraint and women's public influence spread. But the emphasis on self-control circumscribed wives' behavior as well as husbands', and explicit forms of resistance became less common. Beginning in the 1890s, men's violence became more expressive of general male anxieties and misogyny, a trend that became more pronounced with the twentieth century's emphasis on marital intimacy and self-realization. Both husbands' violence and wives' agency increased as the twentieth-century ethos of self-gratification supplanted self-restraint.

The broad social and cultural changes that conditioned the history of violence against wives in Oregon occurred across the United States and much of the world. Isolated couples on the Great Plains at the close of the nineteenth century studied by Betsy Downey behaved similarly to couples in Missouri early in the century and in Oregon at mid-century.[1] Oregon couples in the late nineteenth century behaved similarly to how some central Illinois couples had acted long before the Civil War. The history of violence against wives in a particular place has been conditioned by the timing of its participation in larger cultural transformations.

This is not to say that race, ethnicity, and class have been inconsequential. Oregon's Native Americans suffered a demographic catastrophe beginning in the late eighteenth century and severe sociocultural dislocation ever since. Though documentation is sketchy, Oregon's Native American women clearly experienced domestic violence differently from how Euro-American women did. They have been both more at risk from physical abuse and more able to resist it. The work of Linda Gordon and Pamela Haag suggests something of the same pattern for impoverished women in very large cities.[2] A people's history has its own distinct rhythm and pattern to the degree that they have been insulated or excluded from dominant national developments. A history of violence against wives must always begin with a consideration of its context, very broadly defined.

Like most historians, I have in this book emphasized change, change in culture and change in wife beating. But I have also found a great deal of continuity. For many years, from Oregon's settlement era to the present, husbands have commonly employed violence as a means to enforce their purported authority, an authority that wives have often resisted. Women's widespread economic dependence has operated across time to keep them married to violent men. Respect for familial privacy has, as Elizabeth Pleck argues, consistently undercut community intervention in domestic violence.[3] The actual violence inflicted on wives has been the most consistent factor of all, cutting across eras, social groups, and racial categories. I discovered no place or time in Oregon history that violence toward wives appeared to be rare, or wives' resistance to it unproblematic.

The persistence of violence against wives has profound implications for those interested in stopping or dramatically reducing it. Several obvious steps are long overdue. First of all, wife beating should be treated as a serious crime with serious consequences. Offenders who are not able to respect restraining orders must lose their freedom of movement, and all offenders should be mandated to complete and pay for at least one year of individual and group counseling. The most common way that a wife escapes a violent husband is to leave him. Yet the personal costs of that choice typically remain very high. Full funding for women's shelters and crisis services would help to remedy this. An end to sex discrimination in employment and the assignment and effective collection of fair child support payments would free women from the hard choice of staying with an abusive man or living in poverty. Yet it is far from clear that these changes—which are by no means imminent—would get at the true causes of wife beating. These causes are broadly cultural and social. All men participate in the sexual inequality that makes violence against wives possible, and most men resist a true redistribution of marital power. Furthermore, violence against wives often arises not simply out of a desire to dominate women, but out of a fearful ambivalence over femininity in general, an ambivalence that has long been a staple of mainstream male culture. Even husbands who want to stop acting on violent impulses find themselves swimming against the tide, for the twentieth century's consumption-oriented ethos has made the practice of self-control increasingly difficult.

Exercising self-restraint has become countercultural. External controls imposed by police and the courts can of course help to reduce husbands' violence, just as less formal community oversight sometimes restrained violent husbands in the past. But creating within men the ability to exercise self-control will require a reorientation of modern culture.

Simply returning to the paternalism of the late nineteenth century is neither feasible nor desirable. As discussed in Chapter 2, constraints of women's agency accompanied constraints on men's violence. Judith Hicks Stiehm points out that "the relationship between protector and protected is always asymmetric," for "one has dependents, one is dependent."[4] The cult of domesticity's emphasis on separate spheres was not egalitarian, for men staked out the most remunerative and prestigious sphere for themselves. On the whole, nineteenth-century women were willing to accept this arrangement as an improvement over a gender system in which male authority was more explicit and extensive. But a return to the compartmentalized sex roles of a century ago would mean acquiescing to systematic male dominance. Male dominance, as Linda Gordon points out, does not necessarily cause

wife beating, but it provides the basis for it.[5] Accepting women's sub-
ordination, furthermore, would be a profound tragedy in and of itself,
one that would dwarf even the problem of domestic violence.

We should instead move forward toward a society that is both more
egalitarian and more sensitive to the limitations of modern individualism. As I pointed out in Chapter 5, the cult of self-realization has
been positive in many ways. It is largely responsible for more liberal
divorce laws and perhaps even for the modern feminist movement. It
has spawned reform programs sensitive to marginalized peoples' needs.
But such reform has typically stalled once oppressed people's rights
have impinged on powerful people's privileges. Men have been much
more willing to support women's right to work outside the home than
their wife's right to an equitable division of labor within the home, for
example. The cult of freedom and self-realization has provided
oppressed peoples with a powerful rationale for assertion. But it provides a meager vocabulary with which to address such concepts as
responsibility, accountability, and community. Self-gratification has
abetted protest but diminished the number of people willing to listen
to protest.

It is time for us to qualify our commitment to personal freedom.
Solving such seemingly intractable problems as ecological degradation,
political apathy, poverty, and domestic violence entails recognizing that
we are not atomized human beings, that our individual health and our
collective health cannot be separated one from the other. For men to
expect women, who are still far from realizing the full benefits of individualism, to accomplish this challenging transformation for them
would be perverse and cruel. In many respects women require a larger
dose of self-realization. A movement toward mutuality is the responsibility of the most privileged, not the least.

A collective approach to solving the problem of wife beating would
begin with men's admission that it is the charge not of a few deviant
men but of all of us. Violence toward wives is an extraordinarily prosaic practice. It has been and is practiced by many men and many types
of men. Its foundations, moreover, rest firmly in masculinity. The wife
beater has been inspired by images of women shaped by novelists, ministers, newspaper reporters, and legislators. This is not to say that every
husband is a wife beater or wife abuser, or that those who do not hit
their wives are just as culpable as those who do. But virtually all men

participate in a masculine culture that perpetuates and supports violence against wives. The court-mandated clients I counseled often remarked that I was asking them to reconsider beliefs and actions that they had been raised with and that most if not all of their friends shared. They were right.

The most crucial step in ending or greatly reducing violence against wives, then, is to explore the manifold and intimate interminglings of wife beating and mainstream culture. Oregon's whipping post law for wife beaters in the early twentieth century represents the exact converse of what I am proposing. This law entailed identifying a tiny handful of marginalized violent husbands, hitting them, and declaring the problem of violence toward wives solved. Much contemporary rhetoric about domestic violence mirrors this approach, albeit less crudely. One often hears that wife beating is commonly practiced only by men belonging to certain social groups or that it is caused by alcohol or drug use. Movies like *Sleeping with the Enemy* portray the abusive husband as a psychopath, a man radically different from you, me, and our buddies. Such images commonly prompt a good deal of head-shaking and breast-beating. The subtext of these expressions is that normal men find violence against wives unimaginable and are therefore in no way responsible for it.

I argue otherwise. Violence against wives will remain commonplace until we muster the will to examine how closely it is bound up with some of our most cherished values and most powerful cultural traits. The wife beater is not out there somewhere, on the margins of society and history. He is instead our close companion. He is at the center of our culture. He is at the center of our past.

Appendix: Quantitative Measures

The divorce suits from this study are from Benton, Clackamas, Lane, Marion, Multnomah, and Polk counties through 1870; Baker, Clatsop, Coos, Curry, Grant, Union, and Wasco counties through 1875; Benton, Coos, Crook, Grant, Lane, Marion, Polk, Wasco, and Wheeler counties from 1890 to 1900; Benton, Coos, Crook, Deschutes, Grant, Jefferson, and Wheeler counties from 1924 to 1926 and 1934 to 1936; and Crook, Deschutes, Grant, Jefferson, and Wheeler counties from 1954 to 1956. The date of a divorce petition's signature determined where it fell within these ranges. For Multnomah County I examined the records from 1900 to late 1902, 1905 to late 1907, and 1910 to mid-1911. For 1934 to 1936, 1944 to 1945, 1954 to 1956, and 1968 to 1970 I sampled only portions of Multnomah County's very ample records. I occasionally examined divorce records from dates outside these periods, and I researched some from parts of Missouri and Illinois to the mid-nineteenth century.

Although a number of divorce suits were undoubtedly missing, misfiled, or overlooked, I attempted to examine every one within the time periods, excepting the more recent Multnomah County records, by going through every court case by hand. Cases in which the complaint, answer, or wife's testimony alleged only desertion or adultery and made no hint of marital abuse were not examined further. I did not attempt to read or decipher court testimony in shorthand, which applied to only a small proportion of the cases.

I began this study with high hopes for being able to perform extensive quantitative analysis on the divorce suits. But I reluctantly concluded that only a small number of statistical measures are valid.

In Chapter 3 and even more briefly in Chapter 4 I employ a measure that is the proportion of husbands described as being abusive who were also described as being violent. The nominator, then, is the number of husbands described as being violent, the denominator the number of husbands described as being abusive (whether they used violence or not). A figure of 80 percent, for example, would indicate that 80 percent of abusive husbands employed violence. This measurement does not establish what percentage of husbands in the general population were violent. But it may indicate propensity to violence among men in general. In Chapter 3 it is used to compare husbands' propensity toward violence by class and ethnicity. I had hoped to use this measure to estimate historical shifts in husbands' propensity toward violence but became convinced that informal historical changes in the grounds for divorce made this measurement problematic.

Violence is defined in this study as the intentional infliction of immediate physical pain or a direct threat with a firearm or edged weapon. Abuse is defined as an act of violence, threats of violence, charges of infidelity, or cursing at a person.

Chapter 3 also makes brief reference to the frequency of violence. To determine frequency of violence, I used a five-point scale, essentially a three-point scale (1, 3, and 5) with borderline cases assigned a 2 or a 4. A score of 1 indicates only one example or instance of violence. A score of 3 means that the violence occurred more than once but apparently did not occur frequently. Frequent acts of violence were coded as 5, with "frequent" defined as three acts of violence within a three-month period. Descriptions of violence such as "continually" were coded as 5. A score of 2 was given to cases in which the violence could have occurred more than once or only once. A score of 4 was given to cases in which the violence could have occurred frequently, but may have been only sporadic.

I also occasionally employ statistics measuring which spouse left a marriage. A spouse who literally forced his or her partner out of the home was considered to be the spouse who left, as was one who left of his or her own volition and initiative. Neither spouse was considered to have left if the two disagreed over who left or if a spouse simply ordered the other to leave without using or threatening force.

Third-party interventions are the most commonly used quantitative measures in this study. Interventions were coded only if a person directly intervened against a husband who was using or threatening to use violence, not in response to milder quarrels, drunkenness, or loudness. Running for help was not coded as an intervention, but protecting a wife who had sought shelter or protection from a husband who pursued her to the place of refuge was. Calling the police was coded as a police intervention unless it was clear that the police did not interact with the husband. If a case included interventions from more than one type of third party (a neighbor as well as a child, for example), both of these interventions were coded, not just the most prominent or frequent one.

Abbreviations

Baker Co.	Baker County Circuit Court records, Baker
Bent. Co.	Benton County Circuit Court records, Oregon State Archives, Salem
B.G.A.S.	Boys and Girls Aid Society, Portland
Clack. Co.	Clackamas County Circuit Court records, Oregon State Archives, Salem
Clat. Co.	Clatsop County Circuit Court records, Astoria
Coos Co.	Coos County Circuit Court records, Coquille
C.P.A.R.C.	City of Portland Archives and Records Center, Portland
Crook Co.	Crook County Circuit Court records, Prineville
Desch. Co.	Deschutes County Circuit Court records, Bend
Grant Co.	Grant County Circuit Court records, Canyon City
Jeff. Co.	Jefferson County Circuit Court records, Madras
Lane Co.	Lane County Circuit Court records, Oregon State Archives, Eugene and Salem
Mar. Co.	Marion County Circuit Court records, Oregon State Archives, Salem
M.C.M.E.O.	Multnomah County Medical Examiner's Office, Portland
M.S.A.	Missouri State Archives, Columbia
Mult. Co.	Multnomah County Circuit Court records, Portland

O.H.S.	Oregon Historical Society, Portland
O.S.A.	Oregon State Archives, Salem
Polk Co.	Polk County Circuit Court records, Oregon State Archives, Salem
Sang. Co.	Sangamon County Circuit Court records, Illinois Regional Archival Depository, Sangamon State University, Springfield
Union Co.	Union County Circuit Court records, LaGrande
U.O.S.C.	Special Collections, University of Oregon, Eugene
Wasco Co.	Wasco County Circuit Court records, Oregon State Archives, Salem
Wheel. Co.	Wheeler County Circuit Court records, Fossil

Notes

Prologue

1. Mult. Co. no. 3563.

2. Elizabeth Pleck, *Domestic Tyranny: The Making of American Social Policy against Family Violence from Colonial Times to the Present* (New York: Oxford University Press, 1987); Linda Gordon, *Heroes of Their Own Lives: The Politics and History of Family Violence, Boston, 1880–1960* (New York: Viking, 1988). In addition, Larry Eldridge is researching wife abuse in the seventeenth century, and Jerome Nadelhaft is studying the subject in the nineteenth century. (Eldridge's monograph is scheduled to appear in late 1996.) Violence against wives is not treated in much depth even in books on closely related topics, such as divorce or masculinity: see E. Anthony Rotundo, *American Manhood: Transformations in Masculinity from the Revolution to the Modern Era* (New York: Basic Books, 1993); Elaine Tyler May, *Great Expectations: Marriage and Divorce in Post-Victorian America* (Chicago: University of Chicago Press, 1980); Robert L. Griswold, *Family and Divorce in California, 1850–1890: Victorian Illusions and Everyday Realities* (Albany: State University of New York Press, 1982). The New Western History, led by Patricia Limerick, Donald Worster, and others, is attentive to race and class conflict in the U.S. West, but it seldom treats conflict between men and women.

3. Terrence O'Donnell, *An Arrow in the Earth: General Joel Palmer and the Indians of Oregon* (Portland: Oregon Historical Society Press, 1991), xiv; Richard Maxwell Brown, *Strain of Violence: Historical Studies of American Violence and Vigilantism* (Oxford: Oxford University Press, 1975), 101; Brown,

"Rainfall and History: Perspectives on the Pacific Northwest," in *Experiences in a Promised Land: Essays in Pacific Northwest History*, ed. G. Thomas Edwards and Carlos A. Schwantes (Seattle: University of Washington Press, 1986), 13–27; Brown, "The Great Raincoast of North America: Toward a New Regional History of the Pacific Northwest," in *The Changing Pacific Northwest: Interpreting Its Past*, ed. David H. Stratton and George A. Frykman (Pullman: Washington State University Press, 1988), 39–53; David Alan Johnson, *Founding the Far West: California, Oregon, and Nevada, 1840–1890* (Berkeley: University of California Press, 1992), 7–10, 41–70, 269–278.

4. Gordon, *Heroes of Their Own Lives*; Pamela Haag, "The 'Ill-Use of a Wife': Patterns of Working-Class Violence in Domestic and Public New York City, 1860–1880," *Journal of Social History* 25 (Spring 1992): 447–477; Betsy Downey, "Battered Pioneers: Jules Sandoz and the Physical Abuse of Wives on the American Frontier," *Great Plains Quarterly* 12 (Winter 1992): 31–49.

5. Lionel Tiger and Robin Fox, *The Imperial Animal* (New York: Holt, Rinehart and Winston, 1971), 208. For a feminist assertion of men's seemingly inherent violence see Laurel Holliday, *The Violent Sex: Male Psychobiology and the Evolution of Consciousness* (Guerneville, Calif.: Bluestocking Books, 1978).

6. David Levinson, *Family Violence in Cross-Cultural Perspective* (Newbury Park, Calif.: Sage Publications, 1989), 31, 14–20. Lewis Okun, *Women Abuse: Facts Replacing Myths* (Albany: State University of New York Press, 1986), 78–112; Richard J. Gelles and Murray A. Straus, *Intimate Violence* (New York: Simon and Schuster, 1988), 17–36; R. Emerson Dobash and Russell Dobash, *Violence against Wives: A Case against the Patriarchy* (New York: Free Press, 1979).

7. David Peterson, "Eden Defiled: A History of Violence against Wives in Oregon" (Ph.D. diss., University of Oregon, 1993). This book does, however, treat some themes that the dissertation did not. Note that the material I use from court cases was recorded in a variety of ways. Most is from oral testimony that a court recorder transcribed. Some is from legal documents, such as complaints, written by attorneys. Some is from letters introduced as evidence or, in Chapter 5, from petitions for restraining orders handwritten by women petitioners.

8. One may and should pose the question of how changes in the context in which people pursued divorce and the ways in which the court recorded evidence affected the content of that evidence. Divorce became easier to procure as time passed. Hence early divorce seekers had the most incentive to provide numerous and detailed examples of their spouses' flaws. At the same time, earlier divorce seekers were probably more hesitant than their later counterparts to detail spousal cruelty, for those details would inevitably become general knowledge in a tightly knit community. These two historical trends, increas-

ing acceptance of divorce in court and community and decreasing community interest in and oversight over troubled marriages, therefore exerted somewhat contradictory influences on how divorce seekers presented themselves to the court. The mid-nineteenth-century abused wife might have felt frightened and ashamed to detail the cruelties she had endured, but failure to detail those cruelties could cost her a divorce, property, and children. Her twentieth-century counterpart had less incentive to tell all. Judges almost never denied uncontested suits regardless of a wife's grounds for divorce, and an explicit rendering of a husband's cruelties might prompt him to contest the suit; but such details would little affect a woman's reputation in a disinterested modern community. On the whole, earlier divorce-seeking women had more incentive to describe fully their husbands' abuse than did later women. The fact that Oregon's circuit courts generally recorded and saved less and less material from divorce cases as time passed also suggests that later divorce cases should contain fewer accounts of extreme cruelty than earlier ones, for later accounts tend to contain less details of any sort. All this suggests that, all other factors being equal, more recent divorce cases should contain fewer descriptions of frequent and extreme wife abuse than earlier accounts. The rising proportion of cases describing more vicious assaults in the twentieth century is, therefore, all the more remarkable.

9. Contemporary domestic violence often involves couples who live together but are not married. Chapter 5 occasionally touches on such couples. Until recently, however, unmarried cohabitation was not common in Oregon. Nor do I treat same-sex couples.

1. "To Maintain His Authority": The Settlement Era

1. Helena M. Wall, *Fierce Communion: Family and Community in Early America* (Cambridge: Harvard University Press, 1990); Philip J. Greven, *Four Generations: Population, Land, and Family in Colonial Andover, Massachusetts* (Ithaca, N.Y.: Cornell University Press, 1970); David Hackett Fischer, *Growing Old in America* (New York: Oxford University Press, 1977); Nancy Cott, "Divorce and the Changing Status of Women in Eighteenth Century Massachusetts," *William and Mary Quarterly* 33 (October 1976): 586–614; Cott, "Eighteenth Century Family and Social Life Revealed in Massachusetts Divorce Records," *Journal of Social History* 10 (Fall 1976): 20–43; Jay Fliegelman, *Prodigals and Pilgrims: The American Revolution against Patriarchal Authority, 1750–1800* (Cambridge, England: Cambridge University Press, 1982); Mary Beth Norton, *Liberty's Daughters: The Revolutionary Experience of American Women, 1750–1800* (Boston: Little, Brown, 1980); Norton, "The Evolution of Women's Experience in Early America," *American Historical Review* 89 (June

1984): 593–619; Linda K. Kerber, *Women of the Republic: Intellect and Ideology in Revolutionary America* (New York: W. W. Norton, 1986); Daniel Scott Smith and Michael S. Hindus, "Premarital Pregnancy in America, 1640–1971: An Overview and Interpretation," *Journal of Interdisciplinary History* 5 (Spring 1975): 537–570.

2. Nancy Cott, *The Bonds of Womanhood: "Woman's Sphere" in New England, 1780–1835* (New Haven: Yale University Press, 1977); Carl N. Degler, *At Odds: Women and the Family in America from the Revolution to the Present* (Oxford: Oxford University Press, 1980), 26–51; Steven Mintz and Susan Kellogg, *Domestic Revolutions: A Social History of American Family Life* (New York: Free Press, 1988), 43–65; Barbara Welter, "The Cult of True Womanhood: 1820–1860," *American Quarterly* 18 (Summer 1966): 151–174; Carroll Smith-Rosenberg, "The Female World of Love and Ritual: Relations between Women in Nineteenth-Century America," *Signs* 1 (Autumn 1975): 1–29; Mary P. Ryan, *Cradle of the Middle Class: The Family in Oneida County, New York, 1790–1865* (Cambridge, England: Cambridge University Press, 1981); Joan M. Jensen, *Loosening the Bonds: Mid-Atlantic Farm Women, 1750–1850* (New Haven: Yale University Press, 1986); Paul E. Johnson, *A Shopkeeper's Millennium: Society and Revivals in Rochester, New York 1815–1837* (New York: Hill & Wang, 1978); John Demos, *Past, Present, and Personal: The Family and the Life Course in American History* (New York: Oxford University Press, 1986), 41–67; Robert L. Griswold, *Fatherhood in America: A History* (New York: Basic Books, 1993), 10–33.

3. John Mack Faragher, *Women and Men on the Overland Trail* (New Haven: Yale University Press, 1979); Suzanne Lebsock, *The Free Women of Petersburg: Status and Culture in a Southern Town, 1784–1860* (New York: W. W. Norton, 1984).

4. Peter H. Burnett, *Recollections and Opinions of an Old Pioneer* (1880; reprint, New York: Da Capo Press, 1969), 19. See also Hattie M. Anderson, "The Evolution of a Frontier Society in Missouri, 1815–1828," *Missouri Historical Review* 32 (1938): 304–317; Francis Lea McCurdy, *Stump, Bar, and Pulpit: Speechmaking on the Missouri Frontier* (Columbia: University of Missouri Press, 1969), 5–9.

5. Supreme Court of Illinois, case 1968, Illinois State Archives, Springfield.

6. Sang. Co., box 10, folder 113.

7. Sang. Co., box 7, file 116.

8. Missouri Pardon Papers, box 1, folder 20, M.S.A.

9. Missouri Supreme Court case, box 11, no. 27, M.S.A.

10. Missouri Supreme Court case, box 55, no. 19, M.S.A. Victoria E. Bynum, in *Unruly Women: The Politics of Social and Sexual Control in the Old South* (Chapel Hill: University of North Carolina Press, 1992), 70–72, 82–83, argues

that North Carolina courts, though not uniformly sanctioning violence against wives, emphasized wifely obedience and often tolerated the physical punishment of ones who seemed unruly.

11. Missouri Pardon Papers, box 1, folder 35, M.S.A.; emphasis in the original.

12. Sang. Co., box 13, folder 73. Myra C. Glenn, in *Campaigns against Corporal Punishment: Prisoners, Sailors, Women, and Children in Antebellum America* (Albany: State University of New York Press, 1984), 63–83, treats the lack of determined reform efforts to end wife beating before the Civil War.

13. Ruth Barnes Moynihan, *Rebel for Rights: Abigail Scott Duniway* (New Haven: Yale University Press, 1983), 55. David Alan Johnson, *Founding the Far West: California, Oregon, and Nevada, 1840–1890* (Berkeley: University of California Press, 1992), 7–10, 41–70, 269–278; Peter G. Boag, *Environment and Experience: Settlement Culture in Nineteenth-Century Oregon* (Berkeley: University of California Press, 1992); Samuel N. Dicken and Emily F. Dicken, *The Making of Oregon: A Study in Historical Geography* (Portland: Oregon Historical Society, 1979); William A. Bowen, *The Willamette Valley: Migration and Settlement on the Oregon Frontier* (Seattle: University of Washington Press, 1978).

14. Lillian Schlissel, *Women's Diaries of the Westward Journey*, expanded ed. (New York: Schocken Books, 1992), 13. Faragher, *Women and Men on the Overland Trail;* John Mack Faragher and Christine Stansell, "Women and Their Families on the Overland Trail to California and Oregon, 1842–1867," *Feminist Studies* 2 (1975): 150–166; Julie Roy Jeffrey, *Frontier Women: The Trans-Mississippi West, 1840–1880* (New York: Hill and Wang, 1979); Lillian Schlissel, "Women's Diaries on the Western Frontier," *American Studies* 18 (Spring 1977): 87–100. See Joan Cashin, *A Family Venture: Men and Women on the Southern Frontier* (New York: Oxford University Press, 1991), for women's response to moving to the southern frontier. Sandra L. Myres, in *Westering Women and the Frontier Experience, 1800–1915* (Albuquerque: University of New Mexico Press, 1982), 1–2, 10–11, takes issue with Faragher's interpretation in particular, and argues that women were not so reluctant to go West.

15. "Diary of E. W. Conyers, a Pioneer of 1852," *Transactions of the Thirty-Third Annual Reunion of the Oregon Pioneer Association, June 15, 1905* (1906): 459–460.

16. Kate Morris interview, Fred Lockley Collection, vol. 38, U.O.S.C. U.S. Bureau of the Census, *Seventh Census of the United States: 1850* (Washington, D.C.: Robert Armstrong, Public Printer, 1853), 988.

17. Wasco Co., *Linch v. Linch.*

18. *(Portland) New Northwest,* 2 June 1871, p. 1.

19. [Bethenia] Owens-Adair, *Some of Her Life Experiences* (Portland, Oreg.: Mann & Beach Printers, [1906]), 25.

20. Wasco Co., *Bennett v. Bennett.*

21. Elvina Apperson Fellows interview, Fred Lockley Collection, vol. 18, U.O.S.C.

22. *(Portland) New Northwest*, 16 June 1871, p. 2.

23. W. H. Cole interview, Fred Lockley Collection, vol. 11, U.O.S.C.

24. Susan P. Angell interview, Fred Lockley Collection, vol. 2, U.O.S.C.

25. Lane Co. no. 452.

26. G. W. Kennedy, *The Pioneer Campfire* (Portland, Oreg.: Marsh Printing, 1913), 58.

27. Clat. Co. no. 218.

28. W. F. Rigdon interview, Fred Lockley Collection, vol. 44, U.O.S.C.; Agnes Ruth Sengstacken, *Destination West!* (Portland, Oreg.: Binfords & Mort, 1942), 103–104.

29. *(Portland) New Northwest*, 12 January 1872, p. 2, emphasis in the original. Mary C. Wright, "World of Women: Portland, Oregon, 1860–1880" (master's thesis, Portland State University, 1973), table 30.

30. Margaret Jewett Bailey, *The Grains, or Passages in the Life of Ruth Rover, with Occasional Pictures of Oregon, Natural and Moral*, ed. Evelyn Leasher and Robert J. Frank (1854; reprint, Corvallis: Oregon State University Press, 1986), 220, 12.

31. For divergent views of settler women's work see John Mack Faragher, *Sugar Creek: Life on the Illinois Prairie* (New Haven: Yale University Press, 1986), 96–118; Myres, *Westering Women*, 160–166, 239–252, 262–270; Glenda Riley, " 'Not Gainfully Employed': Women on the Iowa Frontier, 1833–1870," *Pacific Historical Review* 49 (May 1980): 237–264; Susan H. Armitage, "Household Work and Childrearing on the Frontier: The Oral History Record," *Sociology and Social Research* 63 (April 1979): 467–474; Joan M. Jensen, *Promise to the Land: Essays on Rural Women* (Albuquerque: University of New Mexico Press, 1991), 13–14, 186–205.

32. *(Portland) New Northwest*, 8 September 1871, p. 2. [Matthew P. Deady and Lafayette Lane, ed. and comp.], *The Organic and Other General Laws of Oregon: Together with the National Constitution, and Other Public Acts and Statutes of the United States, 1843–1872* (n.p.: Eugene Semple, 1874), 95, 662–663; U.S. Bureau of the Census, *Marriage and Divorce, 1867–1906* (Washington, D.C.: Government Printing Office, 1909), Part 1, 72. On nineteenth-century Oregon women's rights see Sister Miriam Teresa, *Legislation for Women in Oregon* (New York: C. P. Young, 1924).

33. F[rances] F[uller] Victor, *The Women's War with Whisky; or, Crusading in Portland* (Portland, Oreg.: Geo. H. Himes, 1874), 59. G. Thomas Edwards,

"Dr. Ada M. Weed: Northwest Reformer," in *Experiences in a Promised Land*, ed. G. Thomas Edwards and Carlos A. Schwantes (Seattle: University of Washington Press, 1986), 159–178; Edwards, *Sowing Good Seeds: The Northwest Suffrage Campaigns of Susan B. Anthony* (Portland: Oregon Historical Society, 1990), 141–142, 1–142 passim; Moynihan, *Rebel for Rights*, 62–130.

34. Wasco Co., *Marsh v. Marsh*.

35. Union Co. no. 584.

36. Mult. Co. no. 3418.

37. Clack. Co. no. 2494.

38. Grant Co., large cardboard box, *Ford v. Ford*.

39. Mar. Co. no. 339. On prescriptions for women's selflessness see Welter, "Cult of True Womanhood"; Ruth Miller Elson, *Guardians of Tradition: American Schoolbooks of the Nineteenth Century* (Lincoln: University of Nebraska Press, 1964), 301–312.

40. Mar. Co. no. 1732.

41. Polk Co. no. 536.

42. *(Oregon City) Oregon Spectator*, 12 August 1851, p. 1.

43. Orange Jacobs, *Memoirs of Orange Jacobs* (Seattle: Lowman & Hanford, 1908), 71.

44. *(Oregon City) Oregon Spectator*, 2 September 1851, p. 1.

45. Bent. Co. no. 963.

46. *(Eugene) State Republican*, 7 June 1862, p. 1.

47. *(Eugene) State Republican*, 27 September 1862, p. 1.

48. *(La Grande) Blue Mountain Times*, 25 July 1868, p. 1.

49. *Corvallis Gazette*, 18 August 1866, p. 3. Other newspaper humor making fun of women is in: *(Eugene) State Republican*, 22 March 1862, p. 1; 14 June 1862, p. 1; 21 June 1862, p. 1; 8 November 1862, p. 2; 27 December 1862, p. 1; *Portland Oregonian*, 14 March 1867, p. 4; *Corvallis Gazette*, 5 May 1866, p. 4; 11 August 1866, p. 4; *(La Grande) Blue Mountain Times*, 25 July 1868, p. 1; 24 October 1868, p. 1.

50. Nineteenth-century men's ambivalent or contradictory views of women are addressed in several studies: Peter Gay, *The Education of the Senses* (New York: Oxford University Press, 1984), 190–213; David G. Pugh, *Sons of Liberty: The Masculine Mind in Nineteenth-Century America* (Westport, Conn.: Greenwood Press, 1983), 35–36, 45–91; Kim Townsend, "Francis Parkman and the Male Tradition," *American Quarterly* 38 (Spring 1986): 97–113; David Brion Davis, *Homicide in American Fiction, 1798–1860* (Ithaca, N.Y.: Cornell University Press, 1957), 168–170; E. Anthony Rotundo, *American Manhood: Transformations in Masculinity from the Revolution to the Modern Era* (New York: Basic Books, 1993), 92–108.

51. Mult. Co. no. 2860.

52. Mult. Co. no. 3078.

53. Mar. Co. no. 1732.

54. Mult. Co. no. 1973.

55. Union Co. no. 470.

56. Joseph Calvin Wooley interview, Fred Lockley collection, vol. 57, U.O.S.C.

57. Jacobs, *Memoirs of Orange Jacobs*, 33.

58. Louis Albert Banks, *Live Boys in Oregon or An Oregon Boyhood* (Boston: Lothrop, Lee & Shepard, 1900), 61.

59. Joseph Williams, *Narrative of a Tour from the State of Indiana to the Oregon Territory in the Years 1841–2* (1843; reprint, New York: Cadmus Book Shop, 1921), 60.

60. Sarah Morris interview, Fred Lockley collection, vol. 38, U.O.S.C.

61. *(Salem) Oregon Statesman*, 9 November 1863, p. 2. Elliott J. Gorn, " 'Gouge and Bite, Pull Hair and Scratch': The Social Significance of Fighting in the Southern Backcountry," *American Historical Review* 90 (February 1985): 18–43; Rotundo, "Boy Culture: Middle-Class Boyhood in Nineteenth-Century America," in *Meanings for Manhood: Constructions of Masculinity in Victorian America*, ed. Mark C. Carnes and Clyde Griffen (Chicago: University of Chicago Press, 1990), 15–36.

62. Banks, *Live Boys in Oregon*, 29.

63. A. J. McNemee interview, Fred Lockley collection, vol. 35, U.O.S.C.

64. George H. Burnett interview, Fred Lockley collection, vol. 8, U.O.S.C.

65. George E. Cole, *Early Oregon* (Spokane, Wash.: Shaw & Borden, 1905), 72.

66. *(Portland) Oregonian*, 16 September 1864, p. 4.

67. Coos Co. no. 191.

68. Baker Co., drawer 91, *Jack v. Jack*.

69. Mult. Co. no. 3350. Bystanders in violent marriages that did not end up in circuit court were probably less critical of violent husbands, since family and community support was probably an important variable in enabling abused wives to seek divorces, particularly during the settlement era, when divorces were still relatively rare.

70. Baker Co., drawer 21, *Blanchard v. Blanchard*.

71. Coos Co. no. 169; Bent. Co. no. 954.

72. Interview regarding Ferd Patterson, Fred Lockley collection, vol. 41, U.O.S.C. See Margaret Hunt, "Wife Beating, Domesticity, and Women's Independence in Eighteenth-Century London," *Gender and History* 4 (Spring 1992): 14–15, on the relationship between hierarchy, general violence, and wife beating.

73. Mar. Co. no. 1340. *(Salem) Oregon Statesman*, 1850–1866, index located

at O.H.S.; Oregon Mortality Schedule, U.S. Manuscript Census, 1850, 1860, and 1870; Mult. Co. no. 3350. Mult. Co. no. 3638; Wasco Co. no. J-7. Robert D. McGrath, *Gunfighters Highwaymen & Vigilantes: Violence on the Frontier* (Berkeley: University of California Press, 1984), 157–161, 251–252, argues that violence in two western mining towns seldom included women who were not prostitutes, but he relies heavily on newspaper accounts rather than on sources in which violence toward women was more commonly recorded.

74. Clat. Co., *Shively v. Shively;* Clat. Co. nos. 218, 1957, 364; Mult. Co. no. 554.

75. Bent. Co. no. 685.

76. Clack. Co. no. 2390 $^1/_2$.

77. "Diary of Mrs. Elizabeth Dixon Smith Geer," *Transactions of the 35th Annual Reunion of the Oregon Pioneer Association* (1908): 165–166. Mult. Co. nos. 3299, 2080; Mar. Co. no. 1835. Other studies also argue that settler husbands in the West commonly hit their wives: Betsy Downey, "Battered Pioneers: Jules Sandoz and the Physical Abuse of Wives on the American Frontier," *Great Plains Quarterly* 12 (January 1992): 31–49; Downey, "The Underside of American Frontier Violence: The Problem of Male Violence against Wives," unpublished paper, 1992; Melody Graulich, "Every Husband's Right: Sex Roles in Mari Sandoz's *Old Jules,*" *Western American Literature* 18 (Spring 1983): 3–20; and Graulich, "Violence against Women in Literature of the Western Family," *Frontiers* 7, no. 3 (1984): 14–20.

78. Samuel Parker diary, typescript, mss. 1508, O.H.S. Cited in Terrence O'Donnell, *An Arrow in the Earth: General Joel Palmer and the Indians of Oregon* (Portland: Oregon Historical Society Press, 1991), 23.

79. Bent. Co. no. 699.

80. Mar. Co. no. 1670; Mult. Co. no. 3948. Clack. Co. no. 2548; Mult. Co. nos. 3078, 3299. See David Warren Sabean, *Property, Production, and Family in Neckerhausen, 1700–1870* (Cambridge: Cambridge University Press, 1990), 134–138, on the changing context of wife beating in Germany.

81. His wife, on the other hand, said that "he some times abused me worst when he was sober." Mult. Co. no. 2080. See Elizabeth Pleck, *Domestic Tyranny: The Making of Social Policy against Family Violence from Colonial Times to the Present* (New York: Oxford University Press, 1987), 49–66, on public discussions of the relationship between males' intoxication and their abuse. I address this issue elsewhere in this book.

82. Mult. Co. no. 646, emphasis in the original.

83. Baker Co., drawer 76, *Gunson v. Gunson.*

84. Mar. Co. no. 1888.

85. Coos Co. no. 220.

86. Clack. Co. no. 2595.

87. T. C. Elliott, "The Journal of the Ship Ruby," *Oregon Historical Quarterly* 28 (September 1927): 277. This statement cannot simply be taken at face value. Bishop's pointed comparison of the plight of Native American and English women suggested that he was far from an aloof observer. But neither should his remarks be dismissed out of hand. Bishop spent three months among the Chinookans, and not all of his appraisals of them were negative. Anthropologists have identified several factors that appear to be related to violence against wives cross-culturally: a high level of general violence; male control of wealth, household decisions, and divorce; and absence of the father. See David Levinson, *Family Violence in Cross-Cultural Perspective* (Newbury Park, Calif.: Sage Publications, 1989), 43–46, 67–80, 88–90; Wilfred T. Masumura, "Wife Abuse and Other Forms of Aggression," *Victimology* 4 (1979): 46–59; Jacquelyn C. Campbell, "Beating of Wives: A Cross-Cultural Perspective," *Victimology* 10 (1985): 174–185.

88. Albert S. Gatschet, Leo J. Frachtenberg, and Melville Jacobs, "Kalupuya Texts," *University of Washington Publications in Anthropology* 11 (June 1945): 192–193.

89. Doyce B. Nunis, Jr., ed,. *The Golden Frontier: The Recollections of Herman Francis Reinhart, 1851–1869* (Austin: University of Texas Press, 1962), 45–46. See also Gunter Barth, ed., *All Quiet on the Yamhill: The Civil War in Oregon* (Eugene: University of Oregon Books, 1959), 185; Thomas Vaughan, ed., *Paul Kane, the Columbia Wanderer, 1846–47: Sketches and Paintings of the Indians and His Lecture, "The Chinooks"* (Portland: Oregon Historical Society, 1971), 23; Cora Du Bois, "The Wealth Concept as an Integrative Factor in Tolowa-Tututni Culture," in *Essays in Anthropology: Presented to A. L. Kroeber* (Berkeley: University of California Press, 1936), 57–60; Melville Jacobs, "Coos Narrative and Ethnologic Texts," *University of Washington Publications in Anthropology* 8 (April 1939): 117–118; Ivan D. Applegate to A. B. Meacham, 1 December 1870, Superintendency of Indian Affairs, O.S.A.; George Falconer Emmons, "Replies to Inquiries Respecting the Indian Tribes of Oregon and California," in *Information Respecting the History and Prospects of the Indian Tribes of the United States*, ed. Henry R. Schoolcraft (Philadelphia: Lippincott, Grambo, 1854), vol. 3, 211; Verne F. Ray, *Primitive Pragmatists: The Modoc Indians of Northern California* (Seattle: University of Washington Press, 1963), 91–92; Leslie Spier, "Klamath Ethnography," *University of California Publications in American Archaeology and Ethnology* 30 (1936): 50; "Official Report of the Owyhee Reconnaissance Made by Liet. Colonel C. S. Drew, 1st Oregon Cavalry in the Summer of 1864," *Ethnohistory* 2 (Spring 1955): 167; Gustavas Hines, *Wild Life in Oregon* (New York: Hurst, 1881), 113; Lalla Scott, *Karnee: A Paiute Narrative* (Reno: University of Nevada Press, 1966), 18–19.

90. D. Lee and J. H. Frost, *Ten Years in Oregon* (New York: J. Collord, 1844), 314. A. A. Atwood, *The Conquerors: Historical Sketches of the American Settlement of the Oregon Country, Embracing Facts in the Life and Work of Rev. Jason Lee* (Tacoma, Wash.: Jennings and Graham, 1907), 91–92; Cornelius J. Brosnan, *Jason Lee: Prophet of the New Oregon* (New York: Macmillan, 1932), 193; Philip Ashton Rollins, ed., *The Discovery of the Oregon Trail* (New York: Charles Scribner's Sons, 1935), 11; Jacobs, "Coos Narrative," 112; Scott, *Karnee*, 14–15, 38–39; Samuel Parker, *Journal of an Exploring Tour beyond the Rocky Mountains* (1838; reprint, Minneapolis: Ross & Haines, 1967), 252. An article in the *(Oregon City) Oregon Spectator*, 1 May 1851, noted of the local Indians: "If we mistake not, it is a grave offence among them for one male to kill another, but the husband holds the power of life and death over the wife" (p. 2). See Jo-Anne Fiske, "Colonization and the Decline of Women's Status: The Tsimshian Case," *Feminist Studies* 17 (Fall 1991): 526, on marital conflict that arose due to colonization. Levinson, *Family Violence*, 63–66, notes that westernization often leads to wife beating in aboriginal societies.

91. Theodore Stern, *The Klamath Tribe: A People and Their Reservation* (Seattle: University of Washington Press, 1966), 274.

92. A. B. Meacham, *Wigwam and War-Path; or the Royal Chief in Chains* (Boston: John P. Dale, 1875), 130.

93. Leslie Spier and Edward Sapir, "Wishram Ethnography," *University of Washington Publications in Anthropology* 3 (May 1930): 220.

94. Hiroto Zakoji, "Klamath Culture Change" (master's thesis, University of Oregon, 1953), 190.

95. Mar. Co. no. 1341. See also Clifford Merrill Drury, *The Diaries and Letters of Henry H. Spalding and Asa Bowen Smith Relating to the Nez Perce Mission, 1838–1842* (Glendale, Calif.: Arthur H. Clark, 1958), 173.

96. Coos Co. no. 153.

97. Clat. Co. nos. 680, 2418.

98. Martin F. Schmitt, ed., *General George Crook: His Autobiography*, 2nd ed. (Norman: University of Oklahoma Press, 1960), 16.

99. U.S. Congress, House, *Report on the Condition of the Indian Reservations in the Territories of Oregon and Washington*, 35th Cong., 1st sess., 1857–1858, Exec. Doc. no. 39, p. 45.

100. U.S. Congress, House, *Message of the President of the United States*, 38th Cong., 1st sess., 1863, Exec. Doc. no. 1, p. 178.

101. Mult. Co. no. 3392, emphasis in the original. Upon Choate's inquiry, his two friends said the Indian women had yelled because the women were trying to steal from them. See also Elizabeth Kelly interview, Fred Lockley collection, vol. 30, U.O.S.C.; [Ida Pfeiffer], *A Lady's Visit to California, 1853* (Oakland, Calif.: Biobooks, 1950), 50–52; Sara Winnemucca Hopkins, *Life*

among the Piutes: Their Wrongs and Claims, ed. Mrs. Horace Mann (Boston: Cupples, Upham, 1883), 181–182; Stephen Dow Beckham, *Requiem for a People: The Rogue Indians and the Frontiersman* (Norman: University of Oklahoma Press, 1971), 134–151.

102. Mult. Co. no. 2913; Union Co. no. 470; Coos Co. no. 256. White Oregonians used the term "Cayuse" to refer both to a particular Native American group in eastern Oregon and to Native Americans in general. Pugh, *Sons of Liberty*, 66, asserts that native-born white men saw women, African Americans, and immigrants as all being their intellectual and social inferiors but at the same time as sexually potent and hence threatening.

103. Grant Co. no. 1777–319.

104. Clack. Co. no. 2390½.

105. Coos Co. no. 220. Mult. Co. no. 2078.

106. Baker Co., drawer 21, *Blanchard v. Blanchard.*

107. Mult. Co. nos. 3418, 4063; Mar. Co. no. 1789.

108. Coos Co. no. 94.

109. Coos Co. no. 256.

110. Mult. Co. no. 3016.

111. Baker Co., drawer 103, *Liggett v. Liggett.*

112. Baker Co., drawer 21, *Blanchard v. Blanchard.*

113. Baker Co., drawer no. 146, *Rose v. Rose.*

114. Clack. Co. no. 2091.

115. Union Co. no. 382.

116. Baker Co., drawer 146, *Rose v. Rose.* Union Co. no. 314.

117. Clat. Co. no. 167. Downey, "Battered Pioneers," 38–40, argues that a Nebraska settler hit his wife to control her and that he tried to isolate her.

118. Clat. Co. no. 232.

119. Clat. Co. no. 364.

120. Mult. Co. no. 2080.

121. Mult. Co. no. 2745.

122. Clack. Co. no. 2361.

123. Mult. Co. no. 2705.

124. Coos Co. no. 87.

125. Mult. Co. no. 3299.

126. Lane Co. no. 662. Merril D. Smith, in *Breaking the Bonds: Marital Discord in Pennsylvania, 1730–1830* (New York: New York University Press, 1991), argues that Pennsylvania wives often adopted the new companionate ideals more quickly than men, who retained more patriarchal assumptions about marital roles, and that conflict often occurred as a result.

127. Clack. Co. no. 2390½.

128. Mult. Co. no. 327.

129. Mar. Co. no. 1724.

130. Clat. Co. no. 232.

131. Mult. Co. no. 1971.

132. Mult. Co. no. 3043.

133. Clack. Co. no. 2595.

134. Hopkins, *Life among the Piutes*, 228, 231. Gae Whitney Canfield, *Sarah Winnemucca of the Northern Paiutes* (Norman: University of Oklahoma Press, 1983), 77–78, 92, 178–179, 222; A. B. Meacham, *Wi-ne-ma (The Woman-Chief) and Her People* (Hartford, Conn.: American Publishing, 1876), 36–37; Barth, *All Quiet on the Yamhill*, 37. I discuss Native American gender roles in Oregon more fully in "Eden Defiled: A History of Violence against Wives in Oregon" (Ph.D. diss., University of Oregon, 1993), 12–51.

135. Coos Co. no. 153. Linda S. Parker, in "Murderous Women and Mild Justice: A Look at Female Violence in Pre-1910 San Diego, San Luis Obispo, and Tuolumne Counties," *Journal of San Diego History* 38 (Winter 1992): 22–49, finds that minority women, more so than minority men, constituted a disproportionate number of defendants in assault cases in her sample area.

136. Elizabeth Lord, *Reminiscences of Eastern Oregon* (Portland: Irwin-Hodson, 1903), 145. Lord reported that this "high tempered" woman "would get so angry she would threaten to kill herself; then he would say, 'No you won't. If you do, I will tie your body up and whip you after you are dead,' and that seemed to have such a horror for her that she would yield obedience."

137. Mar. Co. no. 362.

138. Mar. Co. no. 1341.

139. S. Parker, *Journal of An Exploring Tour*, 170–171. See also Burt Brown Barker, ed., *Letters of Dr. John McLoughlin, Written at Fort Vancouver, 1829–1832* (Portland: Binfords & Mort for the Oregon Historical Society, 1948), 185.

140. Walter G. West to Commissioner of Indian Affairs, 17 February 1922, Nancy Ben John file, Applegate Collection, U.O.S.C.

141. Minnie E. Corbell file, Applegate collection, U.O.S.C.

142. Clat. Co. no. 364.

143. Mult. Co. no. 3746. Wasco Co., *Schubnell v. Schubnell; Lange v. Lange.*

144. Bent. Co. no. 684.

145. *(Portland) New Northwest*, 26 May 1871, p. 1.

146. *(Portland) New Northwest*, 12 April, 1872, p. 2. Even Duniway generally counseled abused wives to stay with their husbands. *(Portland) New Northwest*, 26 May 1871, p. 1; 2 June 1871, p. 1; Moynihan, *Rebel for Rights*, 116–118. On the stigma of divorce for women in the nineteenth century see Pleck, *Domestic Tyranny*, 88–107.

147. William Thompson, *Reminiscences of a Pioneer* (San Francisco: n.p., 1912), 16–17.

148. Owens-Adair, *Some of Her Life Experiences*, 52.

149. Mult. Co. nos. 3522, 3974.

150. Ed Carr interview, Fred Lockley collection, vol. 9. U.O.S.C.

151. Lillian Schlissel, *Far From Home: Families on the Westward Journey* (New York: Schocken Books, 1989), 33.

152. Mar. Co. no. 1789.

153. Baker Co., drawer 63, *Fredenberg v. Fredenberg.*

154. Bent. Co. no. 881.

155. Wasco Co., second series, *Cooper v. Cooper.* Elizabeth Cooper, the plaintiff in the case, testified that her husband had called her a whore and a bitch and had once slapped her in the face.

156. *(Portland) New Northwest*, 12 January 1872, p. 2. A male witness in one divorce case said that he had counseled the male defendant not to turn his wife out of doors "because if he did he would be holden for her maintenance." Mult. Co. no. 2745. On nineteenth-century women's economic dependence on men see Susan Gonda, "Not a Matter of Choice: San Diego Women and Divorce, 1850–1880," *Journal of San Diego History* 37 (Summer 1991): 194–213. On women's propensity to leave violent husbands who did not support them see Pamela Haag, "The 'Ill-Use of a Wife': Patterns of Working-Class Violence in Domestic and Public New York City, 1860–1880," *Journal of Social History* 25 (Spring 1992): 467–468.

157. Mar. Co. no. 1806.

158. Mult. Co. no. 1971.

159. *Weekly Astorian*, 25 November 1876, p. 3. D. C. Ireland, the newspaper's editor, had been accused in his wife's 1874 divorce suit of hitting her.

160. Mult. Co. no. 3299.

161. Mar. Co. no. 1500. He apparently meant that he believed that the law considered a bruise, not a small cut, as proof of an assault.

162. Clack. Co. no. 2608.

163. City of Portland Recorder's Court record books, 1 June 1867 to 31 July 1868, C.P.A.R.C. On the legal recourse of nineteenth-century abused women see Michael S. Hindus and Lynne E. Withey, "The Law of Husband and Wife in Nineteenth-Century America: Changing Views of Divorce," in *Women and the Law: A Social Historical Perspective*, ed. D. Kelly Weisberg (Cambridge, Mass.: Schenkman, 1982), vol. 2, 133–153; Robert L. Griswold, "Law, Sex, Cruelty, and Divorce in Victorian America, 1840–1900," *American Quarterly* 38 (Winter 1986): 721–745; Elizabeth Pleck, "Criminal Approaches to Family Violence, 1640–1980," in *Family Violence*, ed. Lloyd Ohlin and Michael Tonry (Chicago: University of Chicago Press, 1989), 19–57.

164. Barth, *All Quiet on the Yamhill*, 133.

165. Mar. Co. no. 891.

166. Mar. Co. no. 1727. The importance of wives' kin is addressed in Marilyn Ferris Motz, *True Sisterhood: Michigan Women and Their Kin, 1820–1920* (Albany: State University of New York Press, 1983); Nancy Grey Osterud, *Bonds of Community: The Lives of Farm Women in Nineteenth-Century New York* (Ithaca, N.Y.: Cornell University Press, 1991), 53–85; Faragher, *Sugar Creek*, 79–86.

167. Lane Co. no. 452.

168. Mar. Co. no. 1899. At one point, at least, the brother recommended that she separate from her husband if he again threatened her with a dagger.

169. Owens-Adair, *Some of Her Life Experiences*, 49–50, emphasis in the original. For a biography of Owens-Adair see Carol Kirkby McFarland, "Bethenia Owens-Adair: Oregon Pioneer Physician, Feminist, and Reformer, 1840–1926" (master's thesis, University of Oregon, 1984).

170. Mar. Co. no. 1727. *(Oregon City) Oregon Spectator*, 14 November 1850, p. 1.

171. Mult. Co. no. 3299; Polk Co. no. 627.

172. Nearly one-half of the women in the divorce cases that described a husband's physical violence had married outside the state, and many who had married within the state lived far from their parents or had parents who were deceased.

173. Clack. Co. no. 2561.

174. Mult. Co. no. 2872. The child was age four, at most.

175. Clack. Co. no. 2614.

176. Mar. Co. no. 1500. Of 54 third-party interventions, 25 involved neighbors or friends. Only 17 involved family. See the table in Chapter 5 for a complete breakdown of interventions.

177. Mar. Co. no. 1789.

178. Wasco Co., *Marsh v. Marsh*.

179. Union Co. no. 565.

180. Clack. Co. no. 2608.

181. Coos Co. no. 191.

182. Mar. Co. 1380.

183. Mult. Co. no. 3051.

184. Union Co. no. 455.

185. Wasco Co., *Willett v. Willett*.

186. Wasco Co., *Jaques v. Jaques; Fraser v. Fraser*.

187. Union Co. no. 570.

188. Mult. Co. no. 3043.

189. Mult. Co. no. 4063.

190. Coos Co. no. 71.

191. Christine Stansell, *City of Women: Sex and Class in New York, 1789–1860* (New York: Alfred A. Knopf, 1986), 80–83; Haag, " 'Ill-Use of a Wife.' "

192. Mult. Co. no. 3299.

193. Union Co. no. 542.

194. Olga Freeman, ed., "Almira Raymond Letters, 1840–1880," *Oregon Historical Quarterly* 85 (Fall 1984): 295.

195. Wm. Sharp [Stroup?] to W. W. Raymond, 27 September 1864, William W. Raymond collection, mss. 555, O.H.S.

196. Clat. Co. no. 218. On the relationship between violence and isolation on the frontier, see Downey, "Battered Pioneers," 38–41. Bowen, *Willamette Valley*, 52–53, points out that family and neighborhood ties were surprisingly strong in Oregon around 1850. This was particularly so for women, who had often traveled to Oregon with their parents.

197. Mult. Co. no. 2137.

198. Mult. Co. no. 3350.

199. Clack. Co. no. 2548.

200. *(Portland) New Northwest*, 22 December 1871, p. 2.

201. Canfield, *Sarah Winnemucca*, 163, 172–173.

202. Wasco Co., *Besserer v. Besserer.* Meyer's wife testified that when she heard the Besserers fighting she told Maria "that she had better be quiet and stay here a few days . . . but she would not do so. They kept on fighting." The advantages that meek-appearing wives enjoyed in the nineteenth century are discussed in Marybeth Hamilton Arnold, " 'The Life of a Citizen in the Hands of a Woman': Sexual Assault in New York City, 1790 to 1820," in *Passion and Power: Sexuality in History*, ed. Kathy Peiss and Christina Simmons, with Robert A. Padgug (Philadelphia: Temple University Press, 1989), 35–56; Jane Turner Censer, " 'Smiling Through Her Tears': Ante-Bellum Southern Women and Divorce," *American Journal of Legal History* 25 (1981): 24–47; Myra C. Glenn, "Wife-Beating: The Darker Side of Victorian Domesticity," *The Canadian Review of American Studies* 15 (Spring 1984): 17–33.

203. Owens-Adair, *Some of Her Life Experiences*, 53, 54.

204. First Baptist Church of Eugene, Oregon, records, 29 October 1875, mss. 1560 microfilm, O.H.S., emphasis in the original. Parker was apparently already under scrutiny by the church for his beliefs. He had declared for open communion and had invited the church "to make an Investigation into his character and conduct and if he was guilty of anything inconsistent with his profession as a Baptist and a Christian to turn him out." Dorris then charged him with abusing his wife. West Union Baptist Church records, 3 June 1846 and 8 May 1847, mss. 1560 microfilm, O.H.S. Albert W. Wardin, Jr., *Baptists in Oregon* (Portland, Oreg.: Judson Baptist College, 1969), 37–49, and Ted

Ownby, *Subduing Satan: Religion, Recreation, and Manhood in the Rural South, 1865–1920* (Chapel Hill: University of North Carolina Press, 1990), 127–143, include treatments of church discipline. At least two ministers testified for divorce-seeking wives, even though the wives' complaints did not cite adultery. Mult. Co. nos. 1971, 2745.

205. Bailey, *The Grains*, 185, emphasis in the original.

206. Bailey, *The Grains*, 8–18, 242–311; Mar. Co. no. 180.

207. Linda Gordon, *Heroes of Their Own Lives: The Politics and History of Family Violence, Boston, 1880–1960* (New York: Viking, 1988). To recognize that husbands have often used violence against wives who resist those men's dominance is not to hold those women responsible for that violence. Rather, male dominance has made such resistance necessary.

2. "When a Man Stoops to Strike a Woman": The 1890s

1. U.S. Bureau of the Census: *Thirteenth Census of the United States, 1910: Population by Counties and Minor Civil Divisions, 1910, 1900, 1890* (Washington, D.C.: Government Printing Office, 1912), 436–444; *Twelfth Census of the United States, Taken in the Year 1900, Manufactures, Part 2, States and Territories* (Washington, D.C.: United States Census Office, 1902), 736; *Occupations at the Twelfth Census* (Washington, D.C.: Government Printing Office, 1904), 368, 686. Useful treatments of rural Oregon society in the 1890s include: Gordon B. Dodds, *Oregon: A Bicentennial History* (New York: W. W. Norton; and Nashville, Tennessee: American Association for State and Local History, 1977), 115–151; Samuel N. Dicken and Emily F. Dicken, *The Making of Oregon: A Study in Historical Geography* (Portland: Oregon Historical Society, 1979), 105–133; David Alan Johnson, *Founding the Far West: California, Oregon, and Nevada, 1840–1890* (Berkeley: University of California Press, 1992), 269–278; James Leonard Carson, "A Social History of the Willamette Valley: 1890–1900" (master's thesis, University of Oregon, 1953); Peter G. Boag, *Environment and Experience: Settlement Culture in Nineteenth-Century Oregon* (Berkeley: University of California Press, 1992), 113–154; Margaret Kolb Holden, "The Rise and Fall of Oregon Populism: Legal Theory, Political Culture and Public Policy, 1868–1895" (Ph.D. diss., University of Virginia, 1993), 70–95.

2. U.S. Bureau of the Census: *Report on Population of the United States at the Eleventh Census: 1890, Part 1* (Washington, D.C.: Government Printing Office, 1895), 426, 513; *Reports on the Statistics of Agriculture in the United States, Agriculture by Irrigation in the Western Part of the United States, and Statistics of Fisheries in the United States at the Eleventh Census: 1890* (Washington, D.C.: Government Printing Office, 1896), 174–175.

3. Wasco Co. no. O-57. Coos Co. no. 1192; Wasco Co. nos. S-278, P-76.

4. Christopher Dean Carlson, "The Rural Family in the Nineteenth Century: A Case Study in Oregon's Willamette Valley" (Ph.D. diss., University of Oregon, 1980), 186–193; U.S. Bureau of the Census, *Occupations at the Twelfth Census*, 370, 688; Melinda Tims, "Discovering the Forty-Three Percent Minority: Pioneer Women in Pleasant Hill, Oregon, 1848–1900" (master's thesis, L'Universite de Poitiers, 1982), 39–51. On women's work in this period see Alice Kessler-Harris, *Out to Work: A History of Wage-Earning Women in the United States* (New York: Oxford University Press, 1982), 108–141. The census indicated that over 19 percent of Portland women were employed.

5. Lydia Ann Buckman Carter interview, Fred Lockley collection, vol. 9, U.O.S.C. Holden, "Rise and Fall of Oregon Populism," 242–243, 490–491. Albert W. Wardin, Jr., *Baptists in Oregon* (Portland, Oreg.: Judson Baptist College, 1969), 119–121, 308–311.

6. Lucia H. Faxon Additon, *Twenty Eventful Years of the Oregon Woman's Christian Temperance Union, 1880–1900* (Portland, Oreg.: Gotshall Printing, 1904), 61. *Ninth Annual Convention of the Woman's Christian Temperance Union of Oregon* (Portland, Oreg.: J. F. Gotshall, [1891]), 60–61, 43–44. Treatments of temperance and other late-nineteenth-century women's reform movements include Ruth Bordin, *Women and Temperance: The Quest for Power and Liberty, 1873–1900* (Philadelphia: Temple University Press, 1981); Barbara Leslie Epstein, *The Politics of Domesticity: Women, Evangelism, and Temperance in Nineteenth-Century America* (Middletown, Conn.: Wesleyan University Press, 1981), 115–146; Ellen Carol DuBois and Linda Gordon, "Seeking Ecstasy on the Battlefield: Danger and Pleasure in Nineteenth-Century Feminist Sexual Thought," in *Pleasure and Danger: Exploring Female Sexuality*, ed. Carole S. Vance (Boston: Routledge & Kegan Paul, 1984), 34–37; Karen J. Blair, *The Clubwoman as Feminist: True Womanhood Redefined, 1868–1914* (New York: Holmes & Meier, 1980); Peggy Pascoe, *Relations of Rescue: The Search for Female Moral Authority in the American West, 1874–1939* (New York: Oxford University Press, 1990); Carl Degler, *At Odds: Women and the Family in America from the Revolution to the Present* (New York: Oxford University Press, 1980), 279–327.

7. F[rances] F[uller] Victor, *The Women's War with Whisky; or, Crusading in Portland* (Portland, Oreg.: Geo. H. Himes, 1874), 59. *Oregon Federation of Women's Clubs Year Book, 1902–1903* (n.p., [1903]).

8. Crook Co. no. 429.

9. Wasco Co. no. B-311.

10. E. Anthony Rotundo, *American Manhood: Transformations in Masculinity from the Revolution to the Modern Era* (New York: Basic Books, 1993), 29–30.

11. Ann Douglas, *The Feminization of American Culture* (1977; reprint, New York: Avon Books, 1978), 50–93.

12. *Club Journal* 3 (November 1903): 22.

13. A variety of works discuss the ways that nineteenth-century women benefited from the cult of domesticity, often by expanding its scope: Nancy Cott, *The Bonds of Womanhood: "Woman's Sphere" in New England, 1780–1835* (New Haven: Yale University Press, 1977); Cott, "Passionlessness: An Interpretation of Victorian Sexual Ideology, 1790–1850," *Signs* 4 (Winter 1978): 219–236; Degler, *At Odds*, 26–51; Glenda Gates Riley, "The Subtle Subversion: Changes in the Traditionalist Image of the American Woman," *The Historian* 32 (February 1970): 210–227; Ruth M. Alexander, " 'We Are Engaged as a Band of Sisters': Class and Domesticity in the Washingtonian Temperance Movement, 1840–1850," *Journal of American History* 75 (December 1988): 763–785; Kathryn Kish Sklar, *Catharine Beecher: A Study in American Domesticity* (New York: W. W. Norton, 1976); Daniel Scott Smith, "Family Limitation, Sexual Control, and Domestic Feminism in Victorian America," in *Clio's Consciousness Raised: New Perspectives on the History of Women*, ed. Mary S. Hartmann and Lois Banner (New York: Harper and Row, 1974), 119–136; Carroll Smith-Rosenberg, "The Female World of Love and Ritual: Relations between Women in Nineteenth-Century America," *Signs* 1 (Autumn 1975): 1–29.

14. Coos Co. no. 1012.

15. Joseph A. Hanna papers, U.O.S.C., emphasis in the original.

16. Coos Co. no. 1464.

17. Gail Bederman, " 'Civilization,' the Decline of Middle-Class Manliness, and Ida B. Wells's Antilynching Campaign (1892–94)," *Radical History Review* 52 (Winter 1992): 7.

18. Lane Co. no. 2884. On expanded definitions of marital cruelty by courts and women in the late nineteenth century see Robert L. Griswold, "The Evolution of the Doctrine of Mental Cruelty in Victorian Divorce, 1790–1900," *Journal of Social History* 20 (Fall 1986): 127–148; Griswold, "Divorce and the Legal Redefinition of Victorian Manhood," in *Meanings for Manhood: Constructions of Masculinity in Victorian America*, ed. Mark C. Carnes and Clyde Griffen (Chicago: University of Chicago Press, 1990), 96–110.

19. Karen Lystra, *Searching the Heart: Women, Men, and Romantic Love in Nineteenth-Century America* (New York: Oxford University Press, 1989), 233, 227–258.

20. Coos Co. no. 1839, emphasis in the original.

21. See Rotundo, *American Manhood*, 248–274; Elliott J. Gorn, *The Manly Art: Bare-Knuckle Prize Fighting in America* (Ithaca, N. Y.: Cornell University Press, 1986); Ted Ownby, *Subduing Satan: Religion, Recreation, and Manhood in the Rural South, 1865–1920* (Chapel Hill: University of North Carolina

Press, 1990); Michael S. Kimmel, "The Contemporary 'Crisis' of Masculinity in Historical Perspective," in *The Making of Masculinities: The New Men's Studies,* ed. Harry Brod (Boston: Allen & Unwin, 1987), 137–153.

22. F[rederic] H[omer] Balch, *The Bridge of the Gods: A Romance of Indian Oregon* (1890; reprint, Portland, Oreg,: Binfords & Mort, n.d.), 125–126, 110, 138–139, 148–149, 159.

23. Crook Co. no. 463.

24. Grant Co. no. 1889–1427.

25. Mar. Co. no. 6179.

26. *Reports of Cases Decided in the Supreme Court of the State of Oregon* (San Francisco: Bancroft-Whitney, 1889), 16: 327–328. Elizabeth Pleck, *Domestic Tyranny: The Making of Social Policy against Family Violence from Colonial Times to the Present* (New York: Oxford University Press, 1987), 88–107, treats disapproval of wife beating in the late nineteenth century.

27. Bent. Co. no. 3499; Lane Co. no. 3937.

28. Mar. Co. no. 6656.

29. Lane Co. no. 4609.

30. Lane Co. no. 4332.

31. Lane Co. no. 2884; Coos Co. no. 1069.

32. Bent. Co. no. 3588.

33. Grant Co. no. 22–1363. *Reports of Cases Decided in the Supreme Court of the State of Oregon* (Salem, Oreg.: Frank C. Baker, 1894), 23: 229–230, contains a discussion by Oregon's supreme court on the difference between premeditated spousal violence and that committed while angry and argues that "cruelty is a question of intent."

34. Mult. Co. no. 31651.

35. Bent. Co. no. 3097. In a suit filed four years later, Parilee did complain of physical cruelty.

36. Lane Co. no. 3413.

37. Lane Co. no. 4651.

38. Bent. Co. no. 3222.

39. Crook Co. no. 780.

40. Polk Co. no. 2247.

41. Lane Co. no. 4013; Mar. Co. no. 6475. Jana Lynn Jasinksi, "Physical Violence and Verbal Aggression in Divorcing Couples: 1891–1900" (master's thesis, University of New Hampshire, 1992), 34–35, finds that of people citing cruelty for divorce cases from Rockingham County, New Hampshire, nearly 80 percent indicated that the first act of violence toward them had occurred after the first year of marriage. In general, however, Jasinski asserts that the husbands in her sample were as violent as husbands of the late twentieth century.

42. Lane Co. no. 3503.

43. I have also made this argument in David Peterson, "Wife Beating: An American Tradition," *Journal of Interdisciplinary History* 23 (Summer 1992): 97–118.

44. Roger Lane, "On the Social Meaning of Homicide Trends in America," in *The History of Crime*, ed. Ted Robert Gurr (Newbury Park, Calif.: Sage, 1989), 55–79; Lane, *Violent Death in the City: Suicide, Accident, and Murder in Nineteenth-Century Philadelphia* (Cambridge: Harvard University Press, 1979), 53–76; Lawrence M. Friedman and Robert V. Percival, *The Roots of Justice: Crime and Punishment in Alameda County, California, 1870–1910* (Chapel Hill: University of North Carolina Press, 1981), 30–33.

45. *(Salem) Capital Journal*, 28 May 1891, p. 3.

46. Bent. Co. no. 3285; Polk Co. no. 2654; Coos Co. no. 1464; Lane Co. no. 3856.

47. Coos Co. no. 1593.

48. Wasco Co. no. S-232.

49. Bent. Co. no. 3395.

50. Wasco Co. no. M-273.

51. Lane Co. no. 3856; Bent. Co. no. 3363; Grant Co. no. 1118–1310; Bent. Co. no. 3499; Coos Co. no. 1840; Wasco Co. nos. B-228, Mc-91; Lane Co. no. 3176.

52. Mar. Co. no. 6398; Wasco Co. no. P-89.

53. Coos Co. no. 1714.

54. Wasco Co. no. N-45.

55. Bent. Co. no. 3395.

56. Mar. Co. no. 7064.

57. Bent. Co. no. 3656. Even so, Rhoda reported that her husband "had promised me so many times that he wuld not whip me any more." Some violent men accompanied their abuse of wives with sexual exploitation of their children. At least two men threatened to hurt wives if they told of the men's sexual relationships with the wives' daughters. One child reported that her father "was criminally intimate with both herself & her sister," age thirteen and twelve, that he "would make them come & get into his bed & if the Mother objected he would beat her." B.G.A.S. case 2510. Lane Co. no. 2832.

58. Lane Co. no. 2705.

59. Lane Co. no. 2900.

60. Wasco Co. no. J-39.

61. Lane Co. no. 3508. Hattie said that Millard had threatened to kill her with a pistol, that he had frequently sworn at her, and that she had furnished him with about $2,000 as he had no money or property of his own.

62. Wasco Co. no. W-199.

63. Wasco Co. no. V-56.

64. Wasco Co. no. G-168; Lane Co. no. 3645.

65. Lane Co. no. 3329. Peter N. Stearns, in *Jealousy: The Evolution of an Emotion in American History* (New York: New York University Press, 1989), 82–84, argues that jealousy may well have become more acceptable and common at the century's end, in part due to higher standards for marriage and to greater public roles for women.

66. Lane Co. nos. 3176, 2803, 3398. Elsie Freeman reported that one night her husband, R. P., called her "a whore and a prostitute" and accused her of "having sexual intercourse" with their son after she told him that she would sleep "with our little boy" if R. P. did not stop his vulgar speech. Lane Co. no. 3460.

67. Lane Co. no. 3011.

68. Crook Co. no. 770. Wasco Co. nos. G-144, K-87, B-215; Lane Co. nos. 4066, 4662.

69. Lane Co. no. 3856.

70. Wasco Co. no. G-144.

71. Coos Co. no. 1190. She cited verbal but not physical abuse.

72. Bent. Co. no. 3224.

73. Coos Co. no. 1618.

74. Grant Co. no. 857–1303. As during the settlement era, Oregon husbands mixed sexual and racial images in cursing their wives. Leonia Rinehart testified that her husband, Daniel, "called me a God damned squaw said I was turning myself up to every man who came in the store." Lane Co. no. 2727.

75. Mar. Co. no. 7445.

76. Lane Co. no. 3720.

77. Lane Co. no. 3503.

78. I have also made this argument in Peterson, "Physically Violent Husbands of the 1890s and Their Resources," *Journal of Family Violence* 6 (Winter 1991): 1–15.

79. See Rotundo, *American Manhood;* Gorn, *The Manly Art;* Ownby, *Subduing Satan;* Kimmel, "The Contemporary 'Crisis' of Masculinity."

80. Coos Co. no. 1114.

81. Wasco Co. no. Mc-92. Linda S. Parker, in "Murderous Women and Mild Justice: A Look at Female Violence in Pre-1910 San Diego, San Luis Obispo and Tuolumne Counties," *The Journal of San Diego History* 38 (Winter 1992): 45, contends that the proportion of violent crime committed by women declined sharply in the late nineteenth century.

82. Bent. Co. no. 3363; Lane Co. no. 3937.

83. Grant Co. no. 82–1278.

84. *Reports of Cases Decided in the Supreme Court of the State of Oregon* (Salem,

Oreg.: W. H. Leeds, 1900), 36: 95–96. The court noted that the woman's "conduct was not what marital ethics would approve," but added that "his cruelty to her was entirely out of proportion to the provocation, unjustifiable, and unmerited."

85. Coos Co. no. 1840. U.S. Bureau of the Census, *Marriage and Divorce, 1867–1906* (Washington, D.C.: Government Printing Office, 1909), 1: 72.

86. Coos Co. no. 1565. *Eugene Register*, 1 January 1892, p. 5; 11 April 1894, p. 3; *(Eugene) Oregon State Journal*, 18 June 1892, p. 5; 15 September 1894, p. 1.

87. Coos Co. no. 1618.

88. Lane Co. no. 3583. John Britton, another violent husband, took out legal affidavits promising that he would stop drinking, including one on the day of his wedding to Mary. Wasco Co. no. B-215.

89. Lane Co. no. 3706. U.S. Bureau of the Census: *Occupations at the Twelfth Census*, 370; *Twelfth Census, Manufactures, Part 2*, 737.

90. Wasco Co. no. K-87. Paul H. Jacobson, in collaboration with Pauline F. Jacobson, *American Marriage and Divorce* (New York: Rinehart, 1959), 127, indicates that only 13.4 percent of divorce petitions from 1887 to 1906 in the United States included requests for permanent alimony and that courts awarded alimony in only 9.3 percent of cases. Financial considerations were of course particularly important for wives with children, and wives commonly indicated that they stayed with an abusive husband "on account of our children." Grant Co. no. 1889–1427.

91. Wasco Co. no. B-215.

92. Bent. Co. no. 3363.

93. Divorce-seeking wives of the 1890s who cited physical abuse were more likely to cite intervention by a police officer than were their counterparts from the settlement era. Some 30 percent of the 1890s wives who said that someone had intervened against their violent husband cited the law, compared to 22 percent for the earlier period.

94. Wasco Co. no. B-215.

95. Grant Co. no. 592–1466.

96. Polk Co. no. 2298; Coos Co. no. 1582.

97. Wasco Co. no. B-311.

98. Bent. Co. no. 3232.

99. Lane Co. no. 3643.

100 Coos Co. no. 1111.

101. Lane Co. no. 4332.

102. Lane Co. no. 2803; *Reports of Cases Decided in the Supreme Court of the State of Oregon* (Salem, Oreg.: W. H. Leeds, 1897), 30: 227.

103. Grant Co. no. 857–1303. Neighbors constituted 35 percent of inter-

ventions for the 1890s, down from 46 percent for the settlement period. See the table of third-party interventions in Chapter 5. On household structure, see Carlson, "Rural Family in the Nineteenth Century."

104. Wasco Co., *Lockhart v. Lockhart.*

105. Wasco Co. no. G-144.

106. Coos Co. no. 1907.

107. Lane Co. no. 2832, emphasis in the original.

108. Crook Co. no. 770; Lane Co. no. 4332.

109. Coos Co. no. 1839; Mult. Co. no. 45761. Bryan D. Palmer, "Discordant Music: Charivaris and Whitecapping in Nineteenth-Century North America," *Labour Le Travailleur* 3 (1978): 5–62; Richard Maxwell Brown, "Historical Patterns of Violence," in *Violence in America: Protest, Rebellion, Reform,* ed. Ted Robert Gurr (Newbury Park, Calif.: Sage, 1989), 23–61; Brown, *Strain of Violence: Historical Studies of American Violence and Vigilantism* (New York: Oxford University Press, 1975), 106; Elizabeth Pleck, "Wife Beating in Nineteenth-Century America," *Victimology* 4 (1979): 60–74.

110. B.G.A.S., case 2812.

111. Newspaper clipping, B.G.A.S. case 453–454.

112. Wasco Co., *Lockhart v. Lockhart.*

113. Bent. Co. no. 4087.

114. Polk Co. no. 3027.

115. Coos Co. no. 1840.

116. Nancy Tomes, in "A 'Torrent of Abuse': Crimes of Violence between Working-Class Men and Women in London, 1840–1875," *Journal of Social History* 11 (Spring 1978): 328–345, addresses the trade-offs that mobility from the working class to the middle class brought to women.

3. "His Face Is Weak and Sensual": Portland and the Whipping Post Law

1. Robert Douglas Johnston, "Middle-Class Political Ideology in a Corporate Society: The Persistence of Small-Propertied Radicalism in Portland, Oregon, 1883–1926" (Ph.D. diss., Rutgers University, 1993); Carl Abbott, *Portland: Planning, Politics, and Growth in a Twentieth-Century City* (Lincoln: University of Nebraska Press, 1983), 49–57.

2. U.S. Bureau of the Census, *Thirteenth Census of the United States, 1910: Population by Counties and Minor Civil Divisions, 1910, 1900, 1890* (Washington, D.C.: Government Printing Office, 1912), 436–444.

3. *Portland Oregonian,* 13 November 1904, p. 4. Paul G. Merriam, "The 'Other Portland': A Statistical Note on Foreign Born, 1860–1910," *Oregon Historical Quarterly* 80 (Fall 1979): 258–268.

4. *Portland Oregonian*, 13 December 1904, p. 6.

5. U.S. Bureau of the Census, *Thirteenth Census of the United States Taken in the Year 1910, Abstract of the Census: Statistics of Population, Agriculture, Manufactures, and Mining for the United States, the States, and Principal Cities with Supplement for Oregon* (Washington, D.C.: Government Printing Office, 1913), 665. See also William Toll, *Women, Men and Ethnicity: Essays on the Structure and Thought of American Jewry* (Lanham, Md.: University Press of America and American Jewish Archives, 1991), 85–106. Many of Portland's Russians were Jewish, as were some of its Germans.

6. Abigail Scott Duniway, "Response to Address of Welcome," *The Club Journal* 2 (June 1902): 12.

7. G. Thomas Edwards, *Sowing Good Seeds: The Northwest Suffrage Campaigns of Susan B. Anthony* (Portland: Oregon Historical Society Press, 1990), 212–300; Lauren Kessler, "A Siege of the Citadels: Search for a Public Forum for the Ideas of Oregon Woman Suffrage," *Oregon Historical Quarterly* 84 (Summer 1983): 116–149.

8. *Portland Oregonian*, 9 February 1910, p. 10. U.S. Bureau of the Census: *Occupations at the Twelfth Census* (Washington, D.C.: Government Printing Office, 1904), 368, 370, 686, 688; *Thirteenth Census of the United States, Population, Agriculture, Manufacturing, and Mining*, 587, 593. Elaine Tyler May, *Great Expectations: Marriage and Divorce in Post-Victorian America* (Chicago: University of Chicago Press, 1980).

9. Newspaper clipping from 1899 in scrapbook, Portland Women's Union Papers, box 3, mss. 1443, O.H.S.

10. Mult. Co. no. 45606. On changes in wives' roles during the early twentieth century see Steven Mintz and Susan Kellogg, *Domestic Revolutions: A Social History of American Family Life* (New York: Free Press, 1988), 107–131; Alice Echols, *The Demise of Female Intimacy in the Twentieth Century* (Ann Arbor: Women's Studies Program, University of Michigan, 1978).

11. Mult. Co. no. 30837. On shifts in pre–World War I Portland women's morality see Gloria Elizabeth Myers, "Lola G. Baldwin and the Professionalization of Women's Police Work, 1905–1922" (master's thesis, Portland State University, 1993), 19–39. See also Kathy Peiss, *Cheap Amusements: Working Women and Leisure in Turn-of-the-Century New York* (Philadelphia: Temple University Press, 1986); Joanne Meyerowitz, "Sexual Geography and Gender Economy: The Furnished Room Districts of Chicago, 1890–1930," *Gender & History* 2 (Autumn 1990): 274–296; James R. McGovern, "American Woman's Pre–World War I Freedom in Manners and Morals," *Journal of American History* 55 (September 1968): 315–333.

12. Mult. Co. no. 45471.

13. Henry Marcotte collection, box 7, "Is the Young Man Safe," U.O.S.C.

Kessler, "Ideas of Woman Suffrage"; Edwards, *Sowing Good Seeds*, 242. On men's reaction to women's growing sphere in the early twentieth century see Ava Baron, "Another Side of Gender Antagonism at Work: Men, Boys, and the Remasculinization of Printer's Work, 1830–1920," in *Work Engendered: Towards a New History of American Labor*, ed. Baron (Ithaca, N.Y.: Cornell University Press, 1991), 47–69; Gail Bederman, " 'The Women Have Had Charge of the Church Work Long Enough': The Men and Religion Forward Movement of 1911–1912 and the Masculinization of Middle-Class Protestantism," *American Quarterly* 41 (September 1989): 432–465; Victoria Bissell Brown, "The Fear of Feminization: Los Angeles High Schools in the Progressive Era," *Feminist Studies* 16 (Fall 1990): 493–518; Peter Filene, *Him/Her/Self: Sex Roles in Modern America*, 2nd ed. (Baltimore: Johns Hopkins University Press, 1986), 72–101; Clyde Griffen, "Reconstructing Masculinity from the Evangelical Revival to the Waning of Progressivism: A Speculative Synthesis," in *Meanings for Manhood: Constructions of Masculinity in Victorian America*, ed. Mark C. Carnes and Clyde Griffen (Chicago: University of Chicago Press, 1990), 183–204; Jeffrey P. Hantover, "The Boy Scouts and the Validation of Masculinity," *Journal of Social Issues* 34 (Winter 1978): 184–195; Michael S. Kimmel, "Men's Responses to Feminism at the Turn of the Century," *Gender and Society* 1 (September 1987): 261–283; Angel Kwolek-Folland, "Gender, Self, and Work in the Life Insurance Industry, 1880–1930," in *Work Engendered*, 168–190.

14. Henry Marcotte collection, box 6, "Mothers Old & New," U.O.S.C.

15. Andrew Carrick collection, box 1, sermon no. 767, U.O.S.C., emphasis in the original (it was used as a heading).

16. Henry Marcotte collection, box 6, "Mothers," U.O.S.C.

17. Andrew Carrick collection, box 1, sermon no. 767, U.O.S.C.

18. McGovern, "American Woman's Pre–World War I Freedom," 318–320. See also T. J. Jackson Lears, *No Place of Grace: Antimodernism and the Transformation of American Culture, 1880–1920* (New York: Pantheon, 1981); John Higham, "The Reorientation of American Culture in the 1890s," in *The Origins of Modern Consciousness*, ed. John Weiss (Detroit: Wayne State University Press, 1965), 25–48.

19. Johnston, "Middle-Class Political Ideology in a Corporate Society," 62–69.

20. Elizabeth Pleck, *Domestic Tyranny: The Making of Social Policy against Family Violence from Colonial Times to the Present* (New York: Oxford University Press, 1987), 120; Lears, *No Place of Grace*, 97–139. The whipping post is also treated in Pleck, "The Whipping Post for Wife Beaters, 1876–1906," in *Essays on the Family and Historical Change*, ed. Leslie Page Moch and Gary D. Stark (College Station: Texas A & M University Press, 1983), 127–149; Robert Graham Caldwell, *Red Hannah: Delaware's Whipping Post* (Philadelphia: Uni-

versity of Pennsylvania Press and London: Geoffrey Camberlege, Oxford University Press, 1947).

21. *Portland Oregonian*, 13 January 1905, p. 8.

22. *(Portland) Oregon Daily Journal*, 12 January 1905, p. 10.

23. *Portland Evening Telegram*, 10 December 1917, pp. 1–2.

24. *Portland Evening Telegram*, 26 January 1905, p. 6. *The Journal of the Senate of the State of Oregon, Twenty-Third Legislative Assembly, Regular Session, 1905* (Salem: J. R. Whitney, State Publisher, 1905), 548, 572; *Laws Enacted by the People upon Initiative Petition at the General Election June 6, 1904* (Salem: J. R. Whitney, 1905), 335–336.

25. *Portland Oregonian*, 16 February 1905, p. 4.

26. *Portland Evening Telegram*, 16 February 1905, p. 6.

27. *(Portland) Oregon Daily Journal*, 16 February 1905, p. 3.

28. *Portland Oregonian*, 22 January 1905, p. 4.

29. *Portland Evening Telegram*, 13 January 1905, p. 16.

30. *(Portland) Oregon Daily Journal*, 28 January 1905, p. 4.

31. *Portland Evening Telegram*, 27 January 1909, p. 2. Carl Smith and H. P. Edward, *Behind the Scenes at Salem* (n.p., [1911]), 34–36, 72. [Joseph Gaston], *The Centennial History of Oregon, 1811–1912* (Chicago: S. J. Clarke, 1912), 4: 27–28.

32. *Portland Oregonian*, 27 January 1909, p. 7.

33. *(Portland) Oregon Daily Journal*, 25 January 1909, p. 6.

34. *Portland Oregonian*, 18 January 1911, p. 6; *(Salem) Daily Capital Journal*, 14 February 1911, p. 8.

35. *Roseburg Review*, 15 February 1911, p. 1.

36. *(Portland) Oregon Daily Journal*, 28 January 1911, p. 3.

37. *(Salem) Capital Journal*, 14 February 1911, p. 8.

38. *Roseburg Review*, 15 January 1911, p. 1. *Ashland Tidings*, 2 February 1911, p. 6.

39. *Journal of the House of the Twenty-Sixth Legislative Assembly of the State of Oregon, Regular Session, 1911* (Salem, Oreg.: Willis S. Duniway, 1911), 536–537.

40. *Portland Evening Telegram*, 11 February 1911, p. 9.

41. *Portland Evening Telegram*, 14 February 1911, p. 10.

42. *Portland Evening Telegram*, 18 February 1911, p. 6.

43. *Portland Evening Telegram*, 8 June 1905, p. 8. Negative reactions to whipping appeared in another editorial and in a letter to the editor: *(Portland) Daily News*, 5 August 1907, p. 2; *Portland Oregonian*, 9 June 1905, p. 9.

44. *Portland Oregonian*, 18 January 1911, p. 6.

45. *Portland Oregonian*, 27 November 1906, p. 11. *Oregon City Courier*, 25 August 1905, p. 8.

46. *Portland Oregonian*, 13 February 1911, p. 6. Even the state's most influential newspaper may have missed some instances. But circuit court records for Marion and Clatsop counties, which contained Oregon's second and third largest cities in 1910, indicated that neither area employed the punishment from 1905 to 1910, although a Clatsop County judge sentenced a wife beater to a whipping and then suspended the sentence. I also examined Portland's arrest books for 1905 to 1911 and Multnomah County Circuit Court records for 1905 to late 1907 and for 1910 and found only the three whippings cited by the *Oregonian*.

47. *Portland Oregonian*, 27 January 1909, p. 7.

48. Ibid.

49. *Portland Oregonian*, 27 January 1909, p. 7. *Roseburg Review*, 15 February 1911, p. 1; *(Portland) Oregon Daily Journal*, 16 February 1905, p. 3.

50. W. T. Gardner, Portland, to Prescott F. Hall, Boston, 22 June 1903, outgoing letter book, B.G.A.S.

51. *(Portland) Oregon Daily Journal*, 7 June 1905, p. 1; newspaper clipping, June 1905, scrapbook no. 73, p. 198, O.H.S.

52. *Portland Evening Telegram*, 19 July 1905. pp. 1, 11.

53. *(Portland) Daily News*, 1 August 1907, p. 1; *Portland Oregonian*, 2 August 1907, p. 9.

54. *Portland Evening Telegram*, 1 August 1907, p. 13.

55. *(Portland) Oregon Daily Journal*, 14 August 1907, p. 8.

56. *Portland Evening Telegram*, 29 June 1906, p. 6.

57. Newspaper clipping, June 1905, scrapbook no. 73, p. 198, O.H.S.

58. *Portland Oregonian*, 22 January 1905, p. 4.

59. *(Portland) Oregon Daily Journal*, 16 September 1905, p. 8. *(Portland) Oregon Daily Journal*, 1 August 1907, pp. 1, 12.

60. *(Portland) Daily News*, 1 August 1907, p. 1.

61. Oswald West, "Reminiscences and Anecdotes: Political History," *Oregon Historical Quarterly* 50 (December 1949): 249.

62. *Portland Oregonian*, 20 February 1911, p. 6. James R. McGovern, "David Graham Phillips and the Virility Impulse of the Progressives," *The New England Quarterly* 39 (September 1966): 334–355; Joe L. Dubbert, "Progressivism and the Masculinity Crisis," in *The American Man*, ed. Elizabeth H. Pleck and Joseph H. Pleck (Englewood Cliffs, N.J.: Prentice-Hall, 1980), 305–320; Pleck, "Whipping Post"; E. Anthony Rotundo, *American Manhood: Transformations in Masculinity from the Revolution to the Modern Era* (New York: Basic Books, 1993), 262–274.

63. *Portland Oregonian*, 26 November 1906, p. 9. Pleck, "Whipping Post," points out that legislative debates on the whipping post often featured lighthearted discussions of wife beating.

64. *San Francisco Sunday Call*, ca. 1906, scrapbook no. 88, p. 88, O.H.S.

65. *Portland Oregonian*, 27 November 1906, p. 11.

66. Newspaper clipping, June 1905, scrapbook no. 73, p. 198, O.H.S.

67. *Portland Oregonian*, 19 January 1905, p. 8. *(Portland) Oregon Daily Journal*, 17 February 1905, p. 4; *Portland Evening Telegram*, 24 January 1905, p. 6.

68. *Portland Oregonian*, 5 January 1911, p. 10.

69. *Portland Evening Telegram*, 2 February 1911, p. 6.

70. *Portland Evening Telegram*, 28 January 1911, p. 6; *Portland Oregonian*, 25 July 1909, p. 1.

71. Newspaper clipping, scrapbook no. 88, p. 88, O.H.S. *(Portland) Woman's Tribune*, 4 February 1905, p. 12.

72. *Minutes of the Twenty-Sixth Annual Convention of the Oregon Woman's Christian Temperance Union*, 1909, 42–43; *Minutes of the Twenty-Eighth Annual Convention of the Oregon Woman's Christian Temperance Union*, 1911, 41–42. Pleck, "Whipping Post," indicates that suffrage workers tended to divide on the whipping post.

73. *(Portland) Oregon Daily Journal*, 7 June 1905, p. 1. City of Portland Arrest Books, 1905 to 1911, C.P.A.R.C.; Mult. Co.; Mar. Co.

74. Newspaper clipping, June 1905, scrapbook no. 73, p. 198, O.H.S.

75. *Portland Oregonian*, 2 August 1907, p. 9.

76. *(Portland) Oregon Daily Journal*, 22 July 1905, p. 4.

77. Mult. Co. nos. 34798, 36277.

78. *(Portland) Woman's Tribune*, 8 July 1905, p. 45.

79. Oregon State Association Opposed to the Extension of Suffrage to Women, *An Appeal to Voters and Arguments against Equal Suffrage Constitutional Amendment* (n.p., [1906]), 22.

80. Newspaper clipping, June 1905, scrapbook no. 73, p. 198, O.H.S.

81. *Portland Oregonian*, 26 February 1908, p. 8.

82. *Congressional Record*, 59th Cong., 1st sess., 1906, 40, pt. 3:2448, cited in Pleck, "Whipping Post," 141.

83. *Portland Oregonian*, 13 February 1911, p. 6.

84. *Portland Evening Telegram*, 18 October 1916, p. 6.

85. Newspaper clipping, June 1905, scrapbook no. 73, p. 198, O.H.S.

86. *Portland Evening Telegram*, 20 July 1905, p. 3.

87. Bertram Wyatt-Brown, in *Southern Honor: Ethics and Behavior in the Old South* (New York: Oxford University Press, 1982), 462–493, offers an intriguing Durkheimian analysis of the scapegoating of an antebellum southern wife killer. Oregon wife beaters did not receive public whippings, but reporters from newspapers, the modern equivalent of the town square, made their abasement a public event.

88. The frequency of violence, however, tended to decline as occupational

status rose: 3.18 for laborers, 2.84 for semiskilled and skilled workers, 2.96 for blue-collar proprietors and managers and white-collar workers, and 2.68 for professionals and white-collar proprietors and managers. The occupations for the four categories are as follows (the first two are considered working class):

Laborers: fishermen, helpers in blue-collar occupations, housekeepers, janitors, laborers, loggers, miners, ranch hands, sawmill workers (no skills indicated), scavengers, watchmen.

Semi-skilled and skilled: bakers, barbers, bartenders, bill posters, blacksmiths, boatswains, boiler makers, brewers, bricklayers, butchers, carmen, carpenters, cement makers, chippers with steel companies, cigar makers, conductors, coopers, dispatchers, drivers, electricians, engineers, farmers, finishers, firemen, foremen, grocers, harness makers, horseshoers, hypnotist's assistants, linemen, longshoremen, machinists, mates, millers, millwrights, oilers, painters, peddlers, plumbers, porters, printers, shinglers, sign painters, steam fitters, stewards, stove mounters, switchmen, taxidermists, teamsters, tinners, waiters.

Blue-collar proprietors and managers, white collar workers: actors, advertisers, artists, bookkeepers, clerks, contractors, draftsmen, grocers, blue-collar managers, musicians, small-business owners, photographers, police, postal workers, blue-collar proprietors, real estate, sales, saloonkeepers, secretaries, solicitors, (small) speculators, stenographers, surveyors, teachers, telephone operators.

Professionals and white-collar proprietors and managers: attorneys, dentists, manufacturers, merchandise brokers, ministers, money brokers, physicians, white-collar proprietors.

The men's occupations were determined from city directories and from the divorce suits.

89. Mult. Co. nos. 44918, 45483, 45696.

90. Interpretations emphasizing violence in nineteenth- or early-twentieth-century working-class families include: Ellen Ross, " 'Fierce Questions and Taunts': Married Life in Working-Class London, 1870–1914," *Feminist Studies* 8 (Fall 1982): 575–602; Peter N. Stearns, *Be a Man! Males in Modern Society*, 2nd ed. (New York: Holmes & Meier, 1990), 93–94. Immigrant status was determined from the 1900 manuscript census and occasionally from the divorce suits.

91. City of Portland arrest books, 1905 to 1911. The figures for the non-wife assaults are from two one-year periods, one from 1905 to 1906 and the other from 1910 to 1911. Just over 40 percent of assault and battery cases in both categories were dismissed by the court or by the person assaulted.

92. Working-class men constituted about 79 percent of those arrested,

foreign-born men 33 percent, and African American men 5 percent, all higher figures than their proportion of Portland's husbands. City of Portland arrest books, 1905 to 1911. Occupations were listed in the arrest books or, more commonly, traced through city directories. It is difficult to know if the high number of arrests of men in certain social groups was due largely to police bias or to the wives of such groups being more apt to call on the police. *Portland Oregonian*, 11 November 1907, pp. 1, 4. Karen Taylor, in "Patriarchy and Male Oppression: Suffering the Responsibilities of Manhood," in *Transcending Boundaries: Multi-Disciplinary Approaches to the Study of Gender*, ed. Pamela R. Frese and John M. Coggeshall (New York: Bergin & Garvey, 1991), 62–63, reports that very few battering husbands in Melbourne, Australia, or Boston received more than a fine from 1850 to 1900, and that even wife killers faced relatively light punishments.

93. Mult. Co. no. 31220.

94. Mult. Co. no. 31827.

95. Mult. Co. no. 31026.

96. Mult. Co. no. 37650.

97. Mult. Co. no. 30711. Pamela Haag, " 'The Ill-Use of a Wife': Patterns of Working-Class Violence in Domestic and Public New York City, 1860–1880," *Journal of Social History* 25 (Spring 1992): 468–470 and Christine Stansell, *City of Women: Sex and Class in New York, 1789–1860* (New York: Alfred A. Knopf, 1986), 80–83, argue that working-class women in mid-nineteenth-century New York relied heavily on each other for protection from their husbands and for more general mutual aid. I have found, however, that men intervened more often against violent husbands than women did. See also Ross, " 'Fierce Questions and Taunts.' "

98. Mult. Co. no. 36147.

99. Mult. Co. no. 37847.

100. Mult. Co. no. 37224.

101. Mult. Co. no. 36710.

102. Mult. Co. no. 36104.

103. Mult. Co. no. 36356.

104. *Portland Oregonian*, 7 September 1907, p. 16.

105. *Portland Oregonian*, 13 July 1902, sect. 3, p. 1.

106. *Portland Oregonian*, 7 January 1907, pp. 1, 3.

107. Mult. Co. no. 37500.

108. Mult. Co. no. 36951.

109. Mult. Co. no. 31329.

110. *Portland Oregonian*, 19 February 1910, p. 18. Mult. Co. no. 45340.

111. *Portland Oregonian*, 9 February 1910, p. 10.

112. Multnomah County Circuit Court cases.

113. *Reports of Cases Decided in the Supreme Court of the State of Oregon* (San Francisco: Bancroft-Whitney, 1914), 47: 47.

114. *Report of the Social Survey Committee of the Consumers' League of Oregon on the Wages, Hours and Conditions of Work and Cost and Standard of Living of Women Wage Earners in Oregon with Special Reference to Portland* (Portland, Oreg.: Keystone Press, 1913), 24, passim.

115. Mult. Co. no. 31422.

116. Mult. Co. no. 30730.

117. B.G.A.S., file for case no. 2420. James Allen, "Illusions of Serenity: The Impact of the Judicial System on the Development of Social Policy against Domestic Violence, 1870–1930" (B.A. thesis, Reed College, 1992).

118. Leslie Woodcock Tentler, *Wage-Earning Women: Industrial Work and Family Life in the United States, 1900–1930* (New York: Oxford University Press, 1979), 175.

119. Mult. Co. nos. 31333, 45283.

120. Mult. Co. no. 31827.

121. Multnomah County Coroner's Investigation Books, 1900–1910, M.C.M.E.O.

122. $x2 = 6.133$, $df = 1$, $P < .025$, $N = 38$ for foreign-born versus those with native-born parents.

123. The likelihood of intervention fell as class status rose in the four occupational categories: 39 percent; 38 percent; 31 percent; and 16 percent.

124. Mult. Co. no. 31220. George eventually succeeded in grasping her throat.

125. Mult. Co. no. 36068.

126. Mult. Co. no. 37642.

127. Mult. Co. nos. 36935, 36224. Ross, "'Fierce Questions and Taunts,'" argues that London working-class women of the late nineteenth and early twentieth centuries frequently stood their ground against violent husbands or even precipitated violence.

128. *Portland Oregonian*, 5 May 1908, p. 13.

129. *Portland Oregonian*, 3 March 1909, p. 14.

4. "To Use His Muscle on Her": 1920–1945

1. Warren I. Susman, *Culture as History: The Transformation of American Society in the Twentieth Century* (New York: Pantheon, 1984), 105–149. On society and culture in the 1920s see also Paula S. Fass, *The Damned and the Beautiful: American Youth in the 1920s* (New York: Oxford University Press, 1977); William E. Leuchtenburg, *The Perils of Prosperity, 1914–32* (Chicago: University of Chicago Press, 1958), 140–177; Robert S. Lynd and Helen Merrell

Lynd, *Middletown: A Study in American Culture* (New York: Harcourt, Brace & World, 1929); Henry F. May, *The End of American Innocence: A Study of the First Years of Our Own Time, 1912–1917* (1959; reprint, Chicago: Quadrangle, 1964).

2. Winifred D. Wandersee, *Women's Work and Family Values, 1920–1940* (Cambridge: Harvard University Press, 1981), 27–54. See also: Robert S. Lynd and Helen Merrell Lynd, *Middletown in Transition: A Study in Cultural Conflicts* (New York: Harcourt, Brace, 1937); Richard Polenberg, *War and Society: The United States, 1941–1945* (Philadelphia: J. B. Lippincott, 1972), 136–152.

3. Daniel Bell, *The Cultural Contradictions of Capitalism* (New York: Basic Books, 1976), 18.

4. U.S. Bureau of the Census: *Historical Statistics of the United States, Colonial Times to 1970, Bicentennial Edition, Part 1* (Washington, D.C.: U.S. Government Printing Office, 1975), 33; *Sixteenth Census of the United States, 1940: Population, Volume 2, Characteristics of the Population* (Washington, D.C.: U.S. Government Printing Office, 1943), 5: 964; *Fourteenth Census of the United States Taken in the Year 1920, Volume 2: Population, 1920, General Report and Analytical Tables* (Washington, D.C.: Government Printing Office, 1922), 1284. On the influx of African Americans to Portland see Quintard Taylor, "The Great Migration: The Afro-American Communities of Seattle and Portland during the 1940s," *Arizona and the West* 23 (Summer 1981): 109, 117–126.

5. Desch. Co. no. 1917. U.S. Bureau of the Census: *Fifteenth Census of the United States, 1930: Population, Volume 6, Families* (Washington, D.C.: United States Printing Office, 1933), 1107; *Sixteenth Census of the United States, 1940*, 988–990, 1027, 1034.

6. *Weekly Bend Bulletin*, 10 July 1924, p. 1.

7. Nard Jones, *Oregon Detour* (1930; reprint, Corvallis: Oregon State University Press, 1990), 130–131.

8. On social developments in Oregon during these years see Carl Abbott, *Portland: Planning, Politics, and Growth in a Twentieth-Century City* (Lincoln: University of Nebraska Press, 1983), 93–94, 109–110, 125–130; Samuel N. Dicken and Emily F. Dicken, *The Making of Oregon: A Study in Historical Geography* (Portland: Oregon Historical Society, 1979), 135–139; Gordon B. Dodds, *Oregon: A Bicentennial History* (New York: W. W. Norton and Nashville, Tenn.: American Association for State and Local History, 1977), 185–187; David Horowitz, "The 'Cross of Culture': La Grande, Oregon, in the 1920s," *Oregon Historical Quarterly* 93 (Summer 1992): 147–167; William H. Mullins, " 'I'll Wreck the Town If It Will Give Employment': Portland in the Hoover Years of the Depression," *Pacific Northwest Quarterly* 79 (July 1988): 109–118; David Peterson, "Ready for War: Oregon Mennonites from

Versailles to Pearl Harbor," *The Mennonite Quarterly Review* 64 (July 1990): 213–216; William G. Robbins, *Hard Times in Paradise: Coos Bay, Oregon, 1850–1986* (Seattle: University of Washington Press, 1988), 78–94; William Toll, *Women, Men and Ethnicity: Essays on the Structure and Thought of American Jewry* (Lanham, Md.: University Press and American Jewish Archives, 1991), 119–131.

9. Andrew Carrick collection, box 2, sermon 1652, U.O.S.C., emphasis in the original; box 1, sermon 1055.

10. Henry Guy Goodsell collection, box 2, sermon 351, U.O.S.C.

11. Robert Charlton Lee collection, "My Mother and My Brethren Are Those Which Hear the Word of God and Do It," mss. 2526, O.H.S.

12. Goodsell collection, box 1, sermon 70, U.O.S.C.

13. John Demos, "Images of the American Family, Then and Now," in *Changing Images of the Family*, ed. Virginia Tufte and Barbara Myerhoff (New Haven: Yale University Press, 1979), 43–60. U.S. Bureau of the Census, *Fifteenth Census of the United States*, 1107. David Brion Davis, *From Homicide to Slavery: Studies in American Culture* (New York: Oxford University Press, 1986), 166–183; Fass, *Damned and the Beautiful*, 53–118; Barbara Laslett, "The Family as a Public and Private Institution: An Historical Perspective," *Journal of Marriage and the Family* 35 (August 1973): 480–492; Laslett, "Family Membership, Past and Present," *Social Problems* 25 (June 1978): 476–490; Steven Ruggles, "The Transformation of American Family Structure," *American Historical Review* 99 (February 1994): 103–128.

14. Marion County Circuit Court exhibits, no. 16485, 108/70, O.S.A.

15. Marion County Circuit Court exhibits, no. 17321, 109/50. Elaine Tyler May, "The Pressure to Provide: Class, Consumerism, and Divorce in Urban America, 1880–1920," *Journal of Social History* 12 (Winter 1978): 180–193.

16. Wheel. Co. no. 1237.

17. Marion County Circuit Court exhibits no. 22241, 112/29.

18. Grant Co. no. 3092–6364.

19. Marion County Circuit Court exhibits, no. 16057, 108/27, emphasis in the original.

20. Mult. Co. no. 159894.

21. Desch. Co. no. 4443; Marion County Circuit Court exhibits, no. 17321, 109/50; Mult. Co. no. 156226; Marion County Circuit Court exhibits nos. 18123, 110/5; 22137, 112/25; 22241, 112/29. Marion County Circuit Court exhibits no. 19336, 110/72.

22. Marion County Circuit Court exhibits, no. 22018, 112/20.

23. Desch. Co. no. 4435.

24. Desch. Co. no. 2120. William H. Chafe, *The Paradox of Change: American Women in the 20th Century* (New York: Oxford University Press, 1991),

104–116; Nancy F. Cott, *The Grounding of Modern Feminism* (New Haven: Yale University Press, 1987), 145–174; Steven Mintz and Susan Kellogg, *Domestic Revolutions: A Social History of American Family Life* (New York: Free Press, 1988), 107–131.

25. Mult. Co. no. 159894. John D'Emilio and Estelle B. Freedman, *Intimate Matters: A History of Sexuality in America* (New York: Harper & Row, 1988), 222–264.

26. Desch. Co. no. 1917.

27. Crook Co. no. 3677.

28. Desch. Co. no. 2508.

29. Desch. Co. no. 4495. Nancy Grey Osterud, in *Bonds of Community: The Lives of Farm Women in Nineteenth-Century New York* (Ithaca, N.Y.: Cornell University Press, 1991), 275–288, argues that the absence of gender segregation often empowers women.

30. Desch. Co. no. 1813.

31. Grant Co. no.3020–6290; Bent. Co. no. 8445. Ellen Kay Trimberger, "Feminism, Men, and Modern Love: Greenwich Village, 1900–1925," in *Powers of Desire: The Politics of Sexuality*, ed. Ann Snitow, Christine Stansell, and Sharon Thompson (New York: Monthly Review Press, 1983), 131–152; Alice Echols, *The Demise of Female Intimacy in the Twentieth Century* (Ann Arbor: Women's Studies Program, University of Michigan, 1978). Estelle Freedman, "Separatism as Strategy: Female Institution Building and American Feminism, 1870–1930," *Feminist Studies* 5 (Fall 1979): 512–529; Pamela S. Haag, "In Search of 'The Real Thing': Ideologies of Love, Modern Romance, and Women's Sexual Subjectivity in the United States, 1920–40," *Journal of the History of Sexuality* 2 (April 1992): 547–577. Peter N. Stearns and Mark Knapp, in "Men and Romantic Love: Pinpointing a 20th Century Change," *Journal of Social History* 26 (Summer 1993), 769–795, argue that men's romantic intensity declined early in the twentieth century. Their case is undermined, however, by their heavily relying on a single source (*Esquire* magazine).

32. *Portland Oregonian*, 28 March 1926, sect. 5, p. 5.

33. Joan M. Jensen, *Promise to the Land: Essays on Rural Women* (Albuquerque: University of New Mexico Press, 1991), 194–197, 203–204. U.S. Bureau of the Census: *Occupations at the Twelfth Census* (Washington, D.C.: Government Printing Office, 1904), 368, 370; *Fourteenth Census of the United States Taken in the Year 1920, Volume 4: Population, 1920, Occupations* (Washington, D.C.: Government Printing Office, 1923), 1001, 1003; *Fifteenth Census of the United States, 1930: Population, Volume 4, Occupations, by States* (Washington, D.C.: Government Printing Office, 1933), 1358, 1373; *Sixteenth Census of the United States, 1940: Population, Volume 3, The Labor Force* (Washington, D.C.: Government Printing Office, 1943), 4: 943; Amy Kesselman, *Fleeting Opportuni-*

ties: Women Shipyard Workers in Portland and Vancouver during World War II and Reconversion (Albany: State University of New York Press, 1990), 22–23, 6–7; U.S. Bureau of the Census: *Fifteenth Census of the United States, 1930: Population, Volume 3, Part 2* (Washington, D.C.: Government Printing Office, 1932), 615; *Fifteenth Census of the United States, 1930: Population, Volume 6, Families* (Washington, D.C.: Government Printing Office, 1933), 1105. On women's work from 1920 to 1945 see Carl Degler, *At Odds: Women and the Family in America from the Revolution to the Present* (New York: Oxford University Press, 1980), 395–417; Alice Kessler-Harris, *Out to Work: A History of Wage-Earning Women in the United States* (Oxford: Oxford University Press, 1982), 228–261; Karen Beck Skold, "The Job He Left Behind: Women in the Shipyards During World War II," in *Women in Pacific Northwest History: An Anthology*, ed. Karen J. Blair (Seattle: University of Washington Press, 1988), 107–129.

34. Mult. Co. no. 112930. U.S. Bureau of the Census: *Fourteenth Census of the United States Taken in the Year 1920, Volume 4: Population, 1920, Occupations*, 744; *Fifteenth Census of the United States, 1930: Population, Volume 6, Families*, 1106. Mult. Co. no. 124438.

35. Wandersee, *Women's Work*, 67–102; Susan Levine, "Workers' Wives: Gender, Class and Consumerism in the 1920s United States," *Gender & History* 3 (Spring 1991): 45–64; Lynd and Lynd, *Middletown in Transition*, 180–181.

36. Mult. Co. no. 124583.

37. Marion County Circuit Court exhibits, no. 19447–110/76; Mult. Co. no. 159542.

38. Mult. Co. no. 113095.

39. Dorothy Cobble, *Dishing It Out: Waitresses and Their Unions in the Twentieth Century* (Urbana: University of Illinois Press, 1991), 6, 44–48, 57–58.

40. Desch. Co. no. 2038.

41. Mult. Co. no. 112904.

42. Warren L. Clare, "Big Jim Stevens: A Study in Pacific Northwest Literature" (Ph.D. diss., Washington State University, 1967), 5, 7. *Honey in the Horn*, Davis's Pulitzer prize-winning novel published in 1935, saved its choicest caricatures for Oregon's most modern and comfortable residents and asserted that they achieved dignity only through struggle: "Prosperity brought out everything in them that was childish and pompous and ridiculous and wasteful. But adversity brought them down to cases; it made even the simplest of them get in together and get work done." H. L. Davis, *Honey in the Horn* (New York: Harper & Brothers, 1935), 379.

43. James Stevens, *Brawny-Man* (New York: Alfred A. Knopf, 1926), 53. Clare, "Big Jim Stevens," 87–88, 129.

44. Stevens, *Brawny-Man*, 88–92, 142. In *Mattock* (New York: Alfred A.

Knopf, 1927), based on Stevens's experiences in World War I, the female characters are either shameless manipulators of men or boring churchgoers.

45. Ernest Haycox, *Free Grass* (Garden City, N.Y.: Doubleday, Doran, 1928), 9, 80, 14; Jane Tompkins, *West of Everything: The Inner Life of Westerns* (New York: Oxford University Press, 1992), 33–67. Tompkins, 144, 125–145, offers an intriguing analysis of Owen Wister's life and *The Virginian*, his classic western. She asserts that westerns "stage a moment in the psychosocial development of the male that requires that he demonstrate his independence from and superiority to women, specifically to his mother," and that this passing from mother's boy to manhood explains why the conception of being a dominating man looms so large in westerns. For further information on Haycox, see Richard W. Etulain, *Ernest Haycox* (Boise, Idaho: Boise State University, 1988). See also John Cawelti, *The Six-Gun Mystique*, 2nd ed. (Bowling Green, Ohio: Bowling Green State University Popular Press, 1984), 17–19, 75–76, 85, on the relationship between westerns and gender.

46. Anne Shannon Monroe, *Happy Valley*, (1916; reprint, Corvallis: Oregon State University Press, 1991). Haycox, *Prairie Guns* (1954; reprint, New York: Pocket Books, 1955), 14–29; 94–108; Haycox, *Pioneer Loves* (1947; reprint, Boston: Little, Brown, 1948), 105–123. The three Haycox stories cited in this note originally appeared in magazines in the 1930s.

47. Haycox's *Alder Gulch* (1941; reprint, New York: Dell, 1957) differs from other Haycox novels in that its protagonist learns that reliance on other people is good and necessary. Etulain, *Ernest Haycox*, 24–25.

48. Edison Marshall, *The Isle of Retribution* [New York: A. L. Burt, 1923], 192, 79–80.

49. Charles Alexander, *The Splendid Summits* (New York: Dodd, Mead, 1925), 67, 243.

50. Gail Bederman, " 'Civilization,' the Decline of Middle-Class Manliness, and Ida B. Wells's Antilynching Campaign (1892–94)," *Radical History Review 52* (Winter 1992): 5–30. F. H. Balch, *The Bridge of the Gods: A Romance of Indian Oregon* (1890; reprint, Portland, Oreg.: Binfords & Mort, n.d.). See also E. Anthony Rotundo, *American Manhood: Transformations in Masculinity from the Revolution to the Modern Era* (New York: Basic Books, 1993), 222–283.

51. Carrick collection, box 1, sermon 1335, U.O.S.C.

52. Carrick collection, box 2, sermon 1443, U.O.S.C. On conservative Protestants' views of women's expanding roles see Margaret Lamberts Bendroth, "Fundamentalism and Femininity: Points of Encounter Between Religious Conservatives and Women, 1919–1935," *Church History* 61 (June 1992): 221–233; Betty A. DeBerg, *Ungodly Women: Gender and the First Wave of American Fundamentalism* (Minneapolis: Fortress Press, 1990).

53. Victor Phillips collection, box 3, sermon 413, U.O.S.C.

54. Carrick collection, box 2, sermon 1527, U.O.S.C.

55. Goodsell collection, box 2, sermon 351, U.S.O.C.

56. Phillips collection, box 1, sermon 552, U.S.O.C.

57. John Dale McCormick collection, May folder, 1937, "Found! A Real Mother," U.O.S.C.

58. Carrick collection, box 2, sermon 1443, U.O.S.C.

59. Phillips Collection, box 2, "Woman's Debt to Christ." U.O.S.C.

60. Goodsell collection, box 1, sermons 67, 69, 70 U.S.O.C.

61. Phillips collection, box 3, sermon 413; McCormick collection, May folder, "An Appreciation of Christian Motherhood," U.S.O.C.

62. Goodsell collection, box 4, sermon 605, U.S.O.C.

63. Carrick collection, box 1, sermon 1144, U.S.O.C.

64. Carrick collection, box 2, sermon 1652, U.S.O.C., emphasis in the original.

65. McCormick collection, May folder, "Christian Mothers and Homes," U.O.S.C.

66. McCormick collection, May folder, "For Mothers Day," U.O.S.C.

67. Goodsell collection, box 2, sermon 351, U.O.S.C.

68. Lee collection, "As One Whom His Mother Comforteth," mss. 2526, O.H.S.

69. Goodsell collection, box 1, sermon 52 U.O.S.C.

70. Marshall, *Isle of Retribution*, 141.

71. Marshall, *The Strength of the Pines* (Boston: Little, Brown, and Company, 1921), 209–210.

72. Haycox, *Free Grass*, 250, 251, 245–246. See also Haycox, *Chaffee of Roaring Horse* (1929; reprint, New York: Popular Library, 1930), 202–203.

73. Monroe, *Happy Valley*, 161, 138–139.

74. Grant Co. no. 1306–4481.

75. Wheel. Co. no. 1232.

76. Marion County Circuit Court exhibits, no. 24331, 113/11.

77. Desch. Co. no. 2293.

78. Desch. Co. no. 4796.

79. Desch. Co. no. 4709.

80. Desch. Co. no. 2000.

81. Desch. Co. no. 4882.

82. Stevens, *Brawny-Man*, 191, 199.

83. Carol Zisowitz Stearns and Peter N. Stearns, *Anger: The Struggle for Emotional Control in America's History* (Chicago: The University of Chicago Press, 1986), 69–109; Kevin White, *The First Sexual Revolution: The Emergence of Male Heterosexuality in Modern America* (New York: New York University Press, 1993), 16–56, 89–92, 120–121; Elizabeth Pleck, *Domestic Tyranny: The*

Making of Social Policy against Family Violence from Colonial Times to the Present (New York: Oxford University Press, 1987), 145–163; Linda Gordon, *Heroes of Their Own Lives: The Politics and History of Family Violence, Boston, 1880–1960* (New York: Viking, 1988), 280–282. John Costello, in *Virtue under Fire: How World War II Changed Our Social and Sexual Attitudes* (Boston: Little, Brown, 1985), 76, 76–80, argues that World War II's hypermasculine military environment turned the civilian "into an aggressive soldier" and "often triggered the release of undercurrents of sexual aggression."

84. Goodsell collection, box 1, sermon 67, U.O.S.C.

85. Jones, *Oregon Detour*, 131, 202, 203, 252, 283.

86. Mult. Co. no. 124338.

87. Mult. Co. no. 118661.

88. Mult. Co. no. 156218.

89. Coos Co. no. 11078.

90. Desch. Co. no. 4441; Crook Co. no. 4233.

91. Mult. Co. no. 112930.

92. Mult. Co. no. 156486.

93. Mult. Co. no. 156399.

94. Mult. Co. nos. 156411, 156563.

95. Mult. Co. no. 156411.

96. Mult. Co. no. 159533.

97. Coos Co. no. 7022.

98. Desch. Co. no. 1917.

99. Grant Co. no. 2186–6249.

100. Desch. Co. no. 4810.

101. Desch. Co. no. 4704.

102. Bent. Co. no. 10879; Desch. Co. no. 4485; Mult. Co. nos. 118484, 118770. See Robert L. Griswold, *Fatherhood in America: A History* (New York: Basic Books, 1993), 143–160, on husbands' reaction to the Depression.

103. This generalization is based largely on a qualitative reading of the divorce suits from 1924 to 1945. The quantitative evidence, though problematic, does not indicate a marked rise in violence during the 1930s. The proportion of husbands described as abusive who were also described as violent stood at 63 percent for largely rural counties in the 1920s, 66 percent in the 1930s. It was 71 percent for Multnomah County in the 1930s and 67 percent for 1944–1945.

104. Desch. Co. no. 2508.

105. Desch. Co. no. 1816.

106. Mult. Co. no. 124434.

107. Coos Co. no. 10556. Gordon, *Heroes of Their Own Lives.*

108. Desch. Co. no. 2186.

109. Desch. Co. no. 4443.

110. Grant Co. no. 1306–4481.

111. Desch. Co. no. 2095.

112. Wheel. Co. no. 972.

113. Desch. Co. no. 4675.

114. Desch. Co. no. 1979.

115. Desch. Co. no. 2186.

116. Desch. Co. no. 1926.

117. Desch. Co. no. 2293.

118. Mult. Co. no. 156352.

119. Mult. Co. no. 159534.

120. Wheel. Co. no. 931.

121. Desch. Co. no. 2234; Bent. Co. nos. 8581, 10851; Coos Co. nos. 6946, 6954, 7132, 7310, 7317; Desch. Co. nos. 1819, 1889, 4441, 4800, 4804; Grant Co. nos. 1554–4656, 3126–6373; Mult. Co. nos. 118538, 156325, 156411, 156563, 159581, 159693, 159723; Wheel. Co. no. 1264.

122. Marion County Circuit Court exhibits, no. 11556, 101/26.

123. Desch. Co. no. 2038. Coos Co. no. 10535; Bent. Co. no. 8428; Desch. Co. no. 4611; Coos Co. nos. 7260, 10960; Crook Co. no. 3714; Desch. Co. nos. 2186, 4699; Grant Co. nos. 2188–6261, 3020–6290; Mult. Co. nos. 113081, 124291, 124560, 156411.

124. Mult. Co. no. 124383.

125. Crook Co. no. 3756; Coos Co. no. 7350; Mult. Co. nos. 112896, 118564, 156362. Kathleen M. Blee's *Women of the Klan: Racism and Gender in the 1920s* (Berkeley: University of California Press, 1991), 77–86, treats male Klan members' sadistic treatment of women, including stripping and whipping those suspected of sexual immorality.

126. Coos Co. nos. 6555, 10760, 10757. Violent husbands who accused their wives of wantonness may well have been projecting their own impulses onto their spouses. A Coos County woman whose complaint quoted her husband as saying "you have squatted for many a dog," indicated that he had sexually fondled their sixteen-year-old daughter. Likewise, a husband who had been jailed for harassing women and had reportedly peeked into other people's houses and carried on improper relations with the couple's teenage daughter had accused his wife "of every thing you could think of." Coos Co. no. 7192; Desch. Co. no. 4705.

127. Desch. Co. no. 4796.

128. Desch. Co. no. 1979.

129. Desch. Co. no. 4649; Coos Co. no. 7548.

130. Desch. Co. no. 2077 describes the Christmas incident. Coos Co. nos.

7172, 7260. Bent. Co. nos. 7998, 10558; Coos Co. nos. 7137, 7406, 10461; Desch. Co. no. 1913; Mult. Co. nos. 112930, 124323, 124383, 156355.

131. Grant Co. no. 3127–6388.

132. Mult. Co. no. 124438.

133. Mult. Co. no. 113081.

134. David Riches, "The Phenomenon of Violence," in *The Anthropology of Violence*, ed. Riches (Oxford: Basil Blackwell, 1986), 19–20. Gordon, *Heroes of Their Own Lives*, 264–266; Craig MacAndrew and Robert B. Edgerton, *Drunken Comportment: A Social Explanation* (Chicago: Aldine, 1969), 61–82.

135. Mult. Co. no. 118638.

136. $x2 = 11.430$, $df = 1$, $P < .001$, $N = 280$. Gordon, *Heroes of Their Own Lives*, 280, notes that the police were called in about 49 percent of the wife-beating cases in her study of Boston from 1880 to 1960, and that the rate varied little over time.

137. Desch. Co. no. 1772.

138. Desch. Co. no. 1868.

139. Desch. Co. no. 2361.

140. Desch. Co. no. 2293. The complaint of another eastern Oregon woman stated that her violent husband "has taunted plaintiff by saying that he would be careful to not leave any marks on her, that he knew better than to do that." Desch. Co. no. 2544.

141. Desch. Co. no. 1995.

142. Desch. Co. no. 4605. Gordon, *Heroes of Their Own Lives*, 280–282, states that police tended to identify with husbands in domestic violence altercations, but that they often removed the husbands from their homes for a while.

143. Desch. Co. no. 2226. Family members constituted 34 percent of reported interventions in cases around the turn of the century, but only 26 percent from 1924 to 1945. Assistance against violent husbands by neighbors or friends declined more markedly, from 36 percent to just 23 percent. See the table in Chapter 5 for a complete breakdown of third-party interventions.

144. Desch. Co. no. 2533.

145. Wheel. Co. no. 931.

146. Desch. Co. no. 2003. U.S. Bureau of the Census, *Fifteenth Census of the United States: 1930, Population, Volume 6, Families*, 1107, 1104.

147. Grant Co. no. 2186–6249.

148. Grant Co. no. 3109–6380.

149. Crook Co. no. 3560.

150. David Horowitz, "Social Morality and Personal Revitalization: Oregon's Ku Klux Klan in the 1920s," *Oregon Historical Quarterly* 90 (Winter

1989): 372–373; Jeff LaLande, "Beneath the Hooded Robe: Newspapermen, Local Politics, and the Ku Klux Klan in Jackson County, Oregon, 1921–1923," *Pacific Northwest Quarterly* 83 (April 1992): 46–47. See Nancy Maclean, "White Women and Klan Violence in the 1920s: Agency, Complicity and the Politics of Women's History," *Gender & History* 3 (Autumn 1991): 285–303, and Blee, *Women of the Klan*, 77–86, on Klan measures against husbands.

151. Desch. Co. no. 2520.

152. Goodsell collection, box 1, sermon 159, U.O.S.C. Carrick collection, box 1, sermon 1335, U.O.S.C.; *Portland Oregonian*, 21 February 1931, p. 12.

153. Mult. Co. no. 159812.

154. Mult. Co. no. 156540. In 1933 Oregon's Supreme Court quoted Multnomah County's Court of Domestic Relations on the tendency to award custody to wives: "Every child of tender years should be awarded to its mother unless she is grossly immoral or subjects the child to abuse or gross neglect, provided she is in other respects at least a fairly good parent." *Reports of Cases Decided in the Supreme Court of the State of Oregon* (San Francisco, Calif.: Bancroft-Whitney, 1934), 145: 30.

155. Desch. Co. no. 4593.

156. Desch. Co. no. 1889.

157. Mult. Co. nos. 156318, 156369, 156484, 156479, 156399.

158. *Portland Oregonian*, 14 October 1945, mag. sect., p. 1.

159. Desch. Co. no. 4796.

160. Desch. Co. no. 4705. In contrast, a few divorce-seeking wives cited the children's needs as a reason to leave their husbands.

161. Desch. Co. no. 1917.

162. Bent. Co. no. 10453. Gordon, in *Heroes of Their Own Lives*, 271–274, asserts that the presence of children was the greatest barrier to wives leaving their husbands.

163. Mult. Co. no. 156263.

164. Mult. Co. nos. 156194, 156470.

165. Mult. Co. no. 156379.

166. Tri-County Community Council collection, mss. 1783, box 8, Albertina Kerr Homes, Inc. Publicity—Case Histories 1944–45 file, O.H.S.

167. Mult. Co. no. 118831.

168. Mult. Co. no. 112888.

169. Desch. Co. no. 1889; Bent. Co. no. 8469.

170. Desch. Co. no. 1917.

171. Mult. Co. no. 112896.

172. Desch. Co. no. 2330.

173. Grant Co. no. 3117–6387; Coos Co. no. 6553.

174. Mult. Co. no. 156406.

175. Gordon, *Heroes of Their Own Lives*, 258–260.

176. Grant Co. no. 3125–6366.

177. Grant Co. no. 2186–6249.

178. Mult. Co. no. 156308; Grant Co. no. 3105–6372; Desch. Co. no. 1995. Gordon, *Heroes of Their Own Lives*, 274–276, found that 14 percent of the marital violence in her study contained some sort of violence by women and that it was generally of three types: mutual violence, which was the most common; self-defense with a weapon; and, least commonly, instances in which wives were the primary aggressors. Violence by women appeared to decline over time among her lower-class Bostonians, in part because the women were more likely to leave expeditiously.

5. "We Found That We Were Not Alone": The Years after World War II

1. James Lincoln Collier, *The Rise of Selfishness in America* (New York: Oxford University Press, 1991), 216–261. John C. Burnham, *Bad Habits: Drinking, Smoking, Taking Drugs, Gambling, Sexual Misbehavior, and Swearing in American History* (New York: New York University Press, 1993).

2. Philip Slater, *The Pursuit of Loneliness: American Culture at the Breaking Point*, rev. ed. (Boston: Beacon Press, 1976); Christopher Lasch, *The Culture of Narcissism: American Life in an Age of Diminishing Expectations* (New York: W. W. Norton, 1979). Gary Wills, *Nixon Agonistes: The Crisis of the Self-Made Man* (Boston: Houghton Mifflin, 1969), is an outstanding study of the pervasive nature of individualism in the United States.

3. Daniel Yankelovich, *New Rules: Searching for Self-Fulfillment in a World Turned Upside Down* (New York: Random House, 1981); Peter Clecak, *America's Quest for the Ideal Self: Dissent and Fulfillment in the 60s and 70s* (New York: Oxford University Press, 1983); David Harrington Watt, *A Transforming Faith: Explorations of Twentieth-Century American Evangelicalism* (New Brunswick, N.J.: Rutgers University Press, 1991), 106–117 131–136, 137–154.

4. Joseph Veroff, Elizabeth Douvan, and Richard A. Kulka, *The Inner American: A Self-Portrait from 1957 to 1976* (New York: Basic Books, 1981), 103–139, 529–531.

5. U.S. Bureau of the Census: *Historical Statistics of the United States, Colonial Times to 1970, Part 1* (Washington, D.C.: Government Printing Office, 1975), 33; *1990 Census of Population: General Population Characteristics, Oregon* (Washington, D.C.: U.S. Government Printing Office, 1992), 1; Samuel N. Dicken and Emily F. Dicken, *The Making of Oregon: A Study in Historical Geography* (Portland: Oregon Historical Society, 1979), 171–184; Gordon B. Dodds, *Oregon: A Bicentennial History* (New York: W. W. Norton and

Nashville, Tenn.: American Association for State and Local History, 1977), 187–215; Carlos A. Schwantes, *The Pacific Northwest: An Interpretive History* (Lincoln: University of Nebraska Press, 1989), 347–350.

6. William G. Robbins, *Hard Times in Paradise: Coos Bay, Oregon, 1850–1986* (Seattle: University of Washington Press, 1988), 155–165.

7. Richard M. Steiner collection, mss. 1375, box 6, "Home Sweet Home," O.H.S. Elaine Tyler May, *Homeward Bound: American Families in the Cold War Era* (New York: Basic Books, 1988). Barbara Laslett, "The Family as a Public and Private Institution: An Historical Perspective," *Journal of Marriage and the Family* 35 (August 1973): 480–492; Laslett, "Family Membership, Past and Present," *Social Problems* 25 (June 1978): 476–490.

8. Oregon Bureau of Labor, *Divorced Women in Portland: A Report on an Inquiry* (Salem: Oregon Bureau of Labor, 1978), 70. *Portland Oregonian*, 23 January 1979, p. C1.

9. Howard Gadlin, "Private Lives and Public Order: A Critical View of the History of Intimate Relations in the U.S." *The Massachusetts Review* 17 (Summer 1976): 304–330. John D'Emilio and Estelle B. Freedman, *Intimate Matters: A History of Sexuality in America* (New York: Harper & Row, 1988), 280–288, 301–308; John Demos, "Images of the American Family, Then and Now," in *Changing Images of the Family*, ed. Virginia Tufte and Barbara Myerhoff (New Haven: Yale University Press, 1979), 43–60.

10. *Network News* 9 (Spring 1989): 4. Copies of this newsletter are available at the Oregon Coalition against Domestic and Sexual Violence, Portland.

11. Steven Mintz and Susan Kellogg, *Domestic Revolutions: A Social History of American Family Life* (New York: Free Press, 1988), 186.

12. Mintz and Kellogg, *Domestic Revolutions*, 203; Karen Beck Skold, "The Job He Left Behind: Women in the Shipyards during World War II," in *Women in Pacific Northwest History: An Anthology*, ed. Karen J. Blair (Seattle: University of Washington Press, 1988), 124; Oregon Bureau of Labor, *Divorced Women in Portland*, 33; U.S. Bureau of the Census: *Census of Population: 1950, Volume 2: Characteristics of the Population* (Washington, D.C.: Government Printing Office, 1952), 37: 31; *1980 Census of Population, Volume 1: Characteristics of the Population, Chapter C: General Social and Economic Characteristics, Part 39, Oregon* (Washington, D.C.: Government Printing Office, 1983), 14. On women's work since World War II see also William H. Chafe, *The Paradox of Change: American Women in the 20th Century* (New York: Oxford University Press, 1991), 154–172; 188–192, 223, 231–238; Carl Degler, *At Odds: Women and the Family in America from the Revolution to the Present* (New York: Oxford University Press, 1986), 418–435; Alice Kessler-Harris, *Out to Work: A History of Wage-Earning Women in the United States* (New York: Oxford University Press, 1982), 300–304.

13. Oregon Bureau of Labor, *Divorced Women in Portland*, 82. May, *Homeward Bound*, 193–207. Francesca M. Cancian and Steven L. Gordon, "Changing Emotion Norms in Marriage: Love and Anger in U.S. Women's Magazines Since 1900," *Gender and Society* 2 (September 1988): 308–342; Jean E. Hunter, "Adapting to Changing Familial Roles: 25 Years of 'Can This Marriage Be Saved?' " in *The American Family: Historical Perspectives*, ed. Hunter and Paul T. Mason (Pittsburgh: Duquesne University Press, 1991), 155–167.

14. Barbara Ehrenreich, *The Hearts of Men: American Dreams and the Flight from Commitment* (New York: Anchor Press, 1983), 152, 144–168. Chafe, *Paradox of Change*, 211.

15. Quoted in Timothy Miller, *The Hippies and American Values* (Knoxville: University of Tennessee Press, 1991), 67. Deirdre English, "The Fear that Feminism Will Free Men First," in *Powers of Desire: The Politics of Sexuality*, ed. Ann Snitow, Christine Stansell, and Sharon Thompson (New York: Monthly Review Press, 1983), 477–483; Sylvia Ann Hewlett, *A Lesser Life: The Myth of Women's Liberation in America* (1986; reprint, New York: Warner Books, 1987), 51–69; 207–208; 329–337.

16. Judith Stacey, *Brave New Families: Stories of Domestic Upheaval in Late Twentieth Century America* ([New York]: Basic Books, 1990), 56–57, 59–60, 73–77.

17. Peter N. Stearns, *Be a Man! Males in Modern Society*, 2nd ed. (New York: Holmes & Meier, 1990), 217–222; Ehrenreich, *Hearts of Men*. Robert L. Griswold, *Fatherhood in America: A History* (New York: Basic Books, 1993), 219–242; Hewlett, *A Lesser Life*, 305–322.

18. William H. Chafe, *The Unfinished Journey: America since World War II*, 2nd ed. (New York: Oxford University Press, 1991), 113–117; Peter G. Filene, *Him/Her/Self: Sex Roles in Modern America*, 2nd ed. (Baltimore: Johns Hopkins University Press, 1986), 172–175; Mintz and Kellogg, *Domestic Revolutions*, 191–192; Robbins, *Hard Times in Paradise*, 155–165; Stearns, *Be a Man!*, 177–181; Veroff et al., *Inner American*, 240–241, 280–282.

19. Ehrenreich, *Hearts of Men*, 171, 36–41, emphasis in the original. Rupert Wilkinson, *American Tough: The Tough-Guy Tradition and American Character* (Westport, Conn.: Greenwood Press, 1984), 33–65. Susan Jeffords, *The Remasculinization of America: Gender and the Vietnam War* (Bloomington: Indiana University Press, 1989), 144–167, treats how by 1984 popular interpretations of the Vietnam War feminized the nation's embarrassing loss.

20. Ken Kesey, *One Flew Over the Cuckoo's Nest* (New York: Signet, 1962), 40, emphasis in the original.

21. Ken Kesey, *Sometimes a Great Notion* (1964; reprint, New York: Bantam Books, 1965). Don Berry, a popular Oregon novelist writing in the 1960s, also expressed strong reservations over progress, though his novels were set

in Oregon's settlement period: *Trask* (1960; reprint, Sausalito, Calif.: Comstock, 1969); *Moontrap* (1962; reprint, Sausalito, Calif.: Comstock, 1971).

22. Gerhart Saenger, "Male and Female Relations in the American Comic Strip," in *The Funnies: An American Idiom*, ed. David Manning White and Robert H. Abel (New York: Free Press of Glencoe, 1963), 219–231; Francis E. Barcus, "The World of Sunday Comics," in *The Funnies*, 190–218.

23. May, *Homeward Bound*, 109–112, 62–63.

24. Susan Griffin, *Pornography and Silence: Culture's Revenge against Nature* (New York: Harper & Row, 1981); Neil M. Malamuth and Barry Spinner, "A Longitudinal Content Analysis of Sexual Violence in the Best-Selling Erotic Magazines," *Journal of Sex Research* 16 (August 1980): 226–237; Joyce D. Hammond, "Gender Inversion Cartoons and Feminism," *Journal of Popular Culture* 24 (Spring 1991): 145–160. Edward Donnerstein, Daniel Linz, and Steven Penrod, *The Question of Pornography: Research Findings and Policy Implications* (New York: Free Press, 1987), 88–91.

25. *Network News* 9 (Spring 1989): 3. Saenger, "Male and Female Relations"; Jerome Nadelhaft, "Wife Torture: A Known Phenomenon in Nineteenth-Century America," *Journal of American Culture* 10 (Fall 1987): 39–59.

26. Lasch, *Culture of Narcissism*, 324. Richard Maxwell Brown, "Crime, Law, and Society: From the Industrial to the Information Society," in *The History of Crime*, ed. Ted Robert Gurr (Newbury Park, Calif.: Sage, 1989), 251–268; Brown, *No Duty to Retreat: Violence and Values in American History and Society* (New York: Oxford University Press, 1991), 130–133, 139–142; Gurr, "Historical Trends in Violent Crime: Europe and the United States," in *History of Crime*, 21–54; Roger Lane, "On the Social Meaning of Homicide Trends in America," in *History of Crime*, 55–79; Wesley G. Skogan, "Social Change and the Future of Violent Crime," in *History of Crime*, 235–250; Carol Zisowitz Stearns and Peter N. Stearns, *Anger: The Struggle for Emotional Control in America's History* (Chicago: University of Chicago Press, 1986), 190–210; James Q. Wilson and Richard J. Herrnstein, *Crime and Human Nature* (New York: Simon & Schuster, 1985), 407–438. Linda Gordon, in *Heroes of Their Own Lives: The Politics and History of Family Violence, Boston, 1880–1960* (New York: Viking, 1988), 282–285, notes that post–World War II social workers frequently viewed violence against wives as a side issue that should not distract a couple from dealing with actual problems, commonly defined by the helping professionals as wives' sexual and gender maladjustment. On the relationship between social change and violence against wives see William J. Goode, "Why Men Resist," in *Rethinking the Family: Some Feminist Questions*, ed. Barrie Thorne and Marilyn Yalom (New York: Longman, 1982), 131–150; Stanley Lesse, "The Status of Violence against Women: Past, Present and Future Factors," *American Journal of Psychotherapy* 33 (April 1979): 190–200;

Edward M. Levine, "Sociocultural Causes of Family Violence: A Theoretical Comment," *Journal of Family Violence* 1 (March 1986): 3–12; Rodman Hyman, "Marital Power and the Theory of Resources in Cultural Context," *Journal of Comparative Family Studies* 3 (Spring 1972): 50–69; Kersti Yllö, "Sexual Equality and Violence against Wives in American States," *Journal of Comparative Family Studies* 14 (Spring 1983): 67–86; Yllö, "The Status of Women, Marital Equality, and Violence against Wives," *Journal of Family Issues* 5 (September 1984): 307–320.

27. Jeff. Co. no. 1857.

28. Crook Co. no. 6089.

29. Desch. Co. no. 9429.

30. Jeff. Co. nos. 1698, 1857. Desch. Co. nos. 9111, 9135, 9680, 9687, 9794; Mult. Co. nos. 216735, 216829, 235960.

31. Case code no. A43. As noted in the Prologue, I have taken pains to obscure the identities of people who have recently filed restraining orders.

32. Case code no. A6.

33. Case code no. B23.

34. Case code no. A18.

35. *Escape from Violence: The Women of Bradley Angle House* (n.p.: Olive Press, 1978), 58, 80. *Portland Oregonian*, 2 January 1979, p. C1. McGuire said that she was innocent of hiring the men to kill her husband.

36. Barbara Star, Carol G. Clark, Karen M. Goetz, and Linda O'Malia, "Psychosocial Aspects of Wife Battering," *Social Casework* 60 (October 1979): 479–487; Kathleen H. Hofeller, *Social, Psychological and Situational Factors in Wife Abuse* (Palo Alto, Calif.: R & E Research Associates, 1982), 69, 93; Lewis Okun, *Woman Abuse: Facts Replacing Myths* (Albany: State University of New York Press, 1986), 49; Marilyn G. Miller, Janet S. McCoy, and Barbara Milligan, *Domestic Violence in Oregon* (n.p.: Oregon Educational Association, 1979), 27. Most of the women in the Oregon study had been in contact with a women's organization. Statistics on homicides of wives in Oregon are fragmentary up to 1989. Summaries of murders published in the *Portland Oregonian* for calendar years 1904, 1907, and 1908 indicate a level of 0.67 wife killings per 100,000 females. Multnomah County coroner's records, paired with newspaper accounts of women's murders, indicate a 0.65 rate for 1900 to 1910 and a rate of 0.78 for 1956–1964. The coroner's reports covered only Multnomah County. State Police records for 1989 to 1991 show a level of 0.62 per 100,000, but this rises to 0.97 when one counts women murdered by male partners. Since living together without marriage had become much more common late in the century than early in the century, the 0.97 figure is probably more comparable to the early-twentieth-century figure than the 0.62 figure is. The reader should bear in mind that these statistics are drawn from a

relatively small population of wife killings and that the identity of killers often remained obscured. *Portland Oregonian*, 13 February 1905, p. 1; 6 January 1908, pp. 1, 4; 25 January 1909, p. 9; Multnomah County Coroner's investigation books, 1900–1910, 1956–1964, M.C.M.E.O; annual printouts of the Law Enforcement Data System, Department of State Police, Salem.

37. *Network News* 1 (June 1981): 2.

38. Laurie Hubbard, *From Harassment to Homicide: A Report on the Response to Domestic Violence in Multnomah County* (n.p., 1991), 8.

39. Mary Henderson, *The Story of Henderson House: A Home for Abused Women* (n.p., [ca. 1984]), 14–15.

40. Group of ten people to Gretchen Kafoury, 28 February 1980, City-County Family Violence Program, folder 58/20, C.P.A.R.C. Elizabeth Pleck, in *Domestic Tyranny: The Making of Social Policies against Family Violence from Colonial Times to the Present* (New York: Oxford University Press, 1987), 182–200, treats the revival of concern over wife beating in the 1970s.

41. Family Violence Program, folder 58/22, January 1979 comments by Commissioner Jordan.

42. *Network News* 3 (September–October 1983): 3.

43. *(Portland) Oregon Journal*, 8 May 1955, p. A8.

44. *(Salem) Statesman Journal*, 27 February 1981, p. 6B.

45. *Portland Oregonian*, 2 March 1992, p. B4. Some 2,850 restraining orders were issued in Multnomah County alone during 1990, although not all of them went to wives or even to women. Hubbard, *From Harassment to Homicide*, 25.

46. Randy H. Day of the Portland Police Department to author, 13 April 1994. City of Portland arrest books, 1905–1911, C.P.A.R.C. Portland's population increased 288 percent from 1910 to 1990.

47. Robert Robertson, *Confessions of an Abusive Husband: A How-to Book for "Abuse-Free Living for Everyone"* (Lake Oswego, Oreg.: Heritage Park, 1992), 6; *Portland Oregonian*, 31 January 1993, p. L5; Miller et al., *Domestic Violence in Oregon*, 28; Hubbard, *From Harassment to Homicide*, 35–36.

48. Robertson, *Confessions of an Abusive Husband*, 3, 25.

49. Alisdair MacIntyre, *Secularization and Moral Change* (London: Oxford University Press, 1967), 70–73; Robert N. Bellah, Richard Madsen, William M. Sullivan, Ann Swindler, and Steven M. Tipton, *Habits of the Heart: Individualism and Commitment in American Life* (Berkeley: University of California Press), 1985. Cathy Stein Greenblat, in "A Hit Is a Hit . . . Or Is it? Approval and Tolerance of the Use of Force by Spouses," in *The Dark Side of Families: Current Family Violence Research*, ed. David Finkelhor, Richard J. Gelles, Gerald T. Hotaling (Beverly Hills, Calif.: Sage, 1983), 235–260, finds that men and women alike seldom approve of hitting one's spouse, although

many who deemed it unacceptable indicated a tolerance of it under certain circumstances, such as lack of self-control or in response to sexual infidelity.

50. Jeff. Co. no. 1804.

51. Mult. Co. no. 216686.

52. Case code no. A10.

53. Case code no. A16.

54. *(Portland) Willamette Week*, 30 May 1977, p. 9.

55. Case code no. A39, emphasis in the original.

56. Case code no. A25. Robbins, *Hard Times in Paradise*, 163, 165. Doreen Binder, director of the Women's Crisis Service based in Coos Bay, believes that the area's economic problems are a major contributor to violence against wives, though not its cause: Doreen Binder, interview by author, Coos Bay, Oregon, 26 June 1992. Mirra Komarovsky, in *Blue-Collar Marriage* (1962; reprint, New York: Random House, 1967), 195, found that wife beating was most common among the least educated working-class men that she studied. Several recent studies of violence suggest that men who lacked money, education, and particularly employment were more likely than other husbands to use physical violence on their wives: Okun, *Woman Abuse*, 45–49; Richard J. Gelles and Murray A. Straus, *Intimate Violence* (1988; reprint, New York: Touchstone, 1989), 88–89; Marilyn J. Howell and Karen L. Pugliesi, "Husbands Who Harm: Predicting Spousal Violence by Men," *Journal of Family Violence* 3 (March 1988): 15–27; Albert R. Roberts, "Psychosocial Characteristics of Batterers: A Study of 234 Men Charged with Domestic Violence Offenses," *Journal of Family Violence* 2 (March 1987): 81–93; Mark A. Schulman, *A Survey of Spousal Violence against Women in Kentucky* (Washington, D.C.: Department of Justice, 1979), 16–18. These studies are undercut, however, by the difficulty of detecting violence against wives in the middle class.

57. Robertson, *Confessions of an Abusive Husband*, 3, 2.

58. *Portland Oregonian*, 20 November 1983, p. A1. Mult. Co. nos. 226061, 335753, 335776, 365154; *Portland Oregonian*, 4 February 1980, p. B1; 27 March 1993, p. A1.

59. Robertson, *Confessions of an Abusive Husband*, 36–37, 6–7, 32, 107.

60. *Escape from Violence*, 90–91.

61. *(Salem) Statesman Journal*, 6 July 1982, p. C1.

62. *Escape from Violence*, 96.

63. *Escape from Violence*, 71.

64. Mult. Co. no. 216813.

65. Desch. Co. no. 9119.

66. *Escape from Violence*, 56.

67. Desch. Co. no. 9119.

68. Crook Co. no. 5795.

69. *Escape from Violence*, 7.

70. Case code no. A17.

71. Case code no. B30.

72. *Escape from Violence*, 45–46.

73. *Portland Oregonian*, 21 July 1981, p. C1.

74. Case code no. B9.

75. *Portland Oregonian*, 31 January 1993, p. L4.

76. Robertson, *Confessions of an Abusive Husband*, 137, 41.

77. Crook Co. no. 6155. Case code no. A20; Desch. Co. no. 9251; Mult. Co. nos. 216735, 226061, 235697, 335942.

78. *Network News*, 8 (Winter 1988): 1. This woman used the third person in describing the abuse she had suffered. *Escape from Violence*, 10; case code no. A29.

79. *Network News*, 8 (Winter 1988): 1.

80. Case code no. A40.

81. *Escape from Violence*, 49–50.

82. *Escape from Violence*, 84.

83. Mult. Co. no. 235972.

84. *Escape from Violence*, 84. Miller et al., *Domestic Violence in Oregon*, 29. Richard J. Gelles, in "Violence and Pregnancy: Are Pregnant Women at Greater Risk of Abuse?" *Journal of Marriage and the Family* 50 (August 1988): 841–847, argues that violence against wives does not necessarily increase during pregnancy.

85. J. L. Bernard and M. L. Bernard, "The Abusive Male Seeking Treatment: Jekyll and Hyde," *Family Relations* 33 (October 1984): 543–547; Donald G. Dutton, *The Domestic Assault of Women: Psychological and Criminal Justice Perspectives* (Newton, Mass.: Allyn and Bacon, 1988), 38–42, 75–82; Diane Goldstein and Alan Rosenbaum, "An Evaluation of the Self-Esteem of Maritally Violent Men," *Family Relations* 34 (July 1985): 425–428; Roland D. Maiuro, Timothy S. Cahn, Peter P. Vitaliano, Barbara Wagner, and Joan Zegree, "Anger, Hostility, and Depression in Domestically Violent versus Generally Assaultive Men and Nonviolent Control Subjects," *Journal of Consulting and Clinical Psychology* 56 (February 1988): 17–23; A. R. Mawson, "Aggression, Attachment Behavior, and Crimes of Violence," in *Understanding Crime: Current Theory and Research*, ed. Travis Hirschi and Michael Gottfredson (Beverly Hills, Calif.: Sage, 1980), 103–116; Mildred Daley Pagelow, "Sex Roles, Power, and Woman Battering," in *Women and Crime in America*, ed. Lee H. Bowker (New York: Macmillan, 1981), 239–277; Natalie Shainess, "Psychological Aspects of Wifebattering," in *Battered Women: A Psychosociological Study of Domestic Violence*, ed. Maria Roy (New York: Van Nostrand Reinhold, 1977) 111–119.

86. Nancy Chodorow, "Family Structure and Feminine Personality," in *Woman, Culture, and Society*, ed. Michelle Zimbalist Rosaldo and Louise Lamphere (Stanford, Calif.: Stanford University Press, 1974), 43–66, Chodorow, *The Reproduction of Mothering: Psychoanalysis and the Sociology of Gender* (Berkeley: University of California Press, 1978), 173–209; Dorothy Dinnerstein, *The Rocking of the Cradle and the Ruling of the World* (1976; reprint, London: Women's Press, 1987), 91–114; Lillian B. Rubin, *Intimate Strangers: Men and Women Together* (New York: Harper & Row, 1983); Jean Stockard and Miriam M. Johnson, "The Social Origins of Male Dominance," *Sex Roles* 5 (April 1979): 199–218. Johnson, in *Strong Mothers, Weak Wives: The Search for Gender Equality* (Berkeley: University of California Press, 1988), discusses some pitfalls in identifying women's parenting as the primary cause of sexual inequality and offers some cautions about trying to remedy inequality by immediately having men do equal parenting.

87. Jan Horsfall, *The Presence of the Past: Male Violence in the Family* (North Sydney, Australia: Allen & Unwin, 1991), 91, passim.

88. Jacquelyn C. Campbell, "Beating of Wives: A Cross-Cultural Perspective," *Victimology* 10 (1985): 174–185.

89. Kate Millet, *Sexual Politics* (New York: Ballantine, 1969). Mark C. Carnes, in *Secret Ritual and Manhood in Victorian America* (New Haven: Yale University Press, 1989), 91–127, discusses historical changes in the relationship between parenting and male psychological development, largely among the nineteenth-century middle class.

90. *Escape from Violence*, 7.

91. Case code no. A26. *Portland Oregonian*, 3 December 1964, p. 20.

92. Case code no. A10.

93. Case code no. A22. *Escape from Violence*, 96; Henderson, *Story of Henderson House*, 44; Crook Co. no. 5932; Jeff. Co. no. 1709; Mult. Co. nos. 217022, 226305; case code nos. A28, B9.

94. Packet on domestic violence, Women's Crisis Service, Coos Bay.

95. *Portland Oregonian*, 2 January 1979, p. C1.

96. *Portland Oregonian*, 1 January 1979, p. C1.

97. Annual printouts of the Law Enforcement Data System. Thomas M. Becker, Jonathan M. Samet, Charles L. Wiggins, and Charles R. Key, in "Violent Death in the West: Suicide and Homicides in New Mexico, 1958–1987," *Suicide and Life-Threatening Behavior* 20 (Winter 1990): 328, find that the rate of homicides by Native American women has consistently exceeded that of Spanish-speaking and Anglo women in New Mexico since 1958.

98. Marion County Circuit Court exhibits, case no. 10960.

99. Jeff. Co. nos. 570, 550, 553, 741.

100. Jeff. Co. no. 552.

101. *Portland Oregonian*, 6 January 1972, sect. 2, p. 14.

102. *Reports of Cases Decided in the Supreme Court of the State of Oregon* (Salem, Oreg.: State Printing, 1973), 265: 105.

103. Case code no. B11. Veroff et al., *Inner American*, 483–487; May, *Homeward Bound*, 186.

104. Case code no. A13. Micaela Di Leonardo, "The Female World of Cards and Holidays: Women, Families, and the Work of Kinship," *Signs* 12 (Spring 1987): 440–453; Komarovsky, *Blue-Collar Marriage*, 26–27, 208–209, 236–246; Marion L. Kranichfeld, "Rethinking Family Power," *Journal of Family Issues*, 8 (March 1987): 42–56.

105. *Escape from Violence*, 16–17. This woman indicated that her neighbor later changed her mind and went with her to her house while she got her child and an overnight bag.

106. Genelle Hanken and Ron Whitley, interview by author, Coquille, Oregon, 26 June 1992.

107. Jeff. Co. no. 1975. Divorce-seeking wives of the 1950s who mentioned interventions against violent husbands identified law-enforcement personnel as the interveners 65 percent of the time, up from 52 percent from the 1920s to mid-1940s, and up further still from earlier periods.

108. Hubbard, *From Harassment to Homicide*, 25. Multnomah County courts issued some 2,850 restraining orders in 1990, most to women against their male partners. Hubbard, *From Harassment to Homicide*, 25.

109. Miller et al., *Domestic Violence in Oregon*, 14, 11–13, 27, 30.

110. Binder, interview.

111. Judith Armatta, telephone interview by author, 26 May 1994.

112. *(Portland) Willamette Week*, 30 May 1977, p. 1.

113. Mult. Co. no. 235974.

114. Oregon Bureau of Labor, *"They Carry the Burden Alone . . .": The Socio-Economic Living Pattern of Oregon Women with Dependents* (Salem: Oregon Bureau of Labor, 1968), 104. Oregon Bureau of Labor, *Divorced Women in Portland*, 11–13.

115. Oregon Bureau of Labor, *Divorced Women in Portland*, 26, 18. Oregon Bureau of Labor, *"They Carry the Burden Alone,"* 8; *The Self-Supporting Woman in Oregon: Report on an Inquiry into Her Economic Living Pattern* (n.p.: State of Oregon Bureau of Labor, [1958]). Chafe, *Paradox of Change*, 224–226.

116. Mult. Co. nos. 226271, 235816, 349577, 349353, 336725, 336528, 335965. Some of these wives, or husbands, may have worked less than full time, which would of course have lowered their wages.

117. Crook Co. no. 6177.

118. *Escape from Violence*, 66. By the 1950s, Oregon's Supreme Court openly advocated awarding custody to mothers, unless they were judged to be morally

unfit: *Reports of Cases Decided in the Supreme Court of the State of Oregon* (Salem, Oreg.: State Printing, 1951), 192: 620–623.

119. Case code no. A28.

120. *Portland Oregonian*, 17 December 1977, p. C1.

121. Oregon Bureau of Labor, *Divorced Women in Portland*, 25.

122. Ibid., 9.

123. Oregon Bureau of Labor, *"They Carry the Burden Alone,"* 101, 9.

124. Oregon Bureau of Labor, *Divorced Women in Portland*, 30, 82.

125. Henderson, *Story of Henderson House*, 43–44.

126. Case code no. B19.

127. Case code no. B28.

128. *Portland Oregonian*, 26 February 1984, p. NW16; 2 January 1979, p. C1. Jeff. Co. no. 1975; case code no. A1. Miller et al., *Domestic Violence in Oregon*, 24–25, 28.

129. *Portland Oregonian*, 20 May 1982, p. B8; *Eugene Register-Guard*, 24 March 1991, p. 5B; annual printouts of the Law Enforcement Data System. Faith McNulty, in *The Burning Bed* (New York: Harcourt Brace Jovanovich, 1980), described the most well-known instance of an abused wife killing her husband.

130. *Escape from Violence*, 45–46.

131. Doreen Binder, telephone interview by author, 26 May 1994.

132. *Escape from Violence*, 60.

133. *Portland Downtowner*, 2 March 1992, p. 8. On women's reasons for staying with violent men see Debra S. Kalmuss and Straus, "Wife's Marital Dependency and Wife Abuse," *Journal of Marriage and the Family* 44 (May 1982): 277–286; Martin D. Schwartz, "Marital Status and Woman Abuse Theory," *Journal of Family Violence* 3 (September 1988): 239–248; Michael J. Strube and Linda S. Barbour, "The Decision to Leave an Abusive Relationship: Economic Dependence and Psychological Commitment," *Journal of Marriage and the Family* 45 (November 1983): 785–793; Strube and Barbour, "Factors Related to the Decision to Leave an Abusive Relationship," *Journal of Marriage and the Family* 46 (November 1984): 837–844.

134. Abby Haight and J. E. Vader and the staff of *The Oregonian*, *Fire on Ice: The Exclusive Inside Story of Tonya Harding* (New York: Times Books, 1994), 26, 29, 15–29.

135. Lenore Walker, *The Battered Woman* (1979; reprint, New York: Harper Colophon, 1980), 42–54.

136. Susan Orlean, "Figures in a Mall," *The New Yorker*, 21 February 1994, p. 52.

137. Chodorow, *Reproduction of Motherhood*, 178.

138. Rubin, *Intimate Strangers*, 92–93.

139. Case code no. A11. *(Portland) Network News*, August 1979, pp. 7–8; Hubbard, *From Harassment to Homicide*, 19, 28.

140. Case code no. A36. On the resources used by battered wives who escaped marital violence see Lee H. Bowker, "Coping with Wife Abuse: Personal and Social Networks," in *Battered Women and Their Families: Intervention Strategies and Treatment Programs*, ed. Albert R. Roberts (New York: Springer, 1984), 168–191. Susan Schechter, in *Women and Male Violence: The Visions and Struggles of the Battered Women's Movement* (Boston: South End Press, 1982), surveys the battered women's movement.

141. *Escape from Violence*, 57–58.

142. *Network News* 8 (Winter 1988): 2.

143. Henderson, *Story of Henderson House*, 42.

144. *Network News* 3 (September–October 1983): 1.

Conclusion

1. Betsy Downey, "Battered Pioneers: Jules Sandoz and the Physical Abuse of Wives on the American Frontier," *Great Plains Quarterly* 12 (Winter 1992): 31–49.

2. Linda Gordon, *Heroes of Their Own Lives: The Politics and History of Family Violence, Boston, 1880–1960* (New York: Viking, 1988); Pamela Haag, "The 'Ill-Use of a Wife': Patterns of Working-Class Violence in Domestic and Public New York City, 1860–1880," *Journal of Social History* 25 (Spring 1992): 447–477.

3. Elizabeth Pleck, *Domestic Tyranny: The Making of American Social Policy against Family Violence from Colonial Times to the Present* (New York: Oxford University Press, 1987).

4. Judith Hicks Stiehm, "The Protected, the Protector, the Defender," *Women's Studies International Forum* 5 (1982): 374.

5. Gordon, *Heroes of Their Own Lives*, 251.

Index

Please remember that this is a library book,
and that it belongs only temporarily to each
person who uses it. Be considerate. Do
not write in this, or any, library book.

WITHDRAWN

DATE DUE